Entrepreneurship and
Enterprise Development

We work with leading authors to develop the
strongest educational materials in business studies,
bringing cutting-edge thinking and best
learning practice to a global market.

Under a range of well-known imprints, including
Financial Times Prentice Hall, we craft high quality print and
electronic publications which help readers to understand
and apply their content, whether studying or at work.

To find out more about the complete range of our
publishing, please visit us on the World Wide Web at:
www.pearsoned.co.uk

Small Business, Entrepreneurship and Enterprise Development

Graham Beaver

Professor of Corporate Strategy and Business Development,
Nottingham Business School

FINANCIAL TIMES
Prentice Hall

An imprint of **Pearson Education**

Harlow, England · London · New York · Reading, Massachusetts · San Francisco · Toronto · Don Mills, Ontario · Sydney
Tokyo · Singapore · Hong Kong · Seoul · Taipei · Cape Town · Madrid · Mexico City · Amsterdam · Munich · Paris · Milan

Pearson Education Limited

Edinburgh Gate
Harlow
Essex CM20 2JE
England

and Associated Companies throughout the world

Visit us on the World Wide Web at:
www.pearsoned.co.uk

_____

First published 2002

© Pearson Education Limited 2002

ISBN 0273-65105-6

ISBN-13: 978-0-273-65105-5

British Library Cataloguing-in-Publication Data
A catalogue record for this book is available from the British Library

10 9 8 7 6 5 4 3
08 07 06 05

Typeset in 9.5/12.5pt Stone Serif by 35
Printed and bound by Ashford Colour Press, Gosport

Contents

More information can be found at www.booksites.net/beaver

Preface

Small business is a subject that fascinates society. The people who start up small businesses are often revered as entrepreneurs – the self-made people of today who have generated their own wealth rather than inheriting it. A great deal of serious academic research has been devoted to studying these people and the businesses they create. Similarly, the popular press is often full of stories that describe the personal and invariably very private lives of exceptionally successful small business owner-managers who are cited as the role models that every aspiring business graduate should seek to emulate.

It is still a common fallacy shared by many that small firms are merely large ones in miniature. Nothing could be further from reality. Small businesses differ from their larger counterparts in their motivations, success requirements, management style and philosophy, resource base, scope of operations and expectations. Furthermore, small firms do not just grow into the large companies of tomorrow. They must undertake massive and often brutal evolutionary changes to their structure, ownership and control, management and strategy, financial complexion and invariably their industry and markets. For a majority of small firms, their life span is often short and intense.

The publication of the Commission of Inquiry on Small Firms in 1971 (the Bolton Report) kick-started a new era of research, enlightenment and policy change. For much of the last 25 years the UK government has promoted the small business sector as the way forward out of recession, claiming that small firms create jobs, economic prosperity, structural balance, consumer choice and personal opportunity. They are also regarded as the preferred economic instrument to act as the brake on large company dominance and the misuse of monopoly power for competitive advantage.

However, the reality behind the popular picture is often very different. Successful business development demands careful management, shrewd decision-making, considerable personal risk and a great deal of hard work. The failure rate of new businesses, especially in their first 2 years, is still unacceptably high with the attendant social and economic costs causing real hardship for the unwary.

Furthermore, small firms have not been particularly successful in reducing unemployment (except in special circumstances) or counterbalancing the market domination and influence of large business organisations. Many entrepreneurs do not fit the classic economic stereotype of profit maximisers and seek only independence and control, deliberately ignoring opportunities to grow and develop the enterprise beyond a given point.

This book examines many of the myths which surround the small business legend and takes both an academic and a practical approach to small business management and enterprise development.

Objectives

This text provides an introduction to the establishment, development and managerial issues confronting the smaller enterprise. In particular, it is concerned with the kinds of actions and behaviour – often labelled entrepreneurial – that seem to characterise the launch and growth of a successful business venture.

It examines in some detail the process of new business formation and growth, with particular emphasis on acting and thinking in a strategic framework to maximise the chances of business success and longevity. The process of constructing, using and maintaining a business plan as a management instrument to facilitate the acquisition and deployment of the optimum resources in keeping with the aims and motivations of the principal actors is a central issue.

The text has been written for use on courses on small business and entrepreneurship on final year business and management undergraduate degrees and to accompany comparable elective choices offered on MBA programmes and similar Master's degrees. The text builds on and complements other core programmes in strategy, marketing, finance and management, thus facilitating the application of analytical and managerial skills towards the special set of situations that are peculiar to the establishment, management and development of the smaller enterprise. It includes both reference to and discussion of the latest research findings and evidence together with contemporary enterprise models, concepts and theoretical developments. Most chapters include case illustrations of businesses in different markets and industries to complement the academic and theoretical contribution and to illustrate different approaches, priorities, management problems and operating contexts.

In a work such as this it is clearly impossible to cover the whole catalogue of issues that affect the small business sector together with the fascinating and complex task of enterprise management and development. In determining the issues and content to be included, reference was made to the courses offered by many of the leading business schools and their approaches to enterprise education. However, there is no single text that encapsulates the range of themes in the depth required for both undergraduate and postgraduate programmes. For those students wishing to focus on a particular issue in depth, it is hoped that this text will provide an authoritative and readable introduction to the desired topic.

Author's acknowledgements

Acknowledgements and thanks must go to a number of people that helped with this project, not least my two contributing authors, Caroline Ross of Warwick University and Patricia Carr of Brunel University.

I have been fortunate to have the opportunity to work, research and play with a diverse and inspired group of people over the years and thanks must go to them for their humour, patience and insights into much of the subject matter contained in this book.

At Nottingham Business School thanks are due to Lynette Harris, Chris Prince, Yvonne Harrison, Jim Stewart, David Jennings, Peter Franklin, Paul Brittain, Mike Brown, Tony Watson and Denise Fletcher; at Sheffield Business School, Kevan Scholes, Paul Banfield, the late Bill Richardson (still sadly missed) and Janet Kirkham; at the University of North London and now, I am delighted to report, Nottingham Business School, Paul Joyce; to Conrad Lashley and Rhodri Thomas at Leeds Business School. Adrian Woods and Martyn Pitt of the School of Business and Management, Brunel University; Peter Jennings at The School of Management, University of Southampton; Lew Perren and Aiden Berry at the University of Brighton; Rod Atkin at The University of Greenwich; Ashok Ranchhod and June Fletcher at Southampton Institute; David Rae and Mary Carswell at the University of Derby; Roger Mumby-Croft at the Enterprise Centre, Oxford Bookes University; Shai Vyakarnam at the University of Cambridge; Bill Keogh at Heriot-Watt University; Robin Jarvis and Robert Blackburn at Kingston University Business School; Dean Patton at Leicester Business School; Robert Brown at Cranfield University; Martin Binks at The University of Nottingham; Nigel Sykes, Stephen Batstone, Marc Cowling, Grier Palmer, Francis Green and David Storey at Warwick Business School Centre for SMEs; Elaine White and Richard Welford at European Research Press; Colin Gray at the Open University for a constructive review of some of the early chapters; Sadie McClelland and Geraldine Lyons at Pearson for their encouragement and support; finally, special and sincere thanks to David Hussey.

Publisher's acknowledgements

We are grateful to the following for permission to reproduce copyright material:

Figure 4.1 from Picking Winners: The Art of Identifying Successful Small Firms, by Beaver, G. and Jennings, P. L. from *Rethinking Strategic Management*, John Wiley and Sons Ltd., (Hussey, D. E. (ed.) 1995). Reproduced by permission of John Wiley and Sons Ltd.;

Figure 6.1 from *Strategic Entrepreneurship and Enterprise*, published and copyright by Pearson Education, (Wickham, P. 1998)

Whilst every effort has been made to trace the owners of copyright material, in a few cases this has proved impossible and we take this opportunity to offer our apologies to any copyright holders whose rights we may have unwittingly infringed.

1 The small business sector

Objectives This first chapter seeks to examine the role, position and characteristics of small firms and the small business sector in the economy and the macro-economic environment in which they function.

In this chapter we will:

● discuss the different definitions and perceptions of small firms;

● examine and identify a broad range of issues affecting small firms;

● appreciate the heterogeneous nature of the small business sector;

● consider the relationship between government and the performance of the sector.

Introduction

Small businesses are the lifeblood of the economy. They are at the forefront of this government's efforts to promote enterprise, innovation and increased productivity. Small firms are vitally important because of their role in the supply chain, the competition they stimulate and the ideas and products they bring to the market place.

A few figures illustrate this vividly. The 3.7 million small and medium-sized enterprises represent 99.8% of all UK businesses. They account for over half the UK's economic activities, providing 56% of non-government jobs (excluding financial services) and 52% of turnover.

Small firms are and will continue to be the main providers of new jobs.

Source: Hewitt (2000)

Small enterprises, virtually no matter how they are defined, constitute at least 95% of all enterprises in the European Community.

Source: Storey (1994)

The role and importance of small businesses to the economies of both developed and developing nations have been the subject of increased scrutiny, particularly in the last two decades. This was mainly due to the belief that a prosperous and dynamic small business sector was crucial to the overall performance of a domestic economy. There are many reasons why this belief still dominates the socio-economic, cultural and political agendas of governments in industrialised countries across the world.

First, since the early 1980s, most industrialised nations experienced substantial restructuring of their economies. This led to a considerable growth in the numbers of small enterprises in general and micro-firms in particular (defined here as those employing less than 10 people).

Second, a general decline in manufacturing and the substantial growth of the service sector resulted in smaller-sized businesses becoming more important and efficient both within traditional and emerging industries.

Third, the apparent flexibility of smaller firms in responding to market changes and opportunities placed them at the forefront of economic thought and policy initiatives. The resulting *enterprise culture* (see Chapters 3 and 11 for more information), a popular term articulated by a number of governments across the world, had an important and lasting impact on domestic economic policies aimed at reducing unemployment and inflation rates and revitalising flagging industrial and commercial sectors. For now and the foreseeable future, small businesses are likely to retain their crucial position both within domestic economies and across an increasingly international stage.

Defining and classifying small firms

Small firms are much easier to describe than to define and to this day there is no generally agreed operational or numerical definition of what constitutes a small business. Countries, and in many cases individual institutions within them, have developed classifications and definitions that reflect their own particular requirements. These criteria tend to reflect the nature and composition of that country's economy.

Definitions may also reflect the nature and context of the industrial sector or market under consideration – for example, different criteria would be considered appropriate for firms engaged in manufacturing, construction, retailing, hospitality and tourism, professional services and so on.

Discussions about how to define small firms in the UK invariably begin with reference to the Committee of Inquiry Report on Small Firms (Bolton Report, 1971). This is not surprising because not only was it critical in establishing the importance of smaller enterprises in the minds of officials and academics but its deliberations on the question remain pertinent to some extent to the present day.

The Bolton Committee adopted several definitions of a small firm as follows:

- In *economic terms*, a small firm is one that has a relatively *small market share*.
- It is *managed* by its owners or part owners in a *personalised* way and not through the medium of a formalised management structure.
- It is *independent*, in the sense that it does not form part of a larger enterprise and that the owner/managers should be *free from outside control and interference* in taking their principal decisions.

To the above, the Committee added a series of statistical definitions for use in different sectors. For some, such as manufacturing, a threshold number of employees (200) was used whereas, for retailing, a turnover figure was adopted

(£50 000) and up to five vehicles or less for road transport. The rationale for the multiplicity of definitions was that they might be used for different purposes. For example, a statistical definition would enable international comparisons to be made and it was recognised that degrees of 'smallness' varied between sectors.

During the period since the publication of the Bolton Report, several commentators have noted its shortcomings. Stanworth and Gray (1991), for example, point out that statistical analysis is severely hampered by the use of varying definitions. Furthermore, any definition that uses a financial indicator invariably requires periodic adjustment in order to take account of inflation (Burns and Dewhurst, 1996).

To these, Storey (1994) adds two further problems of accepting the Bolton approach to defining small firms.

First, he notes the incompatibility of a definition which emphasises the personalised nature of management while simultaneously using statistical bands relating to numbers of employees. He argues that there is sufficient research showing that firms employing up to 200 people would inevitably require that business decisions be taken by individuals who were not owners.

Second, in challenging the influence which the notion of perfect competition (where small firms are price takers) had on the deliberations of the Bolton Committee, he argues that many small firms operate in niche markets where premium prices can be charged and superior business growth and performance displayed (see, for example, Storey, 1994, 1998; Beaver and Ross, 2000).

Despite the passing of over 30 years since the publication of the Bolton Report, there is not a single, uniformly acceptable, definition of a small firm (Storey, 1994). This is illustrated clearly by reference to the 16 studies undertaken during the late 1980s and early 1990s, which together formed the UK's largest-ever, small business research project funded by the Economic and Social Research Council. The definitions used for those projects included the following: fewer than 10 employees; fewer than 100 employees; fewer than 200 employees; 1–500 employees; a grounded definition and users of informal venture capital.

What emerges from a comprehensive review of the small business literature is a panoply of definitions that are justified by their users on the basis of their value to particular projects.

In order to meet the perceived imperative of facilitating comparison between sectors and Member States, the European Commission recently adopted a common definition of small and medium-sized enterprises (SMEs) which emphasises numbers of employees as follows:

- *micro-enterprises* (or very small firms): employing less than 10 people;
- *small enterprises*: those with 10–99 people;
- *medium enterprises*: those with 100–499 people.

The major advantage of the EC definition is that, unlike Bolton, it does not use any criteria other than employment and it does not vary its definition according to the sector of the enterprise. The EC definitions have gained considerable currency in recent years and are now used for example by many UK government departments in their reporting and comments. However, it should be noted before leaving this section that the key problem with the EC classification of an SME is that, for a number of countries, it is much too all embracing and therefore loses its focus and distinctiveness. As will be seen in other parts of this book, virtually all firms and the vast bulk of employment and output in countries such as Greece, Ireland, Spain and Portugal fall within the definition of SMEs. Quite obviously, for internal purposes within these countries, the SME definition is not helpful. In these cases, it is the categories within the SME definition which are most relevant.

In conclusion, the issue of small business definition and classification remains a complex one and readers and students are encouraged to use their innate business common sense to dictate suitable criteria that are helpful in a given sector or operating context. However, it is as well to be very mindful of the famous observation from George Bernard Shaw here when he stated:

> To every complex problem there is a simple solution that is wrong.

The interest in small business and enterprise development

It is now an established fact that the small business sector is regarded as a fundamental ingredient in the establishment of a modern, progressive and vibrant economy. The last 30 years or so have seen one of the most sustained and consistent programmes of inquiry into the role and dynamics of the small firm community and its contribution to economic wealth and prosperity in many countries throughout the world.

Mention has already been made of the Bolton Report, which in the UK was a landmark in small business research, providing a comprehensive and rational examination of small firms and their role in the economy. In many other countries there has been a similar interest in the nature and contribution of the small and developing enterprise, as structural economic changes, the development of new industries and markets and the increasing power and sophistication of consumers registered dissatisfaction with many established corporations and their product/service offerings.

There are a number of reasons why there is considerable interest in the creation, management, dynamics and contribution of small businesses:

- Small firms help to diversify a nation's economic base and provide it with the opportunity of responding to a variety of market conditions. The familiar 'acorns to oaks' argument fits well here.
- Small firms assist in employment creation and provide a natural corrective to large corporations undergoing rationalisation programmes and downsizing.
- The establishment of a vibrant and healthy small business sector helps promote an element of local control and accountability.
- The overdependence on large enterprise supported by international finance can be unhealthy and deprives regional economies of their dynamism and independence.
- The creation of a new business venture provides an opportunity to transcend social inequality and the unemployment trap. Enterprise development provides a meaningful expression of meritocracy and opportunity.

- The presence of small firms in an economy is an expression of healthy and necessary competition against the excesses of 'big business' and monopoly power and exploitation.
- Small firms assist in the development and dissemination of new forms of technology and innovation.
- They effectively cater for niche markets which large corporations ignore through strategies of globalisation. (See the research from Storey, Deloitte & Touche, 1997–99, covered in Chapter 8, for a particularly good illustration of this point.)
- Small firms are the natural avenues for self-development and individual achievement, being the natural expression of entrepreneurship.

It should be noted that the above rationale for interest in small firms is neither exhaustive nor definitive. It is merely indicative of the various discussion points associated with the benefits that small businesses potentially bring to an economy.

Claims and statements of the kind listed above have helped researchers, academics, policy-makers and politicians to construct a discourse on small business and enterprise development and to give it a framework of issues. Since the publication of the Bolton Report in the UK, the number of contributors to this discourse has mushroomed as new parties have sought to demonstrate a new set of correlations between a small business as a desirable phenomenon and its effects upon the society around it.

Below are some of the principal issues and questions associated with small business and enterprise development, each of which are considered in greater detail elsewhere in the book. The objective here is to provide a broad overview and introduction to the subject.

How are small firms different from large ones?

Many commentators and academics have gone to considerable trouble to emphasise that small firms are not simply large ones in miniature. They invariably have special characteristics that differentiate them from their larger counterparts and render the business development management process a very different affair (Jennings and Beaver, 1997). These characteristics, some of which are listed below, make many small firms inherently riskier than larger ones:

- Small businesses are frequently *dominated and controlled by one person*. The enterpreneur or owner-manager has an overwhelming influence on all aspects of the firm's direction, development and performance. This, not surprisingly, can be both a strength and a weakness. Business decisions are often personal decisions and the logic of the balance sheet and rational economic criteria may not always apply.
- Many small firms are *heavily reliant on a small number of customers*. This means that they are particularly dependent on the performance and health of any one customer and vulnerable if that business turns elsewhere for its products.
- Most small businesses because of their *small market share* are unlikely to exert much influence on their chosen sector. In the classic economic sense, they

are price takers and may well face significant competition – especially if there is a high threat of new market entrants (Porter, 1985). This means that the threat of failure may well be increased and that attention to strategic management is of paramount importance (see Chapter 5 for a more detailed discussion).

- Many *large organisations are indeed public companies* and as such have access to the stock market in their desire to raise capital. The vast majority of small firms are not quoted businesses and their stock often remains privately held by the owner(s) and/or their nominees. This means they often have problems raising capital and this can significantly restrict their choice of strategies of business development. As we shall see later in the book (Chapter 7 in particular), for many small firms wishing to expand their operations, raising the appropriate finance can become a major impediment to their growth and future competitive existence.

- Small firms may chose to operate in a single market, or limited range of markets with similar customer requirements, i.e. they *deliberately restrict their product/service offering*, often on the grounds of simplicity or focus (Porter, 1985). Provided that operating conditions remain unchanged, this may be the best choice in the short term, but, unlike larger firms, they may find it much more difficult to diversify their business portfolio if conditions change.

It should be noted that *small firms are not a homogenous entity* and that to think otherwise is both dangerous and naive. By their very nature, small businesses are different and have special characteristics, operating contexts and qualities. It makes any attempt to generalise about some 3 million firms in the UK alone an almost impossible affair.

Why do so many small firms fail in the early years?

It is a sobering fact that any business – small or large – can fail and produce quite awful consequences for all the stakeholders concerned. There are many reasons for business failure but in the case of small firms, usually under 3 years old, issues of finance, demand forecasting, management, marketing, capitalisation at start-up and business planning are just some of the issues that suggest themselves.

Whether or not the business owner(s) had a sufficiently viable and robust idea to begin with, the necessary resources, experience and acumen to successfully manage the credibility merry-go-round (Birley, 1996) are also of paramount consideration.

If business start-ups are a desperate response to unemployment, rather than based on sound principles and the committed fashioning of competitive advantage, it is inevitable that many firms will fail. Explanations such as these all seem to suggest that ultimately the key players did not have the talent and abilities necessary to succeed – a personality-based approach.

It should be remembered that all successful economies shed jobs and sometimes whole industries. However, what these economies manage to do is to create the conditions and opportunities for new jobs and businesses in line with market needs.

A successful and progressive economy depends on its constituent firms being innovative, productive and competitive. Perhaps the vulnerability of new businesses can be explained not only in terms of the personal dispositions of their key players but also in terms of bad luck, poor timing, inadequate training and advice, the abuse of entrepreneurial power (see Chapter 6 for a discussion of this issue) and more abstract market economics.

What are the ingredients for small business success?

This subject is rapidly becoming a growth industry in its own right as commentators, business writers and, more recently, successful entrepreneurs seek to provide their own prescriptive formula necessary for successful enterprise development (see, for example, Philips, 1999).

Associated with this question are the recipe-driven, prescriptive approaches frequently adopted in many training manuals and practitioner texts on business development. Clearly, there is a need to assume a foundation of common principles as a starting point for successful business formation and growth but there is much, much more besides. For a start, the subject of *business success* needs clarification here (Jennings and Beaver, 1997).

For many small firm owner/managers, success can be measured in their capacity to sustain a lifestyle business that has been established to provide a measure of independence with an acceptable income at a 'comfort level' of activity. Once that level of activity is reached, management becomes a routine, tactical operation designed to protect the existing business. There is probably little thought about strategic management unless things start to go wrong. The most usual thing is that the market changes without the owner/manager realising it.

The *entrepreneurial* business has a different agenda and a different perception of success that includes business growth, attention to maximising profitability, turnover (or both), management development, innovation in the product–service mix, and so on. These firms present many of the classic change management problems, are not easy to manage and are frequently extremely risky. Most will probably not survive without encountering at least one crisis that will threaten their survival. Timely and effective strategic management is essential if the business is to survive and prosper.

The *family* business may also have a very different success agenda that is understood only by the principal family members (Leach and Bogod, 1999; Scase and Goffee, 1987).

If profitability and growth are to be regarded as the principal measures of small firm success, (i.e. wealth-creating firms), then there may well be generic factors which are transferable and which others would do well to heed.

The ways in which successful businesses use and value strategic management and contemporary marketing practices and pay attention to their ingredients of competitive advantage are of paramount importance here. An interesting question that will be addressed later in the text concerns entrepreneurship. Specifically, can small firms train for entrepreneurship and how does this affect success, performance and longevity?

What is the significance of ownership in small business management and enterprise development?

Business ownership is one of the factors at the very heart of what characterises and differentiates a small business and is probably the key feature of difference (apart from size) between small and large firms.

The ownership of large organisations is usually distanced from its management and control, which are not evident in the majority of small enterprises. The issues and complexities that result from ownership and control in the small firm have been the subject of substantial research over the last 30 years. The outcomes of this have supplied the content of this text on small business and enterprise development, with a great deal of its content and focus.

The relationships between ownership and decision-making, managerial styles, organisational structures and cultures and business development have all formed the basis of extensive research and comment. At the time of writing, a contemporary interest from many commentators and researchers seems to be again focusing around the role of ownership and its connection with enterprise success and failure: not an easy subject on which to offer, or propose, a definitive comment.

Other recent research inquiries have examined the impact and significance for owner/managers of very high levels of personal investment in their business, coupled with issues with personal security and risk. Does this lead, for example, to a greater conservatism and risk aversion in decision-making, acting as a brake to enterprise growth and development?

Other recent projects have examined how managers make the transition from salaried professionals to owners. Indeed, much of the current interest in management buy-outs and buy-ins is focused around this theme.

At the centre of much of the interest in small business ownership are the questions of power, control, culture and patterns of decision-making. It is a common perception that power cultures are thought to decrease with an increase in the size of the firm, when formal delegation and structure become more important. Power and control also feature as an important issue with employees, especially those who do not enjoy some form of trade union protection. Employee dependence, the demands for increased workforce flexibility and performance management, together with changes in deregulation and conditions of service, have resulted in renewed levels of interest in the ramifications of business ownership (Beaver and Harris, 1996).

Ownership and family issues are also very much in vogue. The positives in favour of family ownership tend to be captured in such things as the speed and flexibility with which family-owned firms can make decisions without having to circumvent other stakeholders.

As organisations, they are often said to have a unique atmosphere and set of relationships and can be treated by the family as a long-term investment. They may provide a career path and responsibilities, which may be difficult for family members to obtain outside the business. On the other hand, there may well be a number of negatives associated with family ownership, which may undermine such benefits. For instance, there may be too many overlapping boundaries between family interests and the needs of the business. Rivalries and jealousies may emerge to destabilise the firm. The business may become a source of emotional conflict and may suffer through becoming too inward looking. What was once a source of pride and long-term investment could be destroyed through problems of succession. Authority, power and ambition may well become poisonous issues between competing family members (see Fletcher, 2000, for an informed discussion of this issue).

The business could be the vehicle that exploits family relationships, overworking some members, thus raising the question of family first or business first, a problem which may well find expression in operational friction and value conflicts.

An organisation may find that standards of performance are substituted for standards of satisfaction – the perennial problem of maintaining a lifestyle business rather than concentrating on the efficiencies and new methods that enhance profitability and competitive advantage and take the business forward.

Key positions such as directorships may be used to favour family insiders, thus depleting the firm of the experience and talent of better-qualified outsiders. These factors all have implications for recruitment, selection and retention of the 'right' people and the sustenance of productive business cultures (see Chapter 4 for a more detailed discussion of this theme):

> Appointment and advancement are frequently made on the basis of affiliations, friendship and accidents of birth, than on the basis of ability or qualifications for the job.
>
> *Source*: Beaver and Lashley (1998)

Are small businesses employment generators?

This is a major issue and is the subject of a more rigorous examination later in the text (see Chapters 2–4 and 8 in particular). The relationship of employment generation and the small business sector is at best a controversial one where the evidence is conflicting.

The debate probably started in earnest as a consequence of pioneering studies in the USA; notably, Birch (1979) that showed that some 66% of all new jobs were created by firms employing less than 20 people – a truly breathtaking statistic. Suffice it to say that the evidence for this finding has been vigorously challenged and has certainly not been replicated in the UK or elsewhere.

However, this is not to say that small firms do not create employment opportunities and have been instrumental in doing so in certain industries and sectors. There is a belief that small firms tend to be more labour intensive and therefore more likely to create jobs, while larger organisations are more likely to utilise innovation and new technologies to achieve efficiencies and economies of scale, thus shedding labour. There is certainly substantial evidence to show that many large enterprises have 'exported jobs' by relocating all or part of their manufacturing process to whatever part of the world offers the most favourable (and cost-effective) factors of production.

The quality, substance, remuneration and conditions attached to the jobs created by small firms are also somewhat controversial and comparisons with their large enterprise equivalents are often made. However, the current preoccupation with employment flexibility and deregulation makes such comparisons hard to both analyse and substantiate. Furthermore, the definition of what constitutes a full-time job and the statistical methods used to measure them render the examination of small business employment creation highly problematic.

Questions of employment generation and the role of small firms have more to do with issues of competitive advantage, resource provision, ownership and management dynamics than measures of size per se.

Government support and small business policy

Most governments, irrespective of their political complexion and global position, understand the need for an effective small business policy. For many Western economies, small business policy has indeed come of age. In the UK, for example, it is now such an established feature of the political landscape that during the 1997 and 2001 general elections all the main political parties were at pains to demonstrate their enthusiasm for supporting small business and enterprise development. Barbara Roche – the Shadow Minister for Small Business in 1997 – stated that:

> Labour is dedicated to providing the right conditions in government for small firms to grow and thrive . . . we want strong small businesses because they are crucial to this country's success.
>
> *Source*: Labour Party (1997, p. 4)

This concern to promote the development of small firms is not new or unique to Britain. What some commentators have described as 'a steady stream of measures' during the 1970s became a torrent during the 1980s (Stanworth and Gray, 1991).

The European Union (EU) has, since the mid-1980s, also sought to ensure that small (and medium-sized) enterprises are assisted rather than stifled by the state. If we examine the development of small business policy in the UK as a starting point for international comparisons later in the book (see Chapter 12 in particular), then, in Britain, policy has been articulated to address four main themes:

● creating a favourable economic environment for small firms to thrive;
● initiatives to encourage financial investments in small firms;
● the provision of business information and support;
● sponsoring and developing programmes to encourage business and management development.

The government recently established (April 2000) a new Small Business Service charged with the mandate to improve the delivery, quality and co-ordination of small business interests, assistance, training and support. To quote then Trade and Industry Secretary, Stephen Byers, speaking at the launch of the public consultation stage of the new service:

> For too long, small businesses have been regarded as the Cinderellas of the business world, yet they are some of the most enterprising and ambitious firms. They are the Vodafones and the Pret à Mangers of the future and this government is determined to ensure small businesses have a voice at the heart of government, together with the local support and services they need. The Small Business Service will achieve this.

The Small Business Service has been charged with three main tasks:

● to act as the voice for small business at the heart of government;
● to simplify and improve the quality and coherence of government support for small firms;
● to help small firms deal with regulation and ensure that the interests of the small firm community are properly considered in future regulation.

It comes as no real surprise that the government has reviewed and re-organised its support and service provision, as the previous business support infrastructure attracted substantial criticism in its dealings with the perceived, as opposed to the real, needs of the small business sector.

Furthermore, aspects of quality, consistency, professionalism and organisation have all received less than favourable acclaim. Whatever the outcome and success of the new Small Business Service and its impact on small business support, it is clear that given the multiple and often conflicting objectives pursued by government, it is unlikely to cater for all the needs, wants and deficiencies of the small firm sector:

> Being small can have its price. Many small firms find it difficult to get access to the information and finance they need. They are often unable to draw on the same range of expertise and experience as larger companies. They have fewer resources to get to grips with regulation and fewer opportunities to influence government thinking.
>
> Within the next decade I hope that the UK's small businesses and new entrepreneurs will be leading the rest of the world as champions of commerce.
>
> *Source*: Hewitt (2000)

In his conclusions, Storey (1994, p. 315) was quite clear in recommending that:

> The basic message to government is that, in its dealings with small firms, it needs to do less and better, rather than more and worse. The very clear message, which comes across from discussions with small firms, is in creating a suitable macroeconomic framework within which firms can prosper.

This has been endorsed by other writers (Deakins, 1999) and small business interest groups (for example, the Forum of Private Business, 1999) that confirm that small firms seek an environment in which there are low inflation, low interest rates, steady economic growth and a high level of aggregate demand.

It is the ability of government to deliver these macro-economic conditions which is the main influence on its judgement of competence by the small business sector. In practice, of course, every government would like to achieve these objectives, not only for small firms but also for all firms in the economy. Nevertheless, the macro-economic framework appears to be the acid test by which small firms judge the economic effectiveness of government.

However, notwithstanding the above, substantial progress has been made since a small business policy was first accepted by the UK government and many others as being a necessary item on its agenda. Indeed, the recognition that the sector is in some way disadvantaged (against the larger organisations in the economy) and that its problems are different, special and need attention is now accepted by most enlightened governments as given.

Summary

The principal objective of this first chapter has been to set the framework for small firms and consider their role, nature, characteristics and contribution within the economy. In the chapters that follow, many of the issues raised will be examined in more detail.

References and further reading

Beaver, G. and Harris, L. (1996) 'The Hidden Price of the Disposable Workforce: Issues, Contexts and Approaches in the Search for Competitive Advantage – Lessons for the Smaller Enterprise', *Journal of Business Growth and Profitability*, 2 (1), March, 49–56.

Beaver, G. and Jennings, P. L. (1996) 'The Abuse of Entrepreneurial Power – An Explanation of Management Failure?', *The Journal of Strategic Change*, 5 (3), May–June, 151–64.

Beaver, G. and Lashley, C. (1998) 'Competitive Advantage and Management Development in Small Hospitality Firms: The Need for an Imaginative Approach', *Journal of Vacation Marketing*, 4 (2), April, 145–60.

Beaver, G. and Murphy, M. (1996) 'Carpentry and Joinery (Nottingham) Ltd.: A Case Study in Enterprise Support and Development', *Journal of Small Business and Enterprise Development*, 3 (1), March, 28–33.

Beaver, G. and Ross, E. C. (2000) 'Enterprise in Recession: The Role and Context of Strategy', *The International Journal of Entrepreneurship and Innovation*, 1 (1), February, 23–31.

Birch, D. (1979) 'The Job Generation Process', in *MIT Program on Neighbourhood and Regional Change*. Cambridge, MA: MIT Press.

Birley, S. (1996) 'The Start Up', in Burns, P. and Dewhurst, J. (eds), *Small Business and Entrepreneurship*. Basingstoke: Macmillan, ch. 2.

Bolton Report (1971) *Report of the Committee of Enquiry on Small Firms*. London: HMSO.

Burns, P. and Dewhurst, J. (eds) (1996) *Small Business and Entrepreneurship*, 2nd edn. Basingstoke: Macmillan.

Deakins, D. (1999) *Entrepreneurship and Small Firms*, 2nd edn. Maidenhead: McGraw-Hill.

Fletcher, D. (2000) 'Family and Enterprise', in Carter, S. and Jones-Evans, D. (eds), *Enterprise and Small Business*. London: Financial Times/Pearson, ch. 9.

Hewitt, P. (2000) 'Small is Beautiful', *Enterprise*, May/June, 3.

Jennings, P. L. and Beaver, G. (1997) 'The Performance and Competitive Advantage of Small Firms: A Management Perspective', *International Small Business Journal*, 15 (2), January–March, 63–75.

Labour Party (1997) *Growing and Prospering Your Business and a Labour Government*. London: Labour Party.

Leach, P. and Bogod, T. (1999) *Family Business*, 3rd edn. London: Kogan Page.

Philips, S. (1999) *The Seven Principles for Sustained Growth*. London: Arrow.

Porter, M. E. (1985) *Competitive Advantage*. New York: Free Press.

Scase, R. and Goffee, R. (1987) *The Real World of the Small Business Owner*, 2nd edn. London: Croom Helm.

Stanworth, J. and Gray, C. (eds) (1991) *Bolton 20 Years On: The Small Firm in the 1990s*. London: Paul Chapman.

Storey, D. J. (1994) *Understanding the Small Business Sector*. London: Routledge.

Storey, D. J. (1998) *The Ten Percenters*, 4th Report, *Fast Growing Firms in the UK*, November. Deloitte & Touche.

2

The new business venture

Objectives This chapter discusses and examines some of the important factors that affect the choice and decisions involved in business evaluation and start-up, recognising fully that establishing a new enterprise is essentially a process rather than an event and that it may take a long time to evolve and mature.

In particular, we will discuss:

● the consideration of different factors that affect the establishment of a new business – what are the features and ingredients of a successful start-up?

● the various stages of business creation and the need to assemble and manage the right mix of resources to establish and sustain competitive advantage;

● the various other methods and opportunities available in the business creation process;

● the choice of legal entity that can be selected for business formation.

Introduction

During any single year, the Dun and Bradstreet Corporation lists over 200 000 business start-ups in the UK alone. Every small business start-up is based on the belief (and hope) by the founders that they have recognised an opportunity which no one else has perceived or that they can provide an innovative product/ service which customers will value more highly than the competition (Barrow and Brown, 1997).

Yet, sadly, the success potential of many start-ups remains unfulfilled and the available data suggest that as many as 66% will fail during the first 3 years. Why is it that the success rate of new enterprise creation has been, and still is, so poor and what can be done to enhance the prospects of survival and long-term 'success', however that may be defined?

There is a plethora of both theoretical advice and practical assistance available from academics, industrialists and the business support infrastructure, which suggests that the task of starting a business is well researched, well documented and well understood. Many have put forward extensive checklists of factors which are said to be the basic, underlying causes of small business failure (Beaver and Jennings, 1995).

A close analogy can be drawn between planning a long journey using a map as the guide to the principal routes and choices available and simply setting off with only a rough idea which direction to take. It is a maxim of business folklore but nonetheless a true one that 'If you don't know where you are going, then any road will take you there!' The all too common mistake made by far too many would-be small firm practitioners every year is that it is not enough to simply follow all the well-meaning advice and information to guarantee business success.

The 'golden rules' (such as they are) of new venture management and the associated pitfalls have been well researched and many are covered in this chapter, such as:

- the need for a realistic and detailed business plan;
- managing cash flow as opposed to being content to monitor sales turnover or the number of new or potential prospects;
- selecting, recruiting and motivating the right people;
- listening to customers and catering for their particular requirements;
- etc., etc. – the list is a long and detailed one.

It is relatively easy to list the individual steps and decisions needed before embarking on a new business venture but it is much more difficult to capture and describe the complexity of the process. Every individual decision, while important in its own right, is related to and conditioned by the collective decision tree. Therefore, while there is a logical and systematic progression to the decision-making, it is not a simple sequential process but a dynamic and interactive one.

At the heart of most business start-ups lies the problem of the lack of credibility for the founder in dealing with the new business stakeholder community. It is a fact of life that people find it much easier to recognise and appreciate what you can do after you have done it. A track record is a major source of reassurance in these circumstances – the lack of one is a major obstacle to be overcome.

The *credibility merry-go-round* of Birley, in Burns and Dewhurst (1996), illustrates this point particularly well. The concept clearly shows the inter-related nature of the factors, resources and stakeholders involved in the process and how the event is essentially a dynamic one. How the individual responds to this difficult and unique challenge is also a good indicator of enterpreneurial skill, determination and flair.

The credibility merry-go-round

The inter-related complexities and choices in assembling the mix of business inputs necessary to fashion competitive advantage in the new venture:

Source: Birley (1996)

As an example, a clothing manufacturer was having great difficulty in obtaining finance from his bankers and trade credit from certain suppliers. He required this support to service a major order that had been accepted from an extremely good customer. To obtain what he required, he persuaded the customer to provide him with a cheque for $1 million, which he undertook not to cash and to return within 2 days. The sight of the cheque proved sufficient to gain the confidence of both bankers and suppliers – and the rest is history. The company grew and prospered and is now a leading manufacturing company in Hong Kong.

This chapter concentrates on the more cerebral aspects of starting and evaluating a business venture, while recognising that the creativity and indeed, audacity and innovation of the individual(s) may have a fundamental role in actually making things happen.

The features of a successful business start-up: an overview of the research evidence

It must be recognised that there is no commonly accepted definition or measure of success in business. Generally, it is assumed that success can be measured in quantitative terms such as growth and profitability, while occasionally surrogate measures such as growth in employment are used (Storey, 1994). However, other research suggests that success is measured in a very personalised way by each stakeholder, which necessarily encompasses both quantitative and qualitative measures (Beaver and Jennings, 1995).

Despite this plurality, there are certain common features which are considered to be characteristics that influence the success potential of a new business venture irrespective of exactly how success is defined. The advice that invariably accompanies these features is usually two-fold: first, that the feature in itself and by itself is not sufficient to guarantee success and, second, that careful adaptation of the feature concerned to the specific operating context of the business is essential.

Burns and Dewhurst (1996) discuss success per se and suggest that the principal ingredients arise from the interaction of the founder/entrepreneur with the product/service concept. This is augmented by careful management, the main business functions of which should all be focused directly upon the needs and wants of the customer. While they do not refer explicitly to start-up situations, the implication is that these are the guiding principles that should be followed from start-up and beyond to ensure success. Clearly, the characteristics and motivations of the founder are critical.

Many writers have differentiated between an *entrepreneur* and a *small business owner*. The former founds an enterprise in pursuit of profit and growth and, therefore, engages in innovative behaviour in the practice of strategic management to achieve these objectives. The latter, however, founds the business principally to pursue personal objectives, such as independence, control and a good standard of living. Here the business consumes the majority of the founder's time and resources and provides the primary source of income – and often enjoyment.

Birley also examines new enterprise formation in terms of the factors which influence the founder immediately prior to start-up. She concludes that there are a number of alternative but sometimes complementary *trigger events* that influence the founder and enable action to be taken. Certain trigger events can be regarded as positive influences encouraging start-up while others are negative influences which force action because there seems at the time to be no other reasonable alternative. Specifically, Birley's research focused on several surveys which showed that new firms are not being started in response to a healthy climate for enterprise but because a slack labour market encourages the unemployed to try their hand at entrepreneurial activity.

Not surprisingly, several other studies have also concluded that the motivation to start the business is a critical influencing factor and that unemployment or the threat of unemployment is especially significant.

Other empirical studies have highlighted the fact that individuals setting up in business in which they may have had experience as, say, an employee are more likely to succeed as self-employed business people in the same or related field (Birley and Westhead, 1993). Storey (1994) and Banfield *et al.* (1996) take this a stage further and refer to the importance of managerial competence in determining success. Storey, in particular, refers to the possibility of providing management training to develop knowledge and skills:

> It might therefore be expected that these competencies can be formally taught to entrepreneurs and that those in receipt of this training would perform better in business than untrained individuals.
>
> *Source*: Storey (1994)

It is far from clear, however, whether training prior to start-up, at start-up or following start-up is the most beneficial. While it is possible for one founder/entrepreneur to have a clear vision of the business and the direction it should take, it does not mean that this vision has been documented as a tangible business plan. It is a sad truism that founders rarely plan to fail; they simply fail to plan.

This also embraces the need to undertake suitable market research prior to start-up. It leaves unanswered, however, the question of whether these entrepreneurs could improve their level of success by undertaking and utilising formal market research. There have been several studies during the last 20 years which were unable to show that formalised planning leads to enhanced small firm performance. However, other studies, notably those by Kinsella *et al.* (1993), Joyce *et al.* (1996) and Beaver and Ross (1999), have all noted the relationship between strategic planning and thinking and superior performance, even in a recessionary climate.

As will be seen later in the text, it is usually the case that small firms are required by finance providers to prepare a formal business plan at start-up. However, recent studies (for example, Nayak and Greenfield, 1994) have shown that business planning is almost wholly absent if considering the micro-business segment of the UK small firms sector:

> Many such firms indeed appear to keep few financial records of their business and so would not be in a position to monitor plans even if they had them.
>
> *Source*: Nayak and Greenfield (1994)

17

Access to finance is also an important influence on start-up success and subsequent development and several studies have shown that the choice of sources used and the type of finance forthcoming are likely to be a very important influence on survival and future growth prospects. Commercial banks have been frequently criticised (Stanworth and Gray, 1991; Binks and Ennew, 1996) for failing to provide adequate funds for newly formed enterprises. The banks' usual response to such criticisms is that this is a function of poorly constructed business proposals, rather than a lack of willingness to lend funds.

A wide variety of support agencies and advice centres provide business services which, it is generally believed, will enhance the probability of success. Several studies, notably by Storey *et al.* (1989), the Cambridge Small Business Research Centre (1992), Kerr (1998) and Beaver and Ross (2000), have shown that fast-growing firms made use of services by accountants, financial managers, lawyers business strategy consultants, personnel and recruitment specialists, public relations experts and advertising agencies, the Health and Safety Executive, the Inland Revenue, the Customs and Excise and even the police. In contrast, other research has failed to show any significant correlation between start-up success and future business development and the use of external information and advisory services.

In summary, the following list of critical success factors has been compiled from prominent research findings over the past decade as being instrumental in determining business start-up success:

- owner's goals;
- owner's operational abilities;
- owner's management abilities;
- owner's strategic abilities;
- financial resources;
- personnel resources;
- information technology and systems capabilities;
- business resources.

It may be helpful in concluding this section to consider a short typology that describes the sorts of approaches and attitudes to start-up. It is also easy to remember as each of the categories begins with the letter 'D':

- *Dreamers*. Passively consider start-up as an option. Ideas remain stagnant and unco-ordinated.
- *Deferrers*. Are always finding excuses: a lack of time; dependent children; lack of funds; need to gain experience, skills, training and advice.
- *Diagnosers*. Obsessed with the research of their idea and tend to make little progress; masters of the SWOT and PEST analysis techniques and Porter's five forces model.
- *Doers*. Consider business start-up as a serious option and overcome all the barriers, even the ones that they have been told that they cannot. They have clear and realisable short- and long-term goals.

The stages of business creation

It is normal in larger organisations to evaluate a new business proposal from several perspectives. A typical list would include the fit with existing activities, the demands on existing resources and the requirements for new ones together with the contribution to corporate goals and management aspirations.

All too frequently, this evaluation will fail to consider issues of implementation and control (Hussey, 1998), perhaps because there is some tacit assumption by the incumbent management that suitable people can be found to take the project forward and, if not, then suitable people can be recruited for the purpose.

It should be very clear by now that the nature of the business creation process for the small business demands that clear and unambiguous consideration is given to the personality, motives, abilities and requirements of the key players involved. To do otherwise would be a serious and costly mistake.

Mention has been made above of the statement from Birley, that starting a business is not an event but a process that may take several years to accomplish. This statement emphasises and reflects the incremental, ad hoc and exploratory mechanisms that are characteristic of the business creation process and the nature of entrepreneurial management that is involved.

Very few people get it right the first time, i.e. that the resultant business venture actually appears in the nature and form that it was conceived and delivering the sales and profit expectations that were forecast. If there is one consistent characteristic of the small business sector that we can be certain about, it is the high rates of failure for new and young firms during their early years.

Much that needs to be understood before a new business assumes a predictable form and pattern of trading may only be known in the light of experiment and experience – and monitoring the reaction of customers to the product/service offering. This point is an important one and it is crucial to appreciate it as such. The small business founders that will succeed in this difficult and exacting process are those that will learn from their mistakes and lost opportunities and expect to refine and improve their business venture through an evolutionary process that may take several years.

Every business start-up is a unique event. Circumstances that contribute to its success are often intangible and are invariably different for each individual entrepreneur.

Understanding this point should sound a note of caution about being too dogmatic in any early analysis of a new business idea. If the process of establishing the business is conceived in an appropriate way, there may be many opportunities subsequently to refine and enhance the business concept and sharpen its market focus.

Given the above, the following framework for analysing the process of business creation is discussed which essentially proposes a logical and systematic procedure for assessment, evaluation and commercialisation of the new venture. It is important also to recognise that this framework demands that the questions and decisions to be confronted by the nascent entrepreneur are strategic decisions. The role of strategy is a very important one in business – irrespective of the size of the enterprise (see Chapters 5 and 6, in particular).

In essence, *strategy* relates to the actions that a business takes in order to achieve its goals. This is not to devalue the importance of tactical and operational decisions. To be successful, a new venture must be effective in its marketing, it must manage its finances competently and it must be proficient in its operations. What a strategic approach means is that entrepreneurs must think of all of these things not as isolated functions but as different facets of the venture as a whole, i.e. they must think and plan holistically. They must be seen to function in unison enabling the venture to deliver value to its customers, satisfy stakeholders and develop in the face of competition.

The business creation framework

1 Developing the business idea/concept.
2 Establishing a market.
3 Assessing the competition.
4 Pre-start planning, preparation and assessment.
5 Market entry – trial run or commercialisation.
6 Post-entry development – refinements and the acquisition of resources.

Developing the business idea/concept

The formation of business ideas will be conditional on many things: education, past experience, employment history, levels of training and skill acquisition – to mention but a few. The recognition that a process, product or service could be done better or in a different way has been the idea behind many new business ventures.

Preliminary assessment of the business idea needs to be tolerant. At this stage, it might be quite crudely expressed and not yet ready for the process of refinement and examination that business planning may produce. The history of innovation is full of examples of people whose business ideas have been summarily dismissed as unsuitable or commercially unviable – and who, perhaps motivated into even greater determination by this apparent rejection, have gone on to achieve great success.

Deakins (1999, p. 52) reminds us that:

> It should be recognised that idea formulation can take considerable time. The sudden breakthrough is comparatively rare. Ideas take time to refine; they benefit from discussion with others, from research, from information gathering and from feedback. Thus being creative is only part of the process. Additional skills must be developed that can take basic ideas, then modify and refine them – perhaps involving considerable research – before they become viable start-up ventures.

Some of the important considerations here could include the following.

Timing

The concept of the strategic window is particularly relevant here. Business ideas which anticipate the development of favourable environmental changes – and thus are at the beginning of their life cycle – are launched into a much more favourable climate than those faced by mature or complacent competition.

Entry requirements

The need to start a small and flexible operation, with a commitment to reinforce success as quickly as possible, is the hallmark of many new business ventures. However, for any business idea, there will be some minimum level of entry, which will be a function of the particular market context. Some business ideas by their very nature require substantial resources for their realisation. These may be suited for the large organisation and may preclude the individual. It is crucial to assess what constitutes a minimum efficient level of entry and what resources this is likely to require.

Competition and differential advantage

The business idea must be seen and evaluated in the context of existing competition and the scope to establish sustainable differential advantage. If the principal source of perceived advantage is one based on lower price, then, in all likelihood, this may well be undermined sooner rather than later. Such an idea is unlikely to be a sustainable small business opportunity. In cases such as this, such a perception usually demonstrates a lack of detailed market knowledge on the part of the potential entrepreneur. A focus strategy with the potential for high added value and associated premium pricing is often a far better bet for establishing differential advantage for a small firm.

Core competences

Irrespective of the industry or market context, every business has to have and maintain appropriate core skills and abilities that enable it to relate to the particular requirements of its customers. These need to be identified and accommodated.

Economic viability

Finally, the economics of the proposition must be assessed – and accord with the success requirements of the founder and/or key players. The later stage of developing a business plan should provide a much clearer quantification of factors such as cash flow and return on investment, but a view needs to be formed before deciding whether to invest in this extra time and expense. A very useful guide here is to examine the proposed gross margin and, if possible, test this against the market average.

Establishing a market

This is essentially the research stage. There is no point in pursuing an idea for which there is no market opportunity. Relevant and timely market information is of fundamental necessity to the founder/entrepreneur because they alone make the decision to venture.

Venturing means stepping out into the unknown and market intelligence provides some clues as to how to move forward into this unknown. Information helps to reduce the level of uncertainty and therefore assists in minimising the risks involved. (Do please note that market information gathering does not and never will eliminate risk, as some writers on this subject inaccurately claim.) However, market research by itself is not enough – if it is to be valuable, it must analysed, understood and acted on.

Good market information does not come for free; it has a cost. While the founder/entrepreneur will know many things as a result perhaps of experience within the industry, a lot of additional information may need to be gathered subsequently. Irrespective of the type and nature of the information being collected, it represents an investment in the business venture.

It is used to increase the performance of the enterprise and the pay-off for that investment needs to be appreciated before the information is gathered. Information guides action. However, lack of information should not be an excuse for inaction. While it may be prudent to hold back on a move until more intelligence is available, there are times when the founder/entrepreneur must rely on his/her instincts and make the required move. The judgement between making ill-informed decisions and the inertia caused by the venture becoming more obsessed by information collection and analysis than in taking direct action is one that only the enterprise key players can judge. These two options are often referred to as *extinction by instinct* and *paralysis by analysis*.

Strategic management provides a wide variety of tools and conceptual frameworks to aid decision-making (see Chapter 5). A wide variety of methods, techniques, models and constructs are available to guide resource allocation and competitive positioning. While the founder/entrepreneur would be foolish not to make good use of the insights that can be gained from such analysis, he or she should not be unhealthily dependent on it. Overall, it is the pattern, not the detail, that often matters.

New business creation is as much about the key players learning to develop and respond to their intuition and making judgements based on holistic thinking and their own heuristic approach. Research should be thorough and should focus on the principal market characteristics and operating context of the new venture. Such considerations would necessarily include:

- *General market conditions*:
    - customers' needs and requirements;
    - the size of potential markets;
    - market growth rate and principal trends;
    - structure of customer groups and segments;
    - buying behaviour.

- *Potential competitive reactions*:
    - nature, type, strengths and weaknesses of competition;
    - strategies, tactics and positioning – source and deployment of advantage;
    - barriers to entry and exit.

- *The attractiveness of the innovation/business concept*:
    - current satisfactions/dissatisfactions with current offerings;
    - reactions to the new venture product/service mix;
    - pricing expectations and competitive levels and responses.

- *The creation and maintenance of competitive advantage*:
  - resource requirements for start-up and subsequent refinement;
  - structure of the network in which the venture will be located;
  - sources of investment capital and attitudes to the venture and its operating context;
  - power and influence of existing distribution channels.

Assessing the competition

There is considerable evidence to suggest that established businesses are in a strong position relative to new entrepreneurial entrants (Shepherd and Shanley, 1998). They have gained experience in operating their businesses. They may well have established themselves in a secure network of relationships with customers and suppliers. They face lower risks and so their cost of capital is usually lower – and they may have an established output volume that gives them scale economies.

Despite these considerable advantages, many new ventures do compete effectively against established, even entrenched players. They identify and exploit new opportunities despite the presence of experienced competition. There is always, it seems, a better way of doing things by adding and releasing value in the product/service offering. There are a variety of reasons why existing businesses leave gaps in the market that the innovative entrepreneurial venture can exploit:

- established businesses fail to see and appreciate new opportunities;
- new opportunities are thought to be too small;
- cultural inertia;
- technological inertia;
- competition and anti-trust actions by government which favour new market entrants.

The point that needs to be emphasised here is that it is imperative to anticipate likely competitive retaliation and to have prepared for a considered response. Scenario planning can be of considerable help here. It is the naive or the foolish that believe that competition will be slow or unable to act. The list of factors to consider will depend on the industrial and market context of the venture but is likely to include the following principal issues:

- the number, size, quality, composition and character of competition;
- their major advantages and disadvantages;
- the strategies deployed and realised;
- sources of competitive advantage.

Pre-start planning and assessment

The length and time of this stage will obviously depend on the specific business opportunity and the characteristics and objectives of the new venture. The type and nature of finance required will be a major determinant here. Deakins (1999) embellishes this point by stating:

> If formal venture capital is required, raising such finance may take some time, because of due diligence procedures (12 months), as well as research and preparation . . . If informal or business angel finance is sought, this will still involve a search and matching process

by the entrepreneur before a suitable investor may be found (Mason and Harrison, 1995). Even raising bank finance can entail a search procedure and time to find sufficient bank finance and the best terms and conditions.

Finding the right management team and deciding on the mix of personalities with the talent and commitment to take the venture to the market may well take some considerable time.

Market entry – trial run or commercialisation?

This may be a difficult stage in that many founders/entrepreneurs in the business creation process cannot undertake a trial run without actually being in business. This of course will depend on the venture and the nature of the product offering. The benefits of a trial run could prove to be considerable as it will provide an endorsement (or rejection) of the earlier research undertaken.

Further, the venture key players may learn new and important information on buyer behaviour and attitudes that were hard to discern in the previous stages. (For an example of this, note how the marketing and launch of commercial digital television has had to change in the light of consumer behaviour that took the major companies by surprise.) The sort of issues here will of course be venture specific but may well include the following questions:

- Does the market segment respond to the trial run in the way it was predicted it would?
- Are there any adjustments to be made to the distribution channels?
- Is the credibility merry-go-round established, or are there faults and weaknesses that need correcting and at what cost?

It is as well to note also that the role of serendipity is often an underplayed factor in the start-up and business creation process and it has scarcely been acknowledged, let alone researched, in entrepreneurial development and strategies. The available evidence demonstrates that chance is only one element. The entrepreneur must be prepared to exploit opportunities, recognise and take advantage of them.

Clearly there is going to be a strong relationship between the structure and nature of entry barriers in the market in question and the ability or otherwise in providing a trial run.

Post-entry development – refinements and the acquisition of resources

By this point, the previous stages in the business creation process will have supplied the founder/entrepreneur with much valuable information. As Deakins (1999) rightly notes:

Early stage development is a crucial phase for the novice entrepreneur. The entrepreneur is naive and must learn quickly to understand customers, suppliers, cash-flow and how to deal with other stakeholders in the new business . . . One of the most important issues that a new business faces is credibility. Being new, especially if markets are competitive, means that customers have to take quality on trust, that suppliers will be unwilling to give trade credit and that banks will be unwilling to extend significant credit facilities.

This is a view endorsed by Beaver and Jennings (1995), who note that:

> There is nothing automatic about the birth and development of a winning small business. It has to be planned and managed from the top against a seemingly endless array of internal and external constraints.

In addition to achieving credibility, the establishment of early stage networks (Fletcher, 1999) can be crucial in the development and market acceptance of new ventures.

When it comes to refining the product/service offering and industry position of the new enterprise at this stage, the acquisition of resources is frequently badly managed, with the sad result that too many would-be successful small firms begin their trading existence undercapitalised. Subsequent attempts to create and reinforce the ingredients of differential advantage may well be severely undermined as a consequence.

Although the financial complexion of the business is vitally important, the acquisition of resources involves more than simply questions about money. It goes without saying that to interpret resources only as money is to risk falling at the first hurdle.

The mix of resources necessary for successful trading includes both tangible and intangible elements. Tangible resources include the quality and location of plant and premises, the age and condition of machinery and equipment and the experience and talents of the key players. Intangible resources include such aspects as knowledge, skill levels, motivation and abilities and the quality of business relationships. The qualitative as well as the quantitative character of all resources should be uppermost in the mind of the founder/entrepreneur.

To conclude this section, let us be mindful of the observation by Birley (1996), who notes that:

> A new business entering a hostile environment is a delicate entity – and that the process of assembling the resources is critical.

Methods and opportunities in the business creation and establishment process

There are other methods open to the aspiring small business practitioner other than start-up, which will be briefly discussed in this section. The first is to buy an existing business – invariably called a going concern. This may be either undertaken at arm's length from a third party or related to career employment, such as a management buy-out or buy-in. Another very popular method is to negotiate and acquire a franchise.

Acquiring an existing business

The particular attraction of buying an existing business is that it already has an established customer base and a commercial history which can be evaluated for both its past performance and its future promise. The objective here is to purchase a business with a good trading record, for a consideration that reflects open market value, having regard for the potential that can be realised through the efforts and abilities that the acquiring entrepreneur will invest in it.

If a business is being purchased with the objective of wealth creation and business development, then the acquiring entrepreneur must have a strategic perspective in which he or she knows how added value will be achieved and maintained. The following lists, while not attempting to be comprehensive, examine the main advantages and disadvantages of this method.

Attractions:
- Time, cost and energy of business establishment are saved. Risk should be substantially reduced.
- Resources and capabilities are available for examination – and known in advance.
- Commercial history and track record may make financing easier.
- Established customer base and stakeholder links exist.

Disadvantages:
- The purchaser will inherit any ill-will from the existing business – despite hopes and promises to the contrary.
- The opportunity to add or release value may well involve establishing a new culture and precedents set by the previous owner.
- Employee standards and profile may need changing.
- Established sources of supply may not necessarily be the best.
- There will be issues of modernisation and investment in new technology and plant.
- The consideration paid may not reflect the improvements expected.

Acquiring a going concern is for many nascent entrepreneurs an atypical activity. Therefore the situation demands that professional advice be sought. There are financial, technical, legal, operational, strategic, human and valuation issues in the acquisition process that demand impartial and expert assistance.

Management buy-outs and buy-ins

Both management buy-outs (MBOs) and management buy-ins (MBIs) involve the purchase and transfer of the equity of a company by (usually) the existing management team, invariably financed by a venture capital institution.

MBOs and MBIs have become the single biggest product for the UK venture capital industry throughout the 1980s and early 1990s. Figures from the Centre for Management Buy-Out Research at the University of Nottingham recorded some 5000 MBOs during the period 1979–2000, with an aggregate deal value of over £32 billion.

There were also 1489 MBIs worth £17.5 billion over the same period. There have been many variations on the basic buy-out, in which the top executive managers, (normally some three to eight individuals) take shares in the equity, such as:

- *employee buy-outs*, in which employees are given the opportunity to invest along-side management;
- *'key' employee buy-outs*, in which a layer of key employees below top management are brought in at the front end alongside management;
- *spin-outs*, in which a financing institution backs a project team to acquire a research and development project from a company, typically where that project is outside the company's mainstream activities:

In each of the above variations, there are three essential prerequisites for a buy-out transaction to be successfully concluded:

- a willing seller;
- an effective management team;
- a financially viable proposition.

This is not the forum for a detailed examination of this method of enterprise development as it is a highly technical and complex subject, especially in terms of its financial requirements and management. However, suffice it to say that the process is invariably a long and demanding one, and can rarely be achieved effectively without the experience of professional advice.

Franchising

An accurate and concise introduction to franchising is provided by Colin Barrow (1996) when he states:

> Franchising is something of a halfway house, lying somewhere between entrepreneurship and employment. It holds many of the attractions of running a small business while at the same time eliminating some of the more unappealing risks.

Deakins (1999) also notes that:

> Another entry route . . . not always associated with entrepreneurship is to take on, or take over, a franchise. Franchising still involves new business creation . . . The difference of course is that the franchisor, rather than the franchisee undertakes much of the (business creation) process.

The development and popularity of franchising is comprehensively covered in the small business literature and will not be repeated here. Most detail the advantages and disadvantages for the parties concerned and provide some interesting examples to illustrate the franchising process.

To conclude this section, it is important to note that in taking out a franchise, irrespective of the industry or sector, the business has to embrace a set of rules and procedures which govern its conduct and operations. This will obviously curtail the franchisee's scope for creativity and enterprise and therefore may not offer the same scope for personal satisfaction and independence as the other alternative routes in business creation. However, it must be noted that, despite the considerable disadvantages arising from loss of control in franchises, their popularity has mirrored the growth and popularity of small firms in the economy. The appeal of the reduced risk, while still retaining elements of entrepreneurship, continues to be a powerful motivating factor for many people and the growth of franchising seems likely to continue unabated for some time to come.

Selecting the appropriate legal format

The final section of this chapter is to examine the choices open to the new business proprietor regarding the legal status under which he or she will trade. In some cases there is no choice, as legislation requires the automatic adoption of a particular legal format. For example, some businesses such as certain of the professions can only exist as sole traders or partnerships – they are prohibited from assuming limited liability status.

Apart from the obvious restrictions on the selection of trading format, the choice of status would probably be resolved after evaluating the relative taxation advantages on the one hand and the protection from financial liability on the other.

The principal basic choices available in the UK are:

- sole trader/proprietor;
- partnership;
- (private) limited liability company.

There are in fact other options available, including limited partnerships and companies limited by guarantee. However, in numerical terms these are relatively uncommon and attention will therefore be focused on the three main choices listed above. The discussion will be kept deliberately brief and concentrate on the principal issues as this is a subject that is comprehensively covered throughout the small business management and commercial law literature.

Sole trader

The sole trader or proprietor is a particularly attractive form of legal status for a new business. The benefits include a minimum of formalities and legal requirements. The individual selecting this format retains all the business profits, is able to set all the business expenses against earnings for tax purposes, is not required to make any public disclosure of trading figures and, typically, will receive favourable tax treatment in the early years of the business.

However, because there is no legal distinction between the business and the sole trader, the sole trader is totally responsible, to the extent of his or her personal assets, for the liabilities of the business.

Advantages:	*Disadvantages*:
Simplicity	Lack of experience/ability
Freedom of choice	Potential lack of capital
Full profits	Limited growth
Fewer legal restrictions	
Ease of discontinuance	
Tax advantages	

Partnerships

A partnership enjoys many of the advantages of the sole trader and there are very few restrictions and legal formalities in the creation of a partnership. All that is needed is for two or more people to agree to carry on a business together, intending to share the profits. The law will then recognise the existence of a partnership.

Most of the points mentioned above for the sole trader status apply to partnerships. All the partners are personally liable for the debts of the business even if those debts were incurred by one partner's mismanagement or dishonesty without the other partner(s)' knowledge. Even death may not release a partner from his/her obligations and, in some circumstances, the estate can remain liable.

It is vital, therefore, before entering a partnership, to be absolutely sure of your partner(s) and to take legal advice in drawing up the partnership contract. A partnership offers additional advantages in that it may provide access to capital needed for business growth, to complementary skills required within the business and to additional business experience.

Advantages:	*Disadvantages*:
Ease of organising	Mutual unlimited liability
Access to larger capital provision	Organisation of responsibilities/ authority
Taxation advantages	
Combined talents and business acumen	Potential for conflict
Ease of discontinuance	Succession issues

Limited liability company

The main distinction between a limited company and the two forms of business entity already discussed is that it has a legal identity of its own that is separate from the people who own it. This means that, even in liquidation, creditors' claims are restricted to the assets of the company. The shareholders are not liable as individuals for the business debts beyond the paid-up value of their shares – and this is perhaps the principal advantage. This applies even if the shareholders are working directors, unless the company has been trading fraudulently or wrongfully.

Limited liability companies are required to appoint directors and this may form the basis of a simple management structure. Generally it is easier to raise capital to expand and develop the business because of the greater simplicity of equity participation; also, its longer-term existence is not threatened by the demise or bankruptcy of any one person.

The disadvantages associated with limited companies are that they are more complicated to organise and more expensive to establish. The company accounts must be audited and are subject to public disclosure.

Advantages:	*Disadvantages*:
Limited liability	Expensive to establish
Perpetual life	Subject to corporate taxation
Ease of ownership transfer	Legal requirements for accounting and disclosure
Ease of expansion	
Size no real barrier	Profits divided by shareholders
Potential for business growth	

Concluding remarks

There is no one way to start a business, no set formulae and no simplistic recipes to guarantee success.

There are many ways to prepare for business creation and, for those who choose to follow the stages discussed earlier in this chapter, there is more likelihood of avoiding at least some of the pitfalls. This approach constantly challenges the questions of how to establish business viability and sustain competitive advantage.

For many individuals, starting and managing a small business venture may not be the best answer to their personal circumstances. Unemployment, for example, might be better answered by retraining and a willingness to be mobile, rather than risking everything in a new enterprise. The wrong decision could erode valuable personal assets and leave those involved financially and psychologically marooned at a critical point in their lives.

CASE ILLUSTRATION 2.1

Starting and managing a business

Christopher Wray Lighting

Many people take temporary jobs to earn sufficient money to fund what they really want to do. However, few make such a success with a sideline that they turn it into a multi-million pound business.

Christopher Wray did just that with his business Christopher Wray Lighting. Having started out selling decorative lights from a market stall on London's Kings Road, he now manufactures and sells lights through 18 shops in Britain and Japan.

The son of an agricultural engineer, Wray grew up in Scarborough, North Yorkshire and was sent away to school in Abingdon, Oxford, at 11. He was not academic but had passions for art, swimming and magic and displayed his entrepreneurial talents early. He bought conjuring tricks with money made from selling newts from the bottom of his garden to schoolmates. He also made money at children's parties performing magic tricks, finally abandoning his A-level studies, leaving school at 17 determined to become a magician and working with Windy Blow, a clown. He progressed rapidly to singing and acting and started to develop a promising career as an actor, when he was offered parts in the television series *Z Cars* and *Black Beauty*. Wray started to look for props for repertory theatres when he was performing in the Home Counties. By his own admission, he had no business aspirations but was forced to find an alternative way to earn some cash during the actors' strike in the early 1960s.

Wray states:

My agent told me that it was difficult to find me work and suggested that I find a sideline. A friend suggested that I sell all the rubbish that I had collected in antique shops at a market just off Carlyle Square in London.

Wray paid £10 a week for a stall and among the items he was selling was an old brass oil lamp that sold almost immediately. He went to find some replacements, which he located in junk shops at the Fulham end of the Kings Road. These were bought for 25p, duly polished up, and relocated some few hundred yards to his stall where they were sold for £3 each. He says:

> The people at the Chelsea end of the Kings Road would not be seen dead frequenting the shops at the Fulham end, so I was doing them a service.

Wray was soon doing a good trade in oil lamps and employed 'runners' to locate new stock. The business was soon turning over £45 a week, with very healthy margins.

In 1965, he opened a shop in a former post office on the Kings Road. He could not afford the £4000 to acquire the freehold, so he had no alternative but to rent it for £750 a year, which is what he managed to take in the first week of trading.

Wray had collected his best items in anticipation of the opening and surprised himself by making more money by diversifying into electric lighting. He then travelled to flea markets in Paris in search of products and also to Ireland where he was known as 'The Lamp Man' by the tinkers with whom he would haggle over price.

After 2 years of continuing to play parts in television shows while friends minded the shop, he was finding commuting to regional studios very tough and was forced to choose between careers when the directors of a soap opera asked him to move to Leeds to play a leading role. Lamps won the day.

Wray moved into manufacturing when he was unable to locate the glass shades or chimneys for his lamps. He found old mouldings at Hailwood and Ackroyd, a Yorkshire glass works, and got the company to produce shades for him:

> They took some persuading. It was an old business and the people there were convinced that there was no demand because the designs had gone out of date 40 years before. I did a phenomenal business selling spare parts, while other dealers were still hunting around for old lamps.

In 1967, Wray opened a second shop to handle the growing spare parts business and 3 years after that he had opened a workshop and was employing 10 people. The business was generating sales of £1 million.

In 1975, Wray established a shop in Kilkenny, Ireland, and 3 years later he opened one in Bristol to add to the 10 shops that he had on the Kings Road by the end of the decade as well as other regional stores and glassworks in Wakefield.

Last year (2000), the company made profits of £564 000 on sales of £8.1 million. It now employs 230 people, manufacturing half the products that it sells, including modern lighting alongside the more traditional items. Turnover is also assisted by a telesales business.

Wray states that entrepreneurial achievement comes from identifying a market niche and a lot of grafting:

> The key is to grow the business and not to get in hock by overextending yourself from the start, he says. Keeping my word has always ensured that the future was bright.

Source: Adapted from Steiner (1999)

Starting and managing a business

Bookham Technology and Andrew Rickman

If there was ever a textbook illustration of a successful business start-up then Dr Andrew Rickman and his company Bookham Technology would seem to be the classic example. A graduate in mechanical engineering from Imperial College London, Rickman appears to have planned his route to entrepreneurial success with great care and precision. First he got to know the culture and operating context of Silicon Valley while working for an American high technology company and then he went to work for a seed-corn investment fund.

In 1988, he founded Bookham Technology, named after the Surrey town where he grew up. The business was started in a room above his garage to pioneer the concept of silicon circuits using light and optics rather than electronics. The technology allows Internet access and data networks to work faster and more efficiently.

Rickman carefully researched the market first and was determined to devise the technology that his potential customers required, rather than starting with the technology and trying to find a market for it, which he describes as 'the typical business model'.

Rickman developed his skill base considerably before starting Bookham Technology as a full-time venture. While he was developing the technology and investigating the market and its characteristics, he completed a PhD in integrated optics at Surrey University and an MBA from Cranfield. 'It was not a restful time', states Rickman with some understatement.

The new technology attracted both interest and support as the company grew during the 1990s, attracting 18 research and development awards from the Department of Trade and Industry. The big break came when the US giant Cisco Systems invested £20 million in the company.

Bookham is now based in purpose-built premises in Oxfordshire in the UK and became a public company in April 2000 when its flotation defied the downturn in high technology and Internet-based shares. The initial issue price of £10 a share has risen to £46 (October 2000), making Rickman a paper billionaire. The company has a market capitalisation of over £5 billion and a FTSE 100 index listing. More importantly, it is winning key orders from organisations such as Marconi for its optical components that offer tremendous improvements in both efficiency and cost reduction.

This case illustration is expanded in Chapter 5.

RESEARCH ILLUSTRATION

New research from Barclays Bank, October 2000

On average, entrepreneurs and small business owner/managers take only 1 week's holiday in their first year of trading and put in 53 hours a week according to the latest research by Barclays Bank. Yet 90% said that they would do it all again.

The research, 'Starting up in Business', reveals that 40% believe that being your own boss is the most important motivation. It also shows that 70% of new business owners are male and some 66% are aged between 25 and 44. However, the number of small firm owners who are under 25 and over 45 has shown a noticeable increase.

References and further reading

Banfield, P., Jennings, P. L. and Beaver, G. (1996) 'Competence-Based Training for Small Firms – An Expensive Failure?', *Long Range Planning*, 29 (1), February, 94–102.

Barrow, C. (1996) 'Franchising', in Burns, P. and Dewhurst, J. (eds), *Small Business and Entrepreneurship*, 2nd edn. Basingstoke: Macmillan, ch. 4.

Barrow, C. and Brown, R. (1997) *Principles of Small Business*. London: ITP.

Beaver, G. and Jennings, P. L. (1995) 'Picking Winners: The Art of Identifying Successful Small Firms', in Hussey, D. E. (ed.), *Rethinking Strategic Management – Ways to Improve Competitive Performance*. Chichester: Wiley, ch. 4, pp. 91–106.

Beaver, G. and Ross, C. (1999) 'Recessionary Consequences on Small Business Management and Business Development: The Abandonment of Strategy?', *The Journal of Strategic Change*, 8 (5), August, 251–261.

Beaver, G. and Ross, C. (2000) 'Enterprise in Recession: The Role and Context of Strategy', *The International Journal of Entrepreneurship and Innovation*, February, 23–31.

Binks, M. and Ennew, C. (1996) 'Financing Small Firms', in Burns, P. and Dewhurst, J. (eds), *Small Business and Entrepreneurship*. Basingstoke: Macmillan, ch. 6.

Birley, S. (1996) 'The Start Up', in Burns, P. and Dewhurst, J. (eds), *Small Business and Entrepreneurship*, 2nd edn. Basingstoke: Macmillan, ch. 2.

Birley, S. and Westhead, P. (1993) 'A Comparison of New Businesses Established by "Novice" and "Habitual" Founders in Great Britain', *International Small Business Journal*, 12 (1), 38–60.

Burns, P. and Dewhurst, J. (eds) (1996) *Small Business and Entrepreneurship*, 2nd edn. Basingstoke: Macmillan.

Cambridge Small Business Research Centre (1992) *The State of British Enterprise*. Cambridge: Department of Applied Economics, University of Cambridge.

Deakins, D. (1999) *Entrepreneurship and Small Firms*, 2nd edn. London: McGraw-Hill.

Fletcher, D. (1999) 'Strategic Networks and Small Firms', unpublished PhD thesis, Nottingham Business School, The Nottingham Trent University.

Hussey, D. E. (1998) *Strategic Management – From Theory to Implementation*, 4th edn. Oxford: Butterworth-Heinemann.

Joyce, P., Seaman, C. and Woods, A. (1996) 'The Strategic Management Styles of Small Businesses', in Blackburn, R. and Jennings, P. L. (eds), *Small Firms – Contributions to Economic Regeneration*. London: Paul Chapman, ch. 6.

Kerr, M. (1998) 'Small Businesses and their Competitive Advantage', unpublished PhD thesis, Brunel University Business School, Brunel University.

Kinsella, R. P., Clarke, W., Coyne, D., Mulvenna, D. and Storey, D. J. (1993) *Fast Growth Firms and Selectivity*. Dublin: Irish Management Institute.

Mason, C. M. and Harrison, R. T. (1995) 'Informal Venture Capital and the Financing of Small and Medium Sized Enterprises', *Small Enterprise Research*, 3 (1), 33–56.

Nayak, A. and Greenfield, S. (1994) 'The Use of Management Accounting Information for Managing Micro-Businesses', in Hughes, A. and Storey, D. J. (eds), *Finance and the Small Firm*. London: Routledge.

Shepherd, D. A. and Shanley, M. (1998) *New Venture Strategy*. London: Sage.

Stanworth, J. and Gray, C. (1991) *Entrepreneurship and Education: Action Based Research with Training Policy Implications in Britain*. Singapore: ENDEC.

Steiner, R. (1999) *My First Break*. London: Sunday Times Publishing and News International.

Storey, D. J., Watson, R. and Wynarczyk, P. (1989) 'Fast Growth Small Businesses: Case Studies of Forty Small Firms in Northern England', Research Paper 67. London: Department of Employment.

Storey, D. J. (1994) *Understanding the Small Business Sector*. London: Routledge.

3

Entrepreneurs, owners and managers

Objectives This chapter seeks to examine the frequently misunderstood, inter-related and frequently conflicting roles of the small business entrepreneur, owner and manager. Each has their different perceptions, objectives, motivations, expectations and organisational positions towards the enterprise and its operating context.

In particular, this chapter seeks to examine:

● some of the principal contributions towards understanding entrepreneurship and business ownership;

● the factors that determine the extent of entrepreneurship, and the nature of the process and its impact on enterprise development;

● the personality attributes, characteristics and motivations of small firm owners and managers, recognising the importance of the distinction between ownership and management and its effects on business growth;

● some of the contemporary research evidence that underpins the above.

Introduction

There is no doubt that the individuals who start and run their own business have become, according to Moss Kanter (1989), the 'new cultural heroes' of the Western world – role models to be copied and admired for their innovation, business acumen, risk-taking and daring sense of purpose.

In Burns and Dewhurst (1996), Paul Burns states:

In the 1980s Britain was having a love affair with small business. You could not open a newspaper without reading about some business success story. In fact the love affair was not so much with small businesses as with their owner-managers, or more particularly, the small number of entrepreneurs who started up small firms, made them grow and perhaps became millionaires in the process.

In the first edition of the same text (Burns and Dewhurst, 1989), Burns also wrote that:

We are fascinated by these entrepreneurs as much because most (small) businesses are born to die or stagnate. It is no wonder that we are fascinated by those few that grow.

Entrepreneurs continue to fascinate a variety of publics including economists, sociologists, psychologists, politicians, historians, anthropologists and enterprise academics.

A second and related focal issue was the publication of the Bolton Report (Bolton, 1971), which provided the first comprehensive investigation into the small business sector and remains the single most important document of its kind ever published in the UK. This focused attention on the role and contribution of small firms (and the people who establish and manage them) and their crucial importance to the economic health and prosperity of the country.

The seminal work by Schumacher (1973), *Small is Beautiful: Economics as if People Mattered*, published 2 years later, also contributed significantly in promoting the value and importance of the small enterprise throughout much of the West.

Perhaps one of the most important contributions of the Bolton Report was its use of international comparisons to raise the question of the role of small firms in economic development. At the time the Bolton Committee was appointed, the prevailing orthodoxy in Britain, at least, was that small firms no longer had much relevance to modern economic progress. A principal finding was that, although small businesses survived in large numbers, their share in economic activity was in decline and that this decline had progressed further and faster in the UK than elsewhere. This, the report stated, was a cause for concern:

> We believe that the health of the economy requires the birth of new enterprises in substantial numbers and the growth of some to a position from which they are able to challenge and supplant the existing leaders of industry. We fear that an economy totally dominated by large firms could not for long avoid ossification and decay . . . This 'seedbed' function, therefore, appears to be a vital contribution of the small firms sector to the long run health of the economy.

Apart from the above, the Bolton Committee also stated that from the evidence they collected:

> As to the social standing of the independent businessman, it is our impression that it may now be lower than it has ever been.

It is over 30 years since the publication of the Bolton Report and much has changed including a considerable amount of research that has been undertaken attempting to categorise and classify the determinants and characteristics of small business ownership and entrepreneurship. This research has sought to discover, *inter alia*, whether there are any clear characteristics shared by the owners and controllers of small firms that distinguish them from other members of the economically active population.

The general conclusion appears to be that there is no simple pattern and that the evidence points to a complex set of interrelated factors that increase or decrease the probability that an individual will become an entrepreneur or owner/controller of a small enterprise. The research on this subject is derived from a number of social science disciplines, prominent among which are psychology, economics, geography and sociology. This is not surprising given the factors likely to influence and determine entrepreneurship, self-employment or business ownership.

The Bolton Committee was quite clear in their perception of the small business owner-managed sector, in that it was *heterogeneous*:

> When we come to look at the human and social factors affecting (small firms), we can see that firms are in fact as varied and individual as the men who founded them.
>
> *Source*: Bolton (1971, p. 22)

In describing the 'human and social characteristics' of the small firm owner/manager, however, the Report emphasised their commonalties. For example, small business founders were likely to be both owners and managers and supported by family. Their closeness to the enterprise, Bolton suggests, explains their involvement, flexibility, particular role in innovation and risk-taking and their fervently guarded sense of independence.

Money, although important to any enterprise and its key players, was not the principal source of motivation, according to the Report. There is a quality of life issue – personal involvement in owning and managing a business led to greater satisfaction on a number of fronts all associated with the notion of independence (Chapter 4 develops this theme further).

Indeed, the Report made a central feature of the need to attain and preserve independence, stating that it was the principal factor that distinguished the small business owner/manager from other businessmen:

> The need for independence sums up a wide range of highly personal gratifications provided by working for oneself and not for anybody else. It embraces many important satisfactions which running a small business provided – the personal supervision and control of staff, direct contact with customers, the opportunity to develop one's own ideas, a strong feeling of personal challenge and an almost egotistical sense of personal achievement and pride – psychological satisfactions which appeared to be much more powerful motivators than money or the possibility of large financial gains.
>
> *Source*: Bolton (1971, p. 24)

As Stanworth and Gray (1991) are correct in reminding us, there are two difficulties implied by this passionately guarded need for independence. First, the growth and development of the business might affect the freedoms and methods enjoyed by the owner-manager should he or she be required to delegate authority to others in the pursuit of external finance. Second, attitudes towards government intervention, regulation and assistance would be hostile if they were perceived to be undesirable or unwarranted measures or intrusions.

The Bolton Report also noted that small business owners and practitioners were less likely to have pursued a formal education than their counterparts in managerial positions in large companies. This was because owner/managers were much more likely to have succeeded their fathers in taking over the firm and that the requirements and competences of the corporate manager were substantially different, necessitating the acquisition and application of political and negotiating skills and capabilities, in order to achieve their desired results and outcomes.

Interestingly, the Report mentioned the *craftsman* as a special category of small businessman, stating:

> There is a small and highly specialised segment of the small firm population: the independent craftsman, who may be defined as self-employed, small scale producers of

articles of high quality in a number of different, usually traditional media. An arbitrary definition of 'the crafts' has been sanctioned by long acceptance: it includes for example, pottery, jewellery, stone masonry, woodwork, calligraphy and glassware, but not say, painting sculpture, fashion design and photography.

Source: Bolton (1971, p. 146)

Stanworth and Gray (1991) interpret this type as someone who resents having to spend time on paperwork and administration even more than the 'usual' owner-manager does. They note that:

> Ideally, he would prefer to spend all his time working with his hands and making things of beauty: the independence achieved through self-employment enable him to express his creativity in a way which working for someone else would not allow. However, his salesmanship is weak and this may represent to the continued viability of the business.

It seems, therefore, that the Bolton Report although emphasising the heterogeneity of small business owner/managers ends up painting a very homogenous picture, identifying an atypical type of self-employed craftsman and highlighting certain key features rather than presenting an alternative and more reflective illustration.

In their authoritative review of the small business owner-manager, Stanworth and Gray (1991) rightly ask whether, in the light of all the research undertaken since the Commission published their findings, has this view changed and what differences have emerged? Also, what are the implications for business creation and development and how should policy initiatives be designed to accommodate such changes? They conclude that:

> There would be little point in considering this question of the nature and characteristics of business owners if it were not for the fact that such knowledge might enable us to gain a better understanding of the way in which economic, educational or other conditions might be manipulated in order to stimulate small business behaviour in a socially and economically beneficial way. We therefore have to ask the question: What stance do the economists take on this matter and in what ways have psychologists and sociologists developed useful and explanatory models of business owner characteristics and behaviour?

Source: Stanworth and Gray (1991, p. 153)

The next part of this chapter examines the three principal perspectives on the characteristics of small business ownership and entrepreneurship – psychological, sociological and economic.

A psychological perspective

The majority of studies that adopt a psychological perspective have concentrated on attempting to identify the personality traits and characteristics of the entrepreneur. The focus in the majority of these studies is firmly on the separation of the entrepreneur from the small business owner, a point that will be discussed later in this chapter.

A critical review of the principal research studies that have purported to identify entrepreneurial traits is provided by Stanworth and Gray (1991). They effectively summarise the literature in this area and identify the following traits as being the most commonly discussed and promoting the highest level of agreement:

- need for achievement (McClelland, 1961);
- locus of control (Brockhaus, 1982; Caird, 1990; Chell *et al.*, 1991);
- risk-taking propensity (Quinn, 1980; Carland *et al.*, 1984; Chell *et al.*, 1991);
- need for independence (Bolton, 1971; Collins and Moore, 1970; Kets de Vries, 1977);
- innovative and creative behaviour (Moss Kanter, 1983, 1989; West and Farr, 1990).

There has been robust and sustained criticism of the many attempts to identify personality traits as characteristics of entrepreneurs. These criticisms range over a variety of issues including the need to identify constellations of personality characteristics rather than individual traits, methodological difficulties inherent in the identification of personality characteristics and the conflicting findings of different studies (Chell and Haworth, 1988; Chell *et al.*, 1991).

Stanworth and Gray (1991, p. 158) state that:

> This list of difficulties is now so long and formidable – it might be argued that this is sufficient reason to abandon the trait approach.

The most serious criticism of this approach challenges the assumption that entrepreneurial behaviour is a function of the individual's personality, rather than a response to the environment, context or industry in which the business is operating (see, for example, Goss, 1991). This in turn leads to the inevitable conclusion that the trait approach to entrepreneurship and small business management can at best offer only a partial analysis of behaviour.

In summary, the psychological perspective has resulted in some productive research that has produced some agreement on an amalgam of personality traits which might characterise entrepreneurs and enable the identification of the entrepreneurial personality.

An economic perspective

The primary interest of those examining small business owners and entrepreneurs from an economic perspective is to promote and advance the understanding of the impact of entrepreneurial behaviour on the economy. Stanworth and Gray (1991) ask:

> What function does a business owner/entrepreneur serve in an economy? It is too easy to offer a simplistic answer to such a question when economists since the early 18th Century have put forward differing, closely argued views (Herbert and Link, 1988; Chell *et al.*, 1991).
>
> An emerging view of particular interest is that economists have become increasingly interested in and made shrewd observations about, the crucial characteristics that differentiate types of business owner, and in particular those that characterise the successful entrepreneur.

The first study from this perspective is often attributed to Cantillon, who, as early as the mid 18th century, identified the entrepreneur as someone who confidently pursues profitable exchanges even when faced with uncertain market conditions. He is also credited as being the first to suggest that an entrepreneur can be characterised as both a risk-taker and an innovator and it is these and related issues that have been debated by economists to the present day (see for example Schumpeter, 1934; McClelland, 1961; Carland *et al.*, 1984).

While several schools of thought have emerged over time, the common factor among all of them has been the pursuit of an understanding of the entrepreneur as an instrument of macro-economic change (Hornaday, 1990). More recently, the so-called enterprise culture (see Chapter 11), fostered and developed in the UK during the late 1980s and early 1990s, was underpinned by the assumption that free market economies send signals about economic opportunities to those individuals alert enough to observe them and with the will to act on them (Goss, 1991; Carr, 1999).

In reviewing the work of the economic school of entrpreneurship and business ownership/control, it is very clear that while many researchers have used the term entrepreneur to refer to any business founder or owner, the focus of much of the work in this area has shifted to consider those characteristics which typify entrepreneurial acts (Stanworth and Gray, 1991). In other words, there has been an increasing tendency to separate the 'entrepreneur' – and particularly the successful entrepreneur – from the 'small business owner'.

In this work, the entrepreneurial characteristics that have been identified include innovation, with the entrepreneur being recognised as the agent for change, the willingness to take risks and the ability to make confident, judgemental decisions (Casson, 1982). Indeed there is now some consensus that there is a distinct set of behaviours that characterise entrepreneurial acts and an agreement that such behavioural characteristics are both rare and unusual:

> The rarely gifted person has the power of foresight, is firm and resolute even in the face of disaster, and is able to lead and motivate others.
>
> *Source*: Chell *et al.* (1991)

One fundamental issue in this economic debate is whether all small business owners behave entrepreneurially on particular occasions or whether only a minority might be accurately classified as entrepreneurs. If, as Peter Drucker (1985) has argued, the latter is more precise, the value and utility of the work in this area to those seeking an enhanced understanding of the role of entrepreneurship and its contribution to the development of the small business sector is questionable.

Perhaps more critically, the fact that many of these entrepreneurial characteristics can only be identified with certainty in retrospect raises many poignant questions as to the value and contribution of this identification for those looking to provide assistance in small business creation and enterprise development.

In summary, the contribution of the economists appears to indicate the presence of a distinctive set of behaviours and characteristics which affect entrepreneurial actions and which provide some useful insights into the relationship of the entrepreneur on the economy. It is clear from much of this work that the majority of small business owner/controllers are not entrepreneurs and also that a psychological examination of the nature of entrepreneurship is required if a more balanced understanding is to be achieved (Chell *et al.*, 1991).

A sociological perspective

The majority of studies adopting a sociological perspective have principally concentrated on attempts to differentiate between different categories of entrepreneur and small business owner/controller in order to construct typologies which assist in the contextualisation of the operating environment and the behaviour of the individual. These research studies have sought to examine the social relationships that lie at the heart of the small firm and which allow for a greater tolerance of diversity in small enterprises.

The work of Chell and her colleagues (Chell *et al.*, 1991) offers convincing evidence in support of the following profile of the prototypical entrepreneur:

- opportunistic;
- adventurous;
- ambitious and ideas driven;
- innovative;
- proactive;
- a high-profile image maker;
- a tendency to adopt a broad financial strategy.

It was found by the research team that some business owners (classified as 'caretakers') possessed none of these characteristics, while some others that were studied exhibited a mix. The end result was that a model of small enterprise owner/entrepreneur was developed which classified the entrepreneur, the quasi-entrepreneur, the administrator and the caretaker as the basis of the small firm owner/practitioner.

There have been numerous further attempts to develop and categorise the types of small business owner/entrepreneur, prominent among which is the work of Stanworth and Curran (1982), Dunkleberg and Cooper (1982) and Scase and Goffee (1983).

The three types of business owner that these studies refer to can be summarised as *craft* owners, who are primarily concerned with personal satisfaction, *promoters*, who want to achieve personal wealth and financial reward, and *professional managers*, who are principally driven to construct a successful business which they can manage for both financial gain as well as personal satisfaction. When these are compared, it becomes clear that one of the principal determinants of the type of business owner is the motivations and drives of the small firm owner – regarded by many as critical to an incisive understanding of the performance and behaviour of small firms.

However, the sociological school of business ownership is not without its critics, who have stated that the typologies offered were too simplistic and/or produced contradictory findings and were not methodologically sound (Chell *et al.*, 1991).

To conclude this section, it seems that there is considerable value in the contention advanced by Hornaday (1990) that it is time to leave the search for the entrepreneur and to:

Focus on the legitimate problems of the effects of owner intentions and capabilities on the performance of small firms.

There is much truth in this, for if Drucker's rigorous conditions for the identification of entrepreneurial behaviour are applied then 'very few small business owners, in the UK at least, would merit the title of entrepreneur' (Goss, 1991). Goss concludes that it is preferable to use the term 'entrepreneur' in its loosest and widest form, identifying entrepreneurial behaviour and activity as and when appropriate.

A final consideration – entrepreneur or small business owner?

Michael Gerber (1995) in the second of his highly successful books on small business and entrepreneurship wrote:

There is a myth in this country [the USA] – I call it the E-Myth – which says that small businesses are started by entrepreneurs risking capital to make a profit. This is simply not so. The real reasons that people start businesses have little to do with entrepreneurship. In fact this belief in the entrepreneurial myth is the most important factor in the devastating rate of small business failure today.

Gerber is very clear that there is a substantial difference between the entrepreneur, the manager and the owner, a view that has been endorsed by many writers including Birley (1996), Jennings and Beaver (1997) and Beaver and Lashley (1998). This theme runs through many of the chapters in this book, notably Chapters 4, 5 and 8.

Birley (1996) cites the work of Carland *et al.* (1984) who focus on the essential factors of growth and enterprise development in distinguishing the small business venture from the entrepreneurial venture and the small business owner from the entrepreneur. Their classification is given below:

- A *small business venture* is any business that is independently owned and operated, not dominant in its field and does not engage in any new marketing or innovative practices.
- An *entrepreneurial venture* is one that engages in at least one of Schumpeter's four categories of behaviour. That is, the principal goals of an entrepreneurial venture are profitability and growth and the business is characterised by innovative strategic practices.
- A *small business owner* is an individual who establishes and manages a business for the principal purpose of furthering personal goals. The business must be the primary source of income and will consume the majority of one's time and resources. The owner perceives the business as an extension of his or her personality, intricately bound with family needs and desires.

- An *entrepreneur* is an individual who establishes and manages a business for the principal purpose of profit and growth. The entrepreneur is characterised principally by innovative behaviour and will employ strategic management practices in the business.

Birley and Westhead (1993) also go on to state that:

> The inherent simplicity of these classifications is appealing, yet they are based on two important assumptions: that is possible to dichotomise the whole of the sector by simple motivations and personal drives which, since they do not change, allow us to predict the size and nature of the eventual firm. Recent research conducted in a variety of countries and cultures does not support this view . . . When owner-managers were asked about their reasons for starting their business – seven components were identified.

These components are:

- a need for approval;
- a need for independence;
- a need for personal development;
- welfare considerations;
- perceived instrumentality of wealth;
- tax reduction and indirect benefits;
- following role models.

Birley and Westhead (1993) conclude by stating that:

> These make intuitive sense. More important than this however, they are not mutually exclusive. As we expected, it was possible for entrepreneurs to articulate more than one reason for starting their business. Fine. But does that help us to predict success, to pick winners? Unfortunately not. There was no apparent relationship between the reasons that owner-managers espoused and the subsequent size or performance of their business.

This appears rather too definitive as there must be some limited causal relationship, irrespective of what Birley and Westhead claim. However, the central assertion that there is a major difference between the small business owner and the entrepreneur is a convincing one and has important implications for the design and implementation of enterprise policy as it affects the small business sector (Storey, 1994; Beaver and Jennings, 1995; Beaver and Lashley, 1998; Beaver and Ross, 1999, 2000).

The small business manager

One of the most frequently quoted aspects of the Bolton Report (Bolton, 1971) was the definition that it advanced of the small firm, i.e.:

- relatively small market share;
- independence, in the sense of not being part of a larger enterprise;
- managed by owners or part-owners in a personalised way and not through the medium of a formalised management structure.

The last of these characteristics is now open to challenge both as to its generality and relevance. While the very smallest firms do combine ownership and management within the same individual, this is not the case once the business grows beyond a certain size. There will be some point, depending on the operating context and industry sector, where individuals have to be appointed whose task is, at least in part, to be responsible for the management of others. Since these individuals are often not owners of the business, the concurrence of ownership with management stated by the Bolton Report begins to erode.

Many of the cases contained in this book require this issue (among others) to be addressed and professionally and sensitively accommodated if the business is to progress and develop to its full potential.

Despite the above, the small business literature is dominated by considerations and references to the owner-manager. Probably the best illustration of this is the authoritative review by Curran (1986) of the research undertaken in the 15 years following the publication of the Bolton Report. In Curran's review there are many references to owner-managers but not a single reference to non-owner-managers. Stanworth and Gray (1991) summarise the position clearly when they state:

> This reflects the emphasis of small firm researchers and our consequent ignorance of the role and significance of small firm managers who are not owners. It is only in very recent times – that is, since the Curran review – that the role of the small firm non-owning manager has come to be recognised at all. This may reflect the changing emphasis in research and policy towards smaller firms . . . In the last few years there has been a greater concern with faster growing small firms where non-owning managers are of greater importance.

What is very clear is that the strategic and organisational issues facing the new small firm – especially those new enterprises with ambitions for growth – are fundamentally different from those facing the larger corporate business. Nowhere is this point made more graphically than by Edith Penrose (1959), whose widely quoted observation is now part of small business folklore:

> The differences in the administrative structure of the very small and very large firm are so great that in many ways it is hard to see that the two species are of the same genus . . . We cannot define a caterpillar and then use the same definition for a butterfly.
>
> *Source*: Penrose (1959, p. 19)

This point has been emphasised and re-stated by many prominent writers and researchers since the seminal contribution by Penrose, including Storey (1984), Storey *et al.* (1987), Birley (1996) and Deakins (1999). In part it was the inability and naiveté of the business support infrastructure and those responsible for small enterprise policy generally to appreciate this fundamental issue that led Storey and his research team to state that:

> The recent major upsurge of interest in small firms amongst governments caught researchers unawares. Unfortunately it has meant that public policies to promote small firms have moved well in advance of research. Instead of public policy being grounded

on thorough empirical research, it has in many countries, taken the form of ill-formed acts of faith.

Source: Storey *et al.* (1987)

To contextualize the role of the non-owning manager in the small business (some of the more recent texts and articles refer to these individuals as 'professional managers', which can be an inappropriate and misleading term) requires the analysis to be placed, at least initially, in the more familiar knowledge of the owner/manager. This necessitates attention to two principal issues: first, the personal and socio-economic characteristics of the founders of small firms and their motivations for starting the enterprise; second, and most important in the current context, their styles of management, relationships with employees, forms of internal organisation and ability to plan for competitive advantage.

It is simplistic and naive to think of the owner/manager as the sole managerial resource – consideration must also be given as to how such individuals organise and manage the process of business development through the recruitment and employment of non-owner/managers. This theme is further developed especially in Chapters 4 and 5 that examine the issues of management development and strategic management.

It is apparent from much of the research undertaken in small firms that growth creates significant management and organisational problems (Storey, 1994; Jennings and Beaver, 1997). The principal dimensions of this relate to the need to develop a balanced managerial team, which combines the appropriate functional skills and abilities, with the requirement to create an organisational structure that supports an appropriate delegation of decision-making.

Although this is very well supported in much of the contemporary research studies and literature on small business and enterprise development, there are many different ways of organising the operations and strategic posture of any given small firm and an even wider variety of small business owners and managers with varying motivations, expectations and capabilities.

Many studies have examined the attitudes of owners of small firms to managerial and professional employees and have found a number of interesting and sometimes disturbing findings. Some have found that owners were often reluctant to delegate responsibilities to appointed non-owning (professional) managers because they were fearful that such individuals would start up in business in competition with them, or undermine their authority and position. Other work found that attempts by managers to change working methods and practices led to friction with the business owners who frequently interpreted this as a criticism of their business and management abilities (Banfield *et al.*, 1996; Beaver and Jennings, 1996, 2001; Burns and Dewhurst, 1996).

Cultural, professional and organisational differences between owners and managers in small firms have all been extensively reported as having the potential to generate friction and prejudice growth and enterprise development. However, the presence of small business managers is important in facilitating the expansion of some small businesses and the ability (of the owner/entrepreneur) to construct, maintain and reward a balanced managerial team has been found to be a major factor in the successful growth of many small firms (Jennings and Beaver, 1997).

Concluding remarks

Storey (1994) states that, in attempting to achieve an understanding of the small business sector, there are certain themes which continually emerge from the research that is reviewed and which are highly relevant to the small business entrepreneur, owner and manager.

Case illustration 3.1, taken from Storey's work, provides a brief summary of these themes.

CASE ILLUSTRATION 3.1

The dos and don'ts for small firms

Dos	Don'ts
1 Invest in your own business.	1 Don't take out large sums in the good years.
2 Talk to the bank.	2 Don't surprise the bank.
3 Get private sector advice.	3 Don't blame everyone except yourself.
4 Keep and use current financial data to make key decisions.	
5 Be prepared to consider selling equity.	
6 Grow if you want to survive.	
7 If you want to grow, the key selements are: – product innovation; – management team building; – personnel policy; – marketing.	

In commenting on the above, Storey makes the following observations, which have obvious and significant implications for both entrepreneurs and owners – and the managers that they recruit to assist in running the business:

- Businesses which survive and grow are those where the owner/entrepreneur has invested heavily in the business and has been frugal in removing moneys from the business for personal consumption – as this could lead to under-capitalisation.
- Small firms should seek to maintain good relationships with their banks and maintain regular dialogue – keeping them aware of relevant developments.
- Obtain good quality private sector advice – notably from accountants, banks and solicitors. The research considered by Storey suggests that this is very influential in explaining why some businesses survive and others do not.

- The reluctance of business owners to consider the sale of a proportion of their equity is generally based on their assumption that it would lead to a dilution of their managerial control. The evidence suggests that where the equity is shared the business is likely to exhibit rather faster growth – a point that could be of real significance in attracting and retaining the required professional managerial talent to develop and expand the firm. (This point has been endorsed by Beaver and Ross, 1999, 2000.) The implication on the right-hand side of the above table is that, even where owners are considering selling equity, the price they demand is unrealistically high.
- It is unwise for owners to assume that by not growing there is a higher probability of their business surviving. The research evidence in Storey's text that he considers from the USA suggests that the reverse is the case. Those small firms that grow in terms of employment are more likely to survive than those which do not grow.

Although growth is clearly not an objective for the majority of small firms, certainly in the UK, those that set out to achieve enterprise development appear to share four common characteristics:

1 There is a shift in the product/service markets in which they operate. Rarely are they in the same marketplace a decade later. There are implications here for the ability of the key players to undertake the required strategic positioning to achieve the necessary business posture for the enterprise and achieve sustainable competitive advantage.

2 The ability to develop managerial teams appears to be a key ingredient of the successful business. Businesses which grow are more likely to recruit individuals who are managers and who have previously worked in large firms and to recruit from outside, rather than to promote internally. This point is endorsed by Grieve-Smith and Fleck (1987) in their study of high-technology firms in Cambridge, in the UK.

3 Businesses with between 10 and 50 employees have the greatest difficulty in the recruitment of staff; their personnel procedures are often weak and this is a substantial barrier that has to be overcome to achieve growth and development. Many studies have acknowledged the real problems facing small firms in particular in their search for suitably qualified, capable people (see, for example, Beaver and Harris, 1996).

4 More rapidly growing small firms generally have particular expertise in marketing when the business is started.

Source: Storey (1994, p. 310)

CASE ILLUSTRATION 3.2

Entrepreneurship – an illustration from Charles Handy

Charles Handy's new book, entitled *The New Alchemists* and written with his wife Elizabeth, examines the origins and development of 29 entrepreneurs that fitted his definition and perception of the concept – what Handy calls 'alchemists'

– the people who see a way of turning metaphorical base metal into gold or of creating something out of nothing.

The book includes the famous role models of the current age – Richard Branson, Terence Conran, Tim Waterstone – as well as the less well known, such as Mapi Lucchesi, who runs a translation and voice-over business and has over 1500 linguists and actors on her books. Other less well-known alchemists include Stephen Woodams, who runs a pioneering landscaping and florist business, and Dee Dawson, who started the first residential clinic for anorexics in Britain.

According to Handy, three characteristics defined them. They were dedicated, even passionate, different and determined to make a difference and dogged – prepared for the sheer hard slog that is involved in starting and accomplishing something. These individuals were not in business primarily for the money (although money is important), but for the concept, the fulfilment and the idea. They had something to prove and something that was of major importance to them. For Tim Waterstone, it was (21 years ago) a new way of selling books and for Richard Branson it was his frustration with the bad deals he was getting as a customer in music, on airlines, in personal finance and more recently in car purchasing.

Handy reports that Branson:

> Did not complain and started his own business to show the way it should be done. Only if you are passionate about an idea can you endure the tough times and put up with the setbacks because there are always failures along the way – and put your whole life at risk, because that is what it can take.

Handy has an interesting comment about risk and career choice and its perspective by his alchemists:

> Risk in fact, does not feel like risk if you are passionate – it's the only thing you can bear to do. If you are wise you will try to do it with someone else's money, usually your creditors'. You are passionate because you want to make a difference and because you feel different, so you have to make your own mark on the world. Not for these alchemists the sensible career in the large organisation however exciting this option might be to some. These alchemists are fleas, they live outside the institutions and if they do join them at first to learn their trade, they escape as soon as they can. The are alchemists not careerists.

In his examination of what made these people behave in the way they did, Handy notes that two factors stood out. The first is what he describes as the 'second-child syndrome'. Two-thirds of his sample were the second or third child in their family. He is not the first commentator to notice that second and third children are treated differently – and often very differently – to the first born. In many families the parents are less strict and exercise less control with such children. They are frequently allowed to experiment more and their parents are more disposed to moderate risk-taking. They are allowed more space and learn to be more independent, make mistakes and correct them and acquire self-confidence at an early age.

The alchemists that the Handys studied were also fortunate to be given a nugget of confidence in their formative teenage years, something that Freud called the 'golden seed' syndrome. Someone, perhaps a teacher or a first boss told them that they were special in some way. The example of Dee Dawson is cited. She did not distinguish herself at school and had little self-confidence until her biology teacher told her that she had secured the best grades in the whole region in her biology exams. 'Then I knew that I was clever', she said, and that nugget of self-worth has stuck with her for the rest of her life.

Handy reports on the example of Oswald Boateng, the Ghanaian designer and tailor, and tells how his whole family constantly insisted that he was going to be the successful one – he was the third child – and they did everything to support him. Boateng endured two bankruptcies, a divorce and the break-up of his business partnership without denting his determination.

School appears not to be an important factor in the development of Handy's alchemists. If they were bright they seemed to have gone through the system, passed exams and left. Some found school to be irksome and its restraints frustrating. Others used their schooldays to try out some small business ventures – Julian Richer, for example, bought and sold hi-fi components – or they left as soon as they could – like Richard Branson.

Place and the surrounding environment also have their part to play in shaping the development of the new alchemists. As Handy observes:

> There was something about Athens in the 5th Century, Florence in the 15th Century, Silicon Valley and we believe, Cambridge, Dublin, London and Sydney at the moment. Perhaps Berlin, Glasgow and Barcelona soon. Other studies suggest that for alchemy or entrepreneurship to flourish there has to be a combination of elements in the one place – two or more research based universities to attract the brains and ideas, coupled with a flourishing artistic presence to stimulate the imagination, flexible sources of finance, a good technological and support infrastructure and some uplifting architecture.

There is the obvious yet necessary statement from Handy about the high risks of failure associated with entrepreneurial ventures but it contains an interesting twist on the usual theme:

> Maybe nine out of ten entrepreneurial ventures will fail – look for example at the prospects of many of the dot.com businesses of the moment – but if there are a sufficient number to begin with, enough will survive to keep the economy growing. Failure although uncomfortable, has to be regarded as a learning experience, just as bankruptcy in Silicon Valley is said to be a necessary part of business maturity. Keats coined the phrase, 'negative capability,' meaning the capacity to live with doubt and uncertainty and to keep going in the face of adversity. Entrepreneurs need a big dose of this negative capability if they are to keep going, endure the long hours, the disappointments and the dislocations to their private lives during what seems to the inevitable two years it seems to take for a start-up business to become stable. It also helps at this stage to have a life partner, so long as that partner is committed to the dream as the alchemist is. If he or she is not, then the relationship is almost bound to fail, because there is no room for three – the third being the project.

Entrepreneurs, Handy states do not just dream of what might be, they go out and make it happen. Neither do they go in for deferred gratification meaning that they don't postpone projects until they are richer, wiser or more established. Entrepreneurs are passionate about their dream and they are in a hurry: they do it today, now.

Interestingly, some of Handy's observations about planning and development from his sample of alchemists are worth mentioning here:

> They don't plan much and tend to think short-term, except when bankers demand that they raise their sights. They don't waste time on courses and training, preferring to learn by doing and often failing. Their passion is their charisma and with luck, their enthusiasm is infectious.

To conclude, Handy admits that true entrepreneurship is a rare commodity and that only the few and the gifted have the stuff of alchemy within them – but there is much more going on around us than we give credit for. As an example, he cites the experience of Wharton Business School (one of the most prestigious in the USA) where almost a third of the students leave before the end of their course in order to start their own businesses. He describes these individuals as the 'would-be fleas instead of the aspirational elephants'. There is no doubt that Handy provides some rich and powerful insights into entrepreneurship.

CASE ILLUSTRATION 3.3

Key findings of the MORI report on self-employed professionals (March 2001)

There are approximately 1.6 million self-employed professionals (SEPs) working in the UK and the projections show that there will be 3.2 million by 2010. They represent 6% of the UK working population and contribute £65 billion to the UK economy. However, the evidence collected shows that their voice is unheard, their contribution to the business community remains largely unacknowledged and their services to corporate life are overlooked.

These are some of the findings from a MORI report that was commissioned to investigate the attitudes and beliefs of the SEPs. The report, based on a survey of 500 self-employed professionals, covers a variety of areas including why people become self-employed, how their lives have changed as a result and the degree to which government and official bodies recognise and value self-employed people as a group.

One of the key problems for SEPs is that their very mode of working is individualistic and this militates against traditional collective action. According to the report, SEPs are aware that they lack a voice: their concerns go unheard and their problems remain unanswered. They do not feel supported or listened to by organisations representing small businesses or their individual market contexts.

There are real benefits to be gained from a move to self-employment. The evidence suggests that people think it will make them more productive, better able to innovate and wealthier. Perhaps even more importantly, the move to becoming self-employed provides workers with greater flexibility and a better work–life balance. It also provides a route back into work, as many become self-employed after redundancy.

The move to self-employment has a profound effect on attitudes. It both results from and creates dissatisfaction with traditional structures of support and organisation. There is a lack of support for the self-employed community from government, financial institutions and trade organisations.

The reasons people become self-employed are wide ranging. Some had a long-held desire to work for themselves, while for others being made redundant was the spur required to leave corporate life for good. However, for most people the route to self-employment was conditioned from a dissatisfaction with their previous employment. The variety of reasons cited includes a dislike of their employer and their operating practices, their colleagues, company culture, a hatred of long and inflexible working hours and the pressure of poor management. Some 70% of the sample felt that the absence of office politics was one of the very best aspects of self-employment.

The majority of the sample (some 85%) would take the same decision to become self-employed again. The evidence shows that SEPs are happier and more productive at work, with 78% claiming that working for themselves was about much more than financial rewards. A similar number (85%) felt that their quality of life had improved, felt better motivated and had a more balanced work life. Most stated that they were able to spend more time with their family. Many also found that they had to become more self-disciplined and entrepreneurial and some 66% stated that they had become more personally confident after becoming self-employed.

There are, however, drawbacks to working for yourself. The survey showed SEPs felt the government was not doing enough to reduce the regulations on the self-employed and that the tax system should be fairer. Government was also criticised for not providing effective and relevant training and support. SEPs find it difficult to enact prompt and fair payment for their work and that was cited as a major source of stress. The government passed the Late Payment of Commercial Debts Act in 1998 that allowed small firms to claim interest against their creditors. It is clear from the evidence that this has had a minimal effect as 37% of the survey were not even aware of it. Those that knew of the Act said that it had not made any improvement to their cash flow and stated that they would not charge interest anyway because it would damage their relationship with their customers and clients.

Fundamental to the setting up of a new business has to be sound financial support and advice but the evidence from the survey suggests that the majority received little or no support for their business from banks and financial institutions, especially during the crucial times of establishment. Over half of the SEPs in the survey stated that financial institutions were not supportive to them when their business experienced financial difficulties.

Improvements in information technology are commonly regarded as one of the key enablers in the rise of the SEP sector. While those SEPs in the survey came from a wide variety of sectors and markets, a common fact in their working environment was the emphasis they placed on IT and communications. Some 85% used a computer in the running of the business and 84% have a mobile phone but only 24% had their own company website. This will undoubtedly change rapidly as 61% expected the Internet to become increasingly important to their business success in 2 or 3 years time.

The key findings of the MORI report were as follows:

- *Self-employed professionals lack a voice*:
  - 75% received no support from government;
  - 74% received little or no support from trade bodies;
  - 69% received little or no support for their business from banks and financial institutions.

- *Self-employed professionals like being self-employed*:
  - 70% stated that the absence of office politics was one of the best things about being self-employed;
  - 78% said that they have a better quality of life since becoming self-employed;
  - 90% are fairly or very satisfied with being self-employed;
  - 85% would take the same decision again;
  - 65% felt that they have more time to do the things that they enjoy.

- *Self-employment breeds efficiency and innovation*:
  - 66% feel that being self-employed gives them more time to think;
  - 72% think that they have become more entrepreneurial;
  - 66% have become more confident.

References and further reading

Banfield, P., Jennings, P. L. and Beaver, G. (1996) 'Competence-Based Training for Small Firms – An Expensive Failure?', *Long Range Planning*, 29 (1), February, 94–102.

Beaver, G. and Harris, L. (1996) 'The Hidden Price of the Disposable Workforce: Issues, Contexts and Approaches in the Search for Competitive Advantage – Lessons for the Smaller Enterprise', *Journal of Business Growth and Profitability*, 2 (1), 49–56.

Beaver, G. and Jennings, P. L. (1995) 'Picking Winners: The Art of Identifying Successful Small Firms', in Hussey, D. E. (ed.), *Rethinking Strategic Management – Ways to Improve Competitive Performance*. Chichester: Wiley, ch. 4.

Beaver, G. and Jennings, P. L. (1996) 'The Abuse of Entrepreneurial Power: An Explanation of Management Failure?', *Journal of Strategic Change*, 5 (3), May–June, 151–64.

Beaver, G. and Jennings, P. L. (2001) 'Human Resource Development in Small Firms: The Role of Managerial Competence', *The International Journal of Entrepreneurship and Innovation*, 2 (2), June, 93–101.

Beaver, G. and Lashley, C. (1998) 'Competitive Advantage and Management Development in Small Hospitality Firms: The Need for an Imaginative Approach', *Journal of Vacation Marketing*, 4 (2), 145–60.

Beaver, G. and Ross, E. C. (1999) 'Recessionary Consequences on Small Business Management and Business Development: The Abandonment of Strategy?', *Journal of Strategic Change*, 8 (5), 251–61.

Beaver, G. and Ross, E. C. (2000) 'Enterprise in Recession: The Role and Context of Strategy', *The Journal of Entrepreneurship and Innovation*, 1 (1), February, 23–31.

Birley, S. (1996) 'The Start-Up', in Burns, P. and Dewhurst, J., *Small Business and Entrepreneurship*, 2nd edn. Basingstoke: Macmillan, ch. 2.

Birley, S. and Westhead, P. (1993) 'A Taxonomy of Business Start-up Reasons and their Impact on Firm Growth and Size', *Journal of Business Venturing*, 2 (4), 351–62.

Bolton, J. E. (1971) *Report of the Committee of Inquiry on Small Firms*, Cmnd 4811. London: HMSO.

Brockhaus, R. H. (1982) 'The Psychology of the Entrepreneur', in Kent, C. A., Sexton, D. L. and Vesper, K. H. (eds), *Encyclopedia of Entrepreneurship*. Englewood Cliffs, NJ: Prentice Hall.

Burns, P. and Dewhurst, J. (1989 and 1996) *Small Business and Entrepreneurship*, 1st and 2nd edns. Basingstoke: Macmillan.

Caird, S. (1990) 'What Does it Mean to be Enterprising?', *British Journal of Management*, 1 (3), 137–45.

Cantillon, R. (1931) *Essays on the General Nature of Commerce* (ed. and transl. by H. Higgs). London: Macmillan.

Carland, J. W., Hoy, F., Boulton, W. R. and Carland, J. A. C. (1984) 'Differentiating Entrepreneurs From Small Business Owners: A Conceptualisation', *The Academy of Management Review*, 9 (2), 354–9.

Carr, P. (1999) *The Age of Enterprise: The Emergence and Evolution of Entrepreneurial Management*. Dublin: Blackhall.

Casson, M. (1982) *The Entrepreneur – An Economic Theory*. Oxford: Robertson.

Chell, E. (1985) 'The Entrepreneurial Personality: A Few Ghosts Laid to Rest?', *International Small Business Journal*, 3 (3) 43–54.

Chell, E. and Haworth, J. M. (1988) 'Entrepreneurship and Entrepreneurial Management: The Need for a Paradigm', *Graduate Management Research*, 4 (1), 16–33.

Chell, E., Haworth, J. M. and Brearley, S. A. (1991) *The Entrepreneurial Personality: Concepts, Cases and Categories*. London: Routledge.

Collins, O. F. and Moore, D. G. (1970) *The Organisation Makers*. New York: Appleton Century Crofts.

Curran, J. (1986) *Bolton Fifteen Years On: A Review and Analysis of Small Business Research In Britain 1971–1986*. London: Small Business Research Trust.

Deakins, D. (1999) *Entrepreneurship and Small Firms*, 2nd edn. London: McGraw-Hill.

Drucker, P. F. (1985) *Innovation and Entrepreneurship: Principles and Practice*. London: Heinemann.

Dunkleberg, W. C. and Cooper, A. A. (1982) 'Entrepreneurial Typologies', in Vesper, K. H. (ed.), *Frontiers of Entrepreneurial Research*. Boston, MA: Babson College.

Gerber, M. E. (1995) *The E-Myth Revisited*. New York: HarperCollins.

Goss, D. (1991) *Small Business and Society*. London: Routledge.

Grieve-Smith, A. and Fleck, V. (1987) 'Business Strategies in Small High Technology Companies', *Long Range Planning*, 20 (2), 61–8.

Handy, C. (1999) *The New Alchemists*. London: Hutchinson.

Herbert, R. F. and Link, A. N. (1988) *The Entrepreneur – Mainstream Views and Radical Critiques*, 2nd edn. New York: Praeger.

Hornaday, R. W. (1990) 'Dropping the E-words from Small Business Research', *Journal of Small Business Management*, 28 (4), 22–33.

Jennings, P. L. and Beaver, G. (1997) 'The Performance and Competitive Advantage of Small Firms: A Management Perspective', *International Small Business Journal*, 15 (2), 63–75.

Kets de Vries, M. (1977) 'The Entrepreneurial Personality: A Person at the Crossroads', *Journal of Management Studies*, February, 34–57.

McClelland, D. C. (1961) *The Achieving Society*. Princeton, NJ: Van Nostrand.

McClelland, D. C. (1987) 'Characteristics of Successful Entrepreneurs', *Journal of Creative Behaviour*, 21 (3), 219–33.

MORI (2001) *MORI Report on the Self-Employed*. London: Alodis.

Moss Kanter, R. (1983) *The Change Masters*. New York: Simon and Schuster.

Moss Kanter, R. (1989) *When Giants Learn to Dance*. London: Unwin.

Penrose, E. T. (1959) *The Theory of the Growth of the Firm*. Oxford: Blackwell.

Quinn, J. B. (1980) *Strategies for Change: Logical Incrementalism*. Homewood, IL: Irwin.

Scase, R. and Goffee, R. (1983) 'Class Entrepreneurship and the Service Sector: Towards a Conceptual Clarification', *The Services Industries Journal*, 3, 146–60.

Schumpeter, J. A. (1934) *The Theory of Economic Development*. Cambridge, MA: Harvard University Press.

Schumacher, E. F. (1973) *Small Is Beautiful: Economics as if People Mattered*. New York: Harper and Row.

Stanworth, J. and Curran, J. (1982) 'Growth and the Small Firm', in Gorb, P., Dowell, P. and Wilson, P. (eds), *Small Business Perspectives*. London: Armstrong.

Stanworth, J. and Gray, C. (1991) *Bolton 20 Years On: The Small Firm in the 1990s*. London: Paul Chapman.

Storey, D. J. (1994) *Understanding the Small Business Sector*. London: Routledge.

Storey, D. J., Keasey, K., Watson, R. and Wynarczyk, P. (1987) *The Performance of Small Firms*. London: Croom Helm.

West, M. A. and Farr, J. L. (1990) *Innovation and Creativity at Work*. Chichester: Wiley.

4 Management development

Objectives This chapter examines the nature of management and management development in the small business and demonstrates that there are significant differences in the managerial tasks between small and large firms. Indeed, among small business practitioners there are clearly different aims, objectives and motivations for establishing and managing a small enterprise. Frequently the management of small firms takes place in market sectors where there is a general tendency of low levels of owner/manager and employee development and a lack of pro-active and systematic training. Management development in many small business populations is also at a low level despite the well-meaning intervention and activities of the relevant business support infrastructure.

This chapter seeks to examine:

- the management process in the small firm and comparisons with large organisations;

- the differences in aims, ambitions, motives and objectives pursued by owner/managers and entrepreneurs, building on the evidence discussed in the previous chapter;

- the reasons why so many owner/managers, particularly in the micro-enterprise, do not give priority to their own development – the analysis draws on research by the author from the hospitality industry to illustrate the confusion in management development through inaccurate categorisation;

- frameworks and possibilities for those entrepreneurs who have commercial growth-oriented ambitions and who see their own development as fundamental to securing competitive advantage and attaining business success.

Management in the small business

The management process in the small firm is not simply different from its large counterpart – it is indeed unique. Indeed, it bears little or no resemblance to the management processes found in larger organisations, which have been the subject of substantial academic research, resulting in numerous constructs, prescriptions, theories and models (Beaver, 1984; Jennings and Beaver, 1993, 1995, 1996).

In the larger enterprise, the practice and function of management is principally a predictive process, concerned with the articulation and clarification of long-term objectives, the formation of appropriate policies capable of meeting such objectives and the feedback of information to indicate successful or unsuccessful achievement of the goals established (Faulkner and Johnson, 1992; Johnson and Scholes, 1999).

In contrast, management in the smaller firm is primarily an adaptive process, concerned with adjusting a (usually) limited amount of resources in order to gain the maximum immediate short-term advantage. In the small firm, efforts are concentrated not on predicting but on controlling the operating environment, adapting as quickly as possible to the changing demands of that environment and devising suitable tactics for mitigating the consequences of any changes which occur.

In the small business, the management process is characterised by the highly personalised preferences, prejudices and attitudes of the firm's entrepreneur, owner and/or owner/manager. The nature of managerial activity expands or contracts with the characteristics of the person fulfilling the role(s). Such expansion or contraction is partly conditioned by the adaptive needs of the context in which the business operates and is partly dependent on the personality and the needs of the owner, manager or entrepreneur.

Consequently, the management process in the small enterprise cannot be viewed in isolation from the skills demanded of the three key roles of entrepreneur, owner and manager, together with the technical skills relevant to the industrial setting of the business. However, in the micro-business, all these roles may be enacted by one individual – and it is only following a period of business growth and expansion that separate individuals may enact each role. *Thus the small firm management process cannot be separated from the personality set and experience of the key role-players.*

Another characteristic of the small firm management process is the closeness of the key role-players to the operating personnel and activities being under-taken. This provides the key role-players with extraordinary opportunities to influence these operatives and activities directly. However, these relationships are often informal, there being no precise definition of rights and obligations, duties and responsibilities. Appointment and promotion are often made on the basis of birth or personal friendship rather than on the basis of educational or technical qualifications and abilities.

Organisational structures, in so far as they exist, are likely to develop around the interests and abilities of the key role-players. Such organisational structures are likely to be organic and loosely structured rather than mechanistic and highly formalised. *Thus the management process in the small firm is seldom a readily visible process. It often has an abstract rather than tangible form.*

However, the key role-players must fulfil a number of basic managerial functions, roles and duties for the business to succeed and achieve a measure of competitive advantage. Logically, it follows that a lack of attention to these fundamental man-agerial activities and tasks will, at best, lead to sub-optimal performance and may even threaten the survival of the firm. These essential managerial activities have been defined and refined throughout a long history of management research (Hussey, 1998; Kay, 1993).

Applying these activities specifically to the small firm management process sug-gests that the key skills and abilities outlined in Figure 4.1 need to be utilised. While it may be argued that these attributes are generic to all management situations,

ENTREPRENEURIAL SKILLS   OWNERSHIP SKILLS
(adaptive and organic)   *(predictive and mechanistic)*

Strategic management thinking

Innovation   Objective setting
Risk-taking   Policy formulation
Tactical planning   Strategic planning

Common core skills required

Decision-making
Problem solving
Information-processing

Management skills and abilities

Negotiating   Organising
Trouble-shooting   Co-ordinating
Interpersonal communications   Monitoring
                                              Issues of organisational formality

Figure 4.1 The small firm management process
Source: Beaver and Jennings (1995).

the complexity of the small business operating environment demands a unique blending of these qualities to succeed in exploiting competitive advantage to achieve and sustain superior performance.

It also follows that the inter-relationship of the firm with its specific operating context and the achievement of its strategic ambitions require managerial attention to flexibility and adaptability. Thus the lone small business practitioner may be asked to enact any one of the multiplicity of roles implied by the above at any one time.

It must also be appreciated that, in any given small business management situation, these roles can considered to be mirror reflections of the different stakeholders, each demanding the possession and application of specific skills and abilities. As Mitroff (1983) points out:

> Different stakeholders do not generally share the same definition of an organisation's problems and hence do not share the same solutions.

Each stakeholder approaches the firm's problems from their own unique perspective and demands a solution catering for their particular requirements and expectations. Traditional and contemporary concepts of decision-making have emphasised the need to achieve consensus and agreement between alternative stakeholders in order to produce effective outcomes (Hussey, 1998; Brown and Eisenhardt, 1998).

Mitroff goes on to argue that the individual human psyche or personality contains a 'plurality of selves' – i.e. alternative and sometimes conflicting perceptions of self, which constitute stakeholders, thus influencing behaviour. The small business practitioner is therefore subject to a number of competing and conflicting influences which may cause real dissonance, leading to erratic, unpredictable and unacceptable behaviour, which is in total contrast with the rational, professional and expected management bearing portrayed by Mintzberg (1973) and others. (To be fair Mintzberg has reversed his earlier opinions on this (and many other) positions, which can be seen in Mintzberg *et al.*, 1998.)

Frequently, as Osbourne (1991) and others have pointed out, other stakeholders in the small firm cannot challenge the power that accompanies majority ownership. Therefore the ability of the key role-player(s) to cope with absolute power and leadership responsibility has a significant impact on the survival and development potential of the business.

For any firm to remain successful over a sustained period there must be a capability to adapt to changing circumstances. The much-cited work of Greiner (1972) shows that failure to adapt to a series of crises caused by growth is one of the principal causes of failure for all organisations. *It follows, therefore, that one of the primary ingredients of small business success must be the managerial competence of the owner/manager.*

It is pertinent then to ask, what are these managerial competencies which underpin the successful small firm? A logical first step might be to examine the usual contents of small business training and development programmes. However, there is a need to distinguish between training and development, which might be considered necessary for the employees within a small firm, and that focused on the specific needs of the owner/manager(s).

The small business practitioner requires specific, transferable managerial skills directly related to entrepreneurship and professional management within the operating environment of the business as shown in Figure 4.1. The key role-player(s) needs to be able to initiate and implement strategic change and improvements in services, systems, methods and products. (The article by Tony Watson, 1995, 'Entrepreneurship and Professional Management: A Fatal Distinction', provides an informed and lively discussion of these issues.)

It is very easy to note the obvious. Provided that all the necessary skills and competences are present in the management team that is responsible for the small enterprise, the business should be capable of achieving success. However, this is much too glib and based more on wishful thinking than *The Real World of the Small Business Owner* (see, for example, the work of Scase and Goffee, 1987, whose influential text has this title).

However, adept management is still required to marshall and bring out these abilities and, as Jennings and Beaver (1995, 1996) illustrate, the personality and positional power of the owner/entrepreneur often mean that latent talent within the team goes unrecognised or under-utilised.

This raises the question of whether small firms fail through lack of suitable managerial skills, which lets down otherwise good enterprise competence in providing the product or service, or through the lack of competence in providing the business offering demanded by the customer, despite otherwise competent management in the organisation. Ineffective management cannot simply be identified as the primary cause of small business failure as not only is this rather naive, it is almost certainly inaccurate.

There needs to be a recognition of several factors that are peculiar to the small business operating context. The work by Grieve-Smith and Fleck (1987), using a case study approach to examine the business strategies in small high-technology firms in the Cambridge area, raises several interesting managerial issues.

They note that small enterprises can experience real difficulties in developing or obtaining the appropriate managerial talent, since they cannot provide the salaries and accompanying benefits that managers from large organisations can reasonably expect to obtain. Furthermore, their case studies illustrate several other important issues worthy of note. For example, they refer to the founders of certain companies being conscious, at the outset, of the need to recruit external managers and to appoint these individuals from larger companies, presumably to facilitate business growth and development. Finally, they refer to the need to attract managers with additional skills to those already in the firm, to complement the expertise on which the company was based.

This would suggest that the business founder(s) had the objective to construct a balanced managerial team as one of the prime drivers in attaining business success and performance. It is also a factor that may well dramatically reduce the risk of business failure.

It must be emphasised, however, that there are many types and categories of small business, each with its own distinctive operating context. Equally, there are many ways of organising and managing in the search for competitive advantage and commercial survival. There is an even greater diversity of small firm owners, managers and entrepreneurs with varying motivations, abilities and expectations. Caution, therefore, should be exercised here, for it would be unwise and too simplistic to focus simply on high-technology firms, or indeed any sector-specific research, as a basis on which to make generalisations about management strategies for enterprise growth and failure prevention.

The analysis of the managerial contribution to small business failure must acknowledge the factor of *disadvantage*, owing to not only the size and resource base of the firm but also the nature of the operating context and the relatively ineffective business support infrastructure (Beaver and Harrison, 1994; Beaver and Murphy, 1996; Jennings and Beaver, 1997). This is particularly relevant to certain industries that attract a large small firm population because, among other things, barriers to entry are relatively low.

A good example would be the hospitality industry in the UK. Here is an instance where many potential business practitioners feel that they have the technical competence for success because of the strong link between hospitality and domestic services. For some entrants, the attractions of catering and entertaining friends can be very misguiding. However, successful hospitality management requires an array of competences, which extend way beyond being merely hospitable (Beaver and Lashley, 1998).

There have been many studies reporting on the management customs and practices in small firms. For example, Nicholson and West (1988) illustrate the many significant differences between managers in small and large firms, confirming the presence and nature of disadvantage.

Furthermore, there is some evidence provided by Charles Handy (1988) in his international review of the education, development and training of managers that:

> Small companies are different. In no country do they take the same long-term view of management development, nor are they prepared to spend time and money on any form of training that does not have an almost immediate pay-off.

Management processes in small firms are unique. Much of the contemporary management theory is founded on the empirical analysis of managerial action in large organisations. These principles, no matter how refined, cannot be applied directly to the small enterprise. While common managerial skills need to be in evidence in many organisations, the contextualisation of these skills to meet the requirements of the small business operating environment is distinctive.

Competitive advantage in small firms is an elusive concept and it is easier to describe than to define. It is fashioned by the actions and abilities of the principal role-players and owes much to their personal perception of satisfactory performance and strategic leadership. Growth and development of the small enterprise bring with it many challenges, especially in terms of the separation of ownership and control. The delegation and professionalisation of management activities invariably demand a less personalised and consequently more formal management process.

Labels, classifications and metaphors – confusion in management development through inaccurate categorisation: an example from research undertaken in the hospitality industry

It is clearly impossible in this chapter to consider all the issues and factors influencing management development in the small business community. The small business sector is characterised by heterogeneity, not homogeneity, and any attempt to provide generalisations for the sector as a whole inevitably results in inaccuracies and confusion.

To some extent, the misunderstanding that surrounds the small firm sector is the result of labels, classifications and business metaphors, indiscriminately applied, that have been used to describe the nature and form of the enterprise. In reality such labels serve to disguise, or gloss over, the aims and objectives of the owner/ manager(s) and ignore the particular operating context of the business.

To illustrate this point, recent research undertaken in the UK hospitality industry will be used which shows the lack of real understanding behind the issues and problems of management development that many small firms are currently facing. Accordingly, the following section reports on some insights that have been gained through research at Nottingham Business School (Lashley, 1993; Beaver and Lashley, 1998).

There are two problems for potential providers of management development programmes to small firms in the hospitality industry. The first is that much of the research which might assist training providers focuses on employee development in the hospitality industry as a whole – and thereby includes large organisations which have an array of different realities to face. The second is that all small hospitality firms are being treated as being similar, and there is little recognition of the potential differences in the objectives for and constraints on those managing different types of hospitality business. The research attempted to construct a picture of management needs which recognised and overcame these two deficiencies.

Some 55 semi-structured interviews were undertaken with employers in 10 different categories of hospitality business: hotels (large, medium and small), bed and breakfast establishments, restaurants, cafés, pubs and bars (freehold, tenanted and managed) and clubs. A key theme of the research was to identify the perceived training needs of those taking part and the research instrument asked respondents to identify skill areas where they might have a training need.

The skill areas were arranged under a number of largely functional headings such as finance, marketing, computer skills, legal aspects, general management, staff deficiencies, managing people and so on. Although there was only a relatively small sample in any one category, the research provided some rich data on managerial perceptions of training needs across the small firms in the hospitality sector.

Allowing for the tentative nature of the findings, there were some interesting outcomes in both the nature of the training needs identified and the owner/ manager responses in different establishments. Concern to improve financial performance plus a variety of marketing, human resource management and information technology skills, together with concern about understanding legal responsibilities, particularly in relation to staff, came across quite strongly. More importantly, however, these findings suggested that some hospitality owners appear to be more aware of and concerned by their perceived management deficiencies than others.

Owner/managers in small hotels and tenanted pubs registered the highest level of perceived skill deficiencies. In both cases the respondents running these businesses registered higher levels of perceived skill deficiencies across the range than respondents in other categories. Similarly, respondents running cafés, free houses and bed and breakfast establishments registered significantly lower levels of concern for skill deficiencies.

Given the small sample of establishments in this survey, caution needs to be applied in generalising the findings. However, the general thrust of the findings merits some further discussion because they do raise issues relevant to the provision and take-up of management development in small firms.

The generic term 'owner/manager' covers a wide variety of individuals with different motives and aims for the business. This is discussed in more detail below but the findings do suggest that these variations in motives and material experiences present very different possibilities for the business support infrastructure.

Owner/managers of tenanted pubs and small hotels appeared to be the most aware of their particular training requirements – and both may reflect a sense of vulnerability because of their position in relation to the market. Those running tenanted pubs, for example, may have limited capital to invest in the tenancy and may only have limited additional resources to invest in the business. Often the properties offered by the breweries for tenancy opportunities were marginal in business terms. The best houses were generally kept under the direct managerial control of the brewery. Releasing a pub for tenancy, or more recently for leasing, retained the unit as an outlet for the brewery's sales but simplified the managerial task. In many cases, the brewery received good rents from these units and made profits on the goods supplied but provided minimal assistance to the tenant. In such a situation, it is easy to recognise that the owner/managers running pub tenancies would feel isolated and lack the skills needed to make the business a success and this might raise the awareness of training needs.

Owner/managers of small hotels (defined in the research as 5–16 bed spaces) may well have committed more capital to the venture than some of the pub tenants but they feel equally vulnerable. The entry barriers to running a small hotel are still quite modest, most requiring capital similar to domestic property investment. In many towns and cities, this type of business is located in former Victorian and Edwardian domestic housing. The source of vulnerability might well stem from a limited ability to invest so as to compete with larger firms.

Furthermore, the demand for accommodation has, at almost every level of the market, shifted to a requirement for en suite facilities. The very nature of such properties limits the ability to install full bathroom facilities without a loss of capacity. On the supply side, accommodation is being provided by the large, often multi-national, organisations which may well contribute towards the business threat felt by these individuals and lead to a heightened awareness of their skill deficiencies.

These findings are entirely consistent with general trends in small firm management development, in that it is important to look for business triggers that stimulate the need for training and skills acquisition.

Business start-up, growth and decline are the usual periods in a business's life cycle which create such stimuli. The Hospitality Training Foundation (1996) similarly concludes that few firms have ongoing development plans and that the majority of training and development is sporadic and triggered by some immediate short-term problem.

The second issue to emerge from the interviews with owner/managers is that it is a mistake to assume that they are motivated by the same drives and wants.

The responses from bed and breakfast establishment, cafés and public houses which are freehold, i.e. independent of any one brewery, are very interesting in that all three categories of establishment registered the lowest level of interest in training and development. Common sense dictates that the individuals managing these firms must objectively possess some skill deficiencies but the findings showed conclusively that such deficiencies were not perceived as a problem.

Although this may appear strange to the layman, the practitioners running these businesses see things very differently and clearly have different motives and ambitions for running their businesses. In part, the confusion is located in the generic small business terms which mask a variety of reasons and motives. The indiscriminate use of terms such as 'small business', 'entrepreneur' and 'owner-manager' reflect generalisations which assume homogeneity when heterogeneity is the case. Each term represents an organisational metaphor through which to describe and classify these firms.

Small business implies that the key focus is in relation to the size of the enterprise and the resources available to it, while the term *entrepreneur* suggests that the focus is more to do with the motives, behaviour and composition of the management. The first metaphor suggests that these firms are handicapped, or limited by their size, while the second suggests that those running such businesses are guided by entrepreneurial drives embracing growth and expansion. The fact that many commentators and academic writers use these terms interchangeably reinforces the confusion.

Those responsible for shaping public policy towards these businesses have often been over-concerned with the small business metaphor and have attempted to intervene in such a way as to compensate for their lack of resources through the provision of management training and an array of courses designed to provide the training which the firm itself does not yet have the resources to provide (see, for example, Beaver and Jennings, 1995).

The entrepreneurial metaphor has potential to be of assistance because it suggests that the focus should be concerned with the individual(s) in the business leadership role. However, caution needs to exercised here because the metaphor suggests meanings that embrace growth, individualism, a style of management and of profit maximisation which may, or may not, describe the motives and intentions of those running small firms.

The entrepreneurial metaphor may also imply more homogeneity than is the case. Recent literature on entrepreneurs and entrepreneurship suggests that there are a range of types of entrepreneurs (Curran and Stanworth, 1989; Chell *et al.*, 1991; Cromie and O'Donoghue, 1992) and it is possible to identify some of these within the hospitality context:

- The *entrepreneurial venture* provides a powerful and romantic metaphor for small firms. It suggests that these enterprises are motivated by growth and the seizing of opportunities as and when, they emerge. While the image may well be powerful and widely held, only a minority of firms can be said to entrepreneurial (Morrison *et al.*, 1998).
- The *lifestyle enterprise* is a firm which provides the owner/manager with a means of economic survival within a desired style of living. In the hospitality industry this might include a business set within the countryside, say in rural hotels or public houses. The key motive for running the enterprise is to create sufficient resources to live within the manner and setting desired by the owners.
- The *family enterprise* is very common within the hospitality industry. Many independent hotels, restaurants and public houses represent family concerns, with family members performing different roles within the business. In some cases, the family venture represents just one of several sources of income to the family. A bed and breakfast venture which provides the family home and a source of income in addition to the wage income from family members is a common example.
- The *female enterprise* has witnessed increasing growth over the last decade or so. Female self-employment grew from 20% in 1987 to 32% in 2000. Given the traditional domestic roles of women in the UK, it is not surprising that hospitality ventures have provided some attractive opportunities for women. Bed and breakfast establishments, for example, have provided opportunities for many women to meet domestic role expectations and earn an income.

63

- The *ethnic minority enterprise* provides members of various ethnic minority groups with an opportunity to promote their economic well-being and protection against disadvantage within the host community. The restaurant sector in the UK has several examples where ethnic minority restaurants have successfully developed niche markets for specialist segments of the eating-out market.
- Self-employment and control are important motives for many owner/managers. Self-employment can provide a chance to exercise skills and talents which are personally satisfying to the owners and, given the right market segmentation, can help the individuals to maintain self-employment with a reasonable degree of control over their working lives. Again, the restaurant sector includes examples of individuals who enjoy the skills of food preparation and service and who are not particularly motivated by the desire to increase revenue, profit or the scale of the business beyond certain limits.

While this is not an exhaustive list of different entrepreneurial types, it is sufficient to show that the motives of those establishing and running small hospitality firms are not always compatible with rational economic motives.

Motives associated with personal preferences or which relate to self-image do not automatically lead to levels of self-analysis which suggest that a lack of business skills presents a major threat to their business goals. In many cases, entrepreneurs are commercially satisficing. Provided that the business meets the immediate survival needs, pays the bills and delivers an appropriate level of security, there is limited awareness of, or interest in, the development of skills through which to build a business. In these circumstances, owner/manager interests and concerns are focused on commercial interests in a secondary manner and only become important if the venture is under particular threat or difficulty.

On another level, it may be that the characteristics and personalities of those who start up a business are more inner directed than outer directed (Scase and Goffee, 1995). Attempts to establish a taxonomy of the entrepreneur have produced some interesting and at times very contradictory findings. However, common features in much of the research appear to be an ability to work independently: the limited need for the structure, support systems and positional status found in large organisations and a self-image independent from the opinions of others.

Several surveys of small firms have shown the importance of independence as a primary motive behind venture creation. For example, the National Westminster Bank (1990, 1998) surveys showed that, in firms of one to four employees, 55% and 61% respectively of small business proprietors stated independence as the key ambition for starting the venture, while only 16% and 18% respectively claimed that making money was the important drive.

Similarly, a Leeds Metropolitan University study of over 1000 firms showed that only 11% of respondents stated that 'making more money' was the most important reason for starting the business. Almost 74% stated 'to do what I enjoy' or 'to be my own boss' as the principal reason (Thomas *et al.*, 1997). In these circumstances, the nature of the self-image and the importance of personal independence are likely to create a situation where the business owner's attentions and perceptions are so inner directed as to preclude the consideration of skills and talents that might be developed externally.

Given these differences in aims and motives for starting a business, it is possible to identify the variations in interest in management development mentioned earlier as being associated with a contrast in the reasons for venture creation and the perceptions of commercial threat on the owner/manager.

The individuals who start up many of the small firms outlined in the research have aims and ambitions for the business, which are not driven by immediate commercial gain. For some, the aims are for the maintenance of a particular life-style, while for others the drive is to create opportunities that are not available because of disadvantage due to gender or ethnicity, experienced in the wider society.

Some business practitioners, while still desiring these objectives as primary goals, may feel under some commercial threat because of their specific market position. Thus the owners of small hotels and tenanted pub businesses interviewed in the study are in a position of some vulnerability because of their limited resources and limited market power. Not surprisingly, their perception of the need for improved business skills and abilities is heightened.

These differences in business aims and objectives are also a major factor when analysing the impact of management on small firm performance. Storey and Westhead (1996) report that the relationship between the training and development of managers in small firms and the effects on business performance are weak or hard to establish. (This is not to say that other studies have not shown a more positive association between management training and business improvement/performance.)

In part, the problems are due to the difficulties with research methodologies that attempt to link enhanced performance to a single factor. Additionally, the problem is exacerbated in that attempts to measure improvements in business performance are commercially defined, with success frequently recorded in terms of traditional economic indicators.

Many of the small firms under discussion here are being run by owner/managers that have other motives and, indeed, other perceptions of success. That said, Storey and Westhead do suggest a range of reasons why management in small firms is undertaken with less frequency than in large ones. They report that:

- The price paid by small firms is greater – the market price may well be the same but the opportunity cost of having managers and supervisors away on training programmes will be proportionately greater for the small firm.
- The reduced income through which to spread the cost of management development is a major consideration affecting the small firm.
- The factor of taste is an important variable. The assumption is that many managers in small firms do not purchase training and development programmes for a number of non-price reasons. Such businesses may be driven by short-term aims and do not have an internal labour market. The need to develop managers, together with the presentation and content of training programmes currently available, may well be perceived as inappropriate in both content and mode of delivery. Another consideration due to the size and operating context of many small firms is that many managers and practitioners have to undertake a diversity of business and management responsibilities and do not have the detailed information about the type and nature of training available.

Conclusions

In concluding this chapter, it must be recognised and accepted that management development activity is necessarily different for much of the small firm sector. Traditional methods of training activity may be both inapplicable to the context of the business and inappropriate in catering for the needs, ambitions and success requirements of those managing small enterprises.

Many owner/managers, particularly in the smallest firms in many market settings, have objectives related to life-style and personal control considerations. In these circumstances, personal development needs will give a lower priority to acquiring business-growth-related management skills.

Those organisations that have ambitions to provide management development programmes for the owner/managers of small firms need to target their efforts where there are clear commercial objectives for the enterprise or those sectors where owner/managers are experiencing vulnerability or uncertainty as a result of the pressures of the market-place.

For those small firms that have clear ambitions for growth and business development, there are very real issues of how best to initiate and implement sensitive and timely management development training and practices.

There are a number of factors which need to be examined here, principally concerned with what Jones and Woodcock (1985) refer to as 'organisation readiness'. This general term encompasses a number of variables which will affect decisions on methods and approaches. The following list is indicative:

● top management commitment;
● aims, ambitions and priorities of the business and its key players;
● resource availability and allocation – short term and long term;
● understanding and acceptance of managerial roles and needs:
● the nature of the firm, its operating context and managerial composition.

Many of these variables are self-explanatory and they are of course connected and inter-related. For example, top management commitment will be influenced by business priorities and how they can be supported and achieved by management development. This in turn will have an impact on resource availability and allocation.

Whatever view is taken of the role and meaning of management development and whatever approaches and methods are applied consequent to that view, one thing seems clear from the majority of the research and comment on the subject. This is that management development in practice relies on self-development, or, at least, self-managed development (Pedlar *et al.*; Jennings and Beaver, 1993a). The point here that is of particular relevance to the small firm sector is that self-managed development does not necessarily require formalised systems or the allocation of significant resources. Indeed, many training providers in the business support community have both the capability and the potential to be of real assistance to those firms wishing to improve their performance and to develop their management talent.

References and further reading

Beaver, G. (1984) 'The Entrepreneurial Ceiling: A Discussion of the Small Business Management Process', in 7th UKEMRA National Small Firms Policy and Research Conference, Nottingham, September.

Beaver, G. and Harrison, Y. (1994) 'TEC Support for Women Entrepreneurs: Help or Hindrance?', in 17th National Small Firms Policy and Research Conference, Sheffield, November.

Beaver, G. and Jennings, P. L. (1995) 'Picking Winners: The Art of Identifying Successful Small Firms', in Hussey, D. E. (ed.), *Rethinking Strategic Management – Ways to Improve Competitive Performance*. Chichester: Wiley, ch. 4.

Beaver, G. and Lashley, C. (1998) 'Competitive Advantage and Management Development in Small Hospitality Firms: The Need for an Imaginative Approach', *Journal of Vacation Marketing*, 4 (2), April, 145–60.

Beaver, G. and Murphy, M. (1996) 'Carpentry and Joinery (Nottingham) Limited: A Case Study in Enterprise Support and Development', *Journal of Small Business and Enterprise Development*, 3 (1), March, 28–33.

Brown, S. L. and Eisenhardt, K. M. (1998) *Competing on the Edge: Strategy as Structured Chaos*. Boston, MA: Harvard Business School Press.

Chell, E., Haworth, J. and Brierley, S. (1991) *The Entrepreneurial Personality, Concepts, Cases and Categories*. London: Routledge.

Cromie, S. and O'Donoghue, J. (1992) 'Assessing Entrepreneurial Inclinations', *International Small Business Journal*, 10 (2), 66–71.

Curran, J. and Stanworth, J. (1989) 'Education and Training for Enterprise: Some Problems of Classification, Evaluation, Policy and Research', *International Small Business Journal*, 7 (2), 11–22.

Faulkner, D. and Johnson, G. (1992) *The Challenge of Strategic Management*. London: Kogan Page.

Greiner, L. (1972) 'Evolution and Revolution as Organisations Grow', *Harvard Business Review*, July/August, 24–36.

Grieve-Smith, A. and Fleck, V. (1987) 'Business Strategies in Small High Technology Companies', *Long Range Planning*, 20 (2), 61–8.

Handy, C. (1988) *Making Managers*. London: Pitman.

Hospitality Training Foudation (1996) *Training: Who Needs It?*, Report. London: HTF.

Hussey, D. E. (1998) *Strategic Management: From Theory to Implementation*, 4th edn. Oxford: Butterworth-Heinemann.

Jennings, P. L. and Beaver, G. (1993a) 'Improving the Role of Accreditation in the Training and Development of Owner/Managers', in Richardson, W. (ed.), *Managing in Enterprise Contexts*. Sheffield: Pavic, pp. 233–74.

Jennings, P. L. and Beaver, G. (1993b) 'The Abuse of Entrepreneurial Power', in Small Business and Enterprise Development Conference, Leicester University, April. European Research Press.

Jennings, P. L. and Beaver, G. (1995) 'The Managerial Dimension of Small Business Failure', *Journal of Strategic Change*, 4 (4), 185–200.

Jennings, P. L. and Beaver, G. (1996) 'Managerial Competence and Competitive Advantage in the Small Business: An Alternative Perspective', in 26th European Small Business Seminar, Vaasa, Finland.

Jennings, P. L. and Beaver, G. (1997) 'The Performance and Competitive Advantage of Small Firms: A Management Perspective', *International Small Business Journal*, 15 (2), January–March, 63–75.

Johnson, G. and Scholes, K. (1999) *Exploring Corporate Strategy*, 5th edn. London: Prentice Hall.

Jones, J. E. and Woodcock, M. (1985) *A Manual of Management Development*. Aldershot: Gower.

Kay, J. (1993) *Foundations of Corporate Success: How Business Strategies Add Value*. Oxford: Oxford University Press.

Lashley, C. (1993) 'Management Development Needs of Small Hotel and Catering Firms', Discussion Papers in Hospitality Management, Paper 7, Spring. Leeds Metropolitan University.

Mintzberg, H. (1973) *The Nature of Managerial Work*. New York: Harper and Row.

Mintzberg, H., Ahlstrand, B. and Lampel, J. (1998) *Strategy Safari: A Guided Tour Through the Wilds of Strategic Management*. London: Prentice Hall.

Mitroff, I. (1983) *Stakeholders of the Organisational Mind*. San Francisco, CA: Jossey Bass.

Morrison, A., Rimmington, M. and Williams, C. (1998) *Entrepreneurship in the Hospitality, Tourism and Leisure Industries*. London: Butterworth.

National Westminster Bank (1990, 1998) *National Survey of Small Businesses*. London.

Nicholson, N. and West, M. (1988) *Managerial Job Change*. Cambridge: Cambridge University Press.

Osbourne, R. L. (1991) 'The Dark Side of the Entrepreneur', *Long Range Planning*, 24 (3), 26–31.

Pedlar, M., Burgoyne, J. and Boydell, T. (1994) *A Manager's Guide to Self Development*, 3rd edn. London: McGraw-Hill.

Scase, R. and Goffee, R. (1987) *The Real World of the Small Business Owner*, 2nd edn. Beckenham: Croom Helm.

Scase, R. and Goffee, R. (1995) *Corporate Realities in Large and Small Organisations*. London: Routledge.

Storey, D. J. and Westhead, P. (1996) 'Management Training and Small Firm Performance: Why is the Link so Weak?', *International Small Business Journal*, 14 (4), 13–24.

Thomas, R., Friel, M., Jameson, S. and Parsons, D. (1997) *The National Survey of Small Tourism and Hospitality Firms: Annual Report, 1996–97*. Leeds: Centre for the Study of Small Tourism and Hospitality Firms, Leeds Metropolitan University.

Watson, T. J. (1994) *In Search of Management*. London: Routledge.

Watson, T. J. (1995) 'Entrepreneurship and Professional Management: A Fatal Distinction', *International Small Business Journal*, 13 (2), January–March.

5 Strategy and management

Objectives Strategic management is a central concept in modern management practice. This chapter examines business strategy from the small firm and enterprise development perspective. The value of a well-considered and well-defined strategy for the venture is advocated for superior business performance and the ways in which entrepreneurs can devise, control and communicate strategy are considered.

In particular we will examine:

- the use and value of strategic management in small business and enterprise development;
- key issues in strategy formulation, evaluation and implementation;
- the role of strategy in enterprise success and performance;
- case study evidence of strategy in the entrepreneurial venture;
- contemporary research evidence on the role and contribution of strategy, including its value in managing in a recession;
- case study illustration of effective recessionary management.

The role of strategic management

Strategic management as a field of study typically deals with large and established businesses and their relationship with their market environment and operating context. However, knowing where the business is going, together with the opportunities and routes available to get it there, is as important to a small enterprise as to a large one. Despite the importance and growing recognition of small firms and entrepreneurial ventures and their contribution to economic vitality, employment generation, innovation and business development, the value and importance of strategic management and thinking to the small firm community have only been recognised and acknowledged comparatively recently.

Despite the contribution and significance of small firms, however, every year tens of thousands of small enterprises fail or cease trading. According to the USA Small Business Administration, some 25% fail within 2 years and 63% fail within 6 years (SBA, 1998). Similar rates of failure occur in the UK, the Netherlands, Ireland, Japan and Hong Kong. Although some studies indicate that the survival rate of new enterprises is higher, small businesses are definitely risky. The causes of small enterprise failure (depending on the study cited) range from inadequate accounting procedures to the inability to manage growth (see, for example, Carland *et al.*, 1984; Jennings and Beaver, 1996, 1997).

The underlying problem appears to be an overall lack of strategic management skills and abilities – beginning with an inability to articulate a strategy to reach the customer(s) and ending with a failure to develop an adequate system of performance measurement and control. According to a much cited study of small business failures:

> In nearly all cases, the practice of strategic planning by small firm owners and managers was found to be scanty and perfunctory.
>
> *Source*: El-Namacki (1990)

Contemporary research has shown repeatedly that strategic thinking and planning is strongly related to small business financial performance. This has been confirmed by a recent study of small firms in the UK Midlands by Beaver and Ross (2000) that showed quite conclusively that strategic thinking is an essential ingredient in enterprise survival, performance and growth (see also Storey, 1998, 1999).

It is important here to again distinguish between a small firm and an entrepreneurial venture as the concepts and operating realities are frequently very different (refer to Chapter 3 for an earlier discussion of this issue):

- The *small firm* is independently owned and operated, not dominant in its field and does not engage in innovative strategic practices.
- The *entrepreneurial venture*, by contrast, is any business whose primary goals are profitability and growth and that can be characterised by innovative strategic management practices.

The basic difference then between the small business and the entrepreneurial venture as it affects the discussion here lies not in the type or nature of the products/services provided but in the fundamental perspectives on innovation, growth and business development. Indeed, many commentators and researchers have noted that strategic management is more likely to be an integral part of an entrepreneurial venture than the 'typical' small firm and that it is the approach to planning that separates the entrepreneur from the small business owner/manager.

However, many small enterprise managers and practitioners still refuse to embrace the strategy process, with four reasons usually cited for the apparent lack of strategic management practice in many new and established small firms:

- *Not enough time*. Day-to-day operating issues and decisions absorb the time necessary for long-term planning. Avoidance of strategic management is justified on the basis of everyday operational and administrative decisions, which by their nature may be complex and demanding and often leave little time for anything else.
- *Unfamiliarity with strategic management techniques and process*. The route into small business management may make the owner/manager distrust or reject the value of strategic planning – also, it does not (usually) have a short-term pay-off, which may go against the mind set of many practitioners, especially if resources are limited.

- *Lack of skills.* Strategic management is perceived by many small firm practitioners as both complex and demanding with limited applicability to the operating context of the enterprise. Small business managers often lack the necessary skills and confidence to begin strategic planning and lack the motivation or resources to commission consultants or outside assistance. The small business support infrastructure may also lack the calibre and experience of suitably qualified individuals to advise on strategic matters (Banfield *et al.*, 1996).

- *Lack of trust and openness.* Many small firm owner/managers are very sensitive about business information (especially financial matters) and are unwilling to share strategic planning with employees or other stakeholders. For this reason also, boards of directors (if they exist) are often composed of close friends and relatives of the owner/manager – people unlikely to provide an objective viewpoint or effective professional advice (Aram and Cowan, 1990).

Irrespective of the above, the entrepreneur is a strategic manager as quite obviously he or she, at least initially, makes all the strategic and operational decisions. All three levels of strategy – corporate, business and functional – are the concerns of the founder and owner-manager of the enterprise. As one commentator states, 'Entrepreneurs are strategic planners without realising it' (Wickham, 1998).

The nature of corporate strategy

The notion that an organisation has a strategy lies at the centre of much contemporary management thinking. A strategy can be defined as the actions an organisation takes to pursue its business objectives. Strategy drives performance and an effective strategy should result in a good performance. An organisation's strategy is, therefore, multi–faceted. It can be viewed from a number of perspectives depending on which aspects of its actions are of interest. A basic distinction exists between the content of a firm's strategy and the strategy process that the business adopts to maintain and succeed with that strategy. The *strategy content* relates to what the business actually does while the *strategy process* relates to the way the business decides what it is going to do.

The strategy content has three distinct decision areas:

- the products and/or services to be offered;
- the markets to be targeted;
- the approach taken to secure and retain competitive advantage.

Applying the above to the operating context of the small business, it is first necessary to understand the motivations of the owner(s) or principal stakeholders of the enterprise, since the two are frequently indistinguishable – certainly in the early days of the firm's start-up.

The pressures and reasons which determine these objectives may well embrace personal life-style and family considerations as well as commercial ones. Furthermore, the entrepreneur often starts the business with the declared intention of becoming independent and, once established, may have a clear intention of maintaining this independence by keeping day-to-day operational control. To achieve this, the strategic goal may become one of no growth or indeed of minimum growth consistent with survival and an acceptable level of financial reward. Moreover, the choices that are made may well take into account personal life-styles, interests and family considerations. To the outside observer, this can produce a company with a very strange profile but one which is in fact pursuing a strategy which is internally consistent.

As the operating environment changes over time and adjustments are made to preserve and enhance competitive vitality, the owner-manager or entrepreneur may well be forced to consider issues of retirement, divestment, succession and family considerations and, not surprisingly, personal objectives may well change.

Irrespective of the needs of the business or, indeed, the desires and skills of the family members, priority may well be given to continue the family name in the firm and to continue to provide employment for a loyal workforce. The list of possible outcomes and consequences here is considerable but what is clear is that the goals and direction of the business may need to change. Ownership and control of the enterprise, once in the hands of the few, may well become increasingly divorced and fragmented and the complexion of the business together with the strategic choices being made may bear little resemblance to the original venture.

The formation and development of strategy in the smaller enterprise can be more easily understood if a simple example is provided comparing the management, ownership and competitive environment of a large organisation, as shown below.

Example 5.1: Strategy in the large and the small enterprise

The large organisation

- A chairman/chief executive officer is appointed on the basis of corporate track record and credibility with the 'City' and principal stakeholders and shareholders. Political skills and the ability for holistic thinking are essential attributes.

- There is a requirement to balance the various and often competing requirements of stakeholders. The stakeholder web of the organisation is driven by economic, social and political considerations.

- Strategic choices and actions are invariably driven by managerial motives and ambitions that may be at variance with preferred shareholder choice(s).

The small business

- The owner-manager/entrepreneur is the principal stakeholder and ultimate strategic manager. Usually, there is little separation of ownership and control.

- Personal, family and life-style considerations dictate strategy, which may be at variance with conventional economic criteria. Managerial competence and independence may deliberately curtail business development. Ambitions may be limited or modest.

- Notions and perceptions of business success are dependent on the owner/entrepreneur's orientation towards the enterprise and can be expected to change over time.

Entrepreneurs and owner-managers inhabit a very different world from that of their counterparts in large organisations. They frequently have limited resources to draw upon and operate with the knowledge that the difference between success and failure can be their willingness to risk all their personal possessions in a venture and to work extremely hard.

However, a well-defined and well-communicated strategy can help the small business to succeed whatever its principal goals and ambitions happen to be. The following gains can be expected to accrue to the enterprise that has invested in developing a strategy that is both realistic and achievable – and communicated it to stakeholders:

- It encourages the entrepreneur to assess and articulate their vision.
- A strategy provides the starting point for the setting of objectives.
- It acts as a guide to decision-making.
- A strategy guides the organisation and design of the enterprise and relates it to the operating environment.
- A strategy illuminates new possibilities for business development.
- A strategy acts as a common language for stakeholders.

Example 5.2: Formal and informal strategy formulations

Define mission	What do we stand for?
Set objectives	What are we trying to achieve?
Formulate strategy	How are we going to get there? How can we beat the competition?
Determine policies	What sort of ground rules should we be following to get the job done right?
Establish programmes	How should we organise this operation to get what we want done as cheaply as possible with the highest quality?
Prepare pro-forma budgets	How much is this going to cost us and where can we get the cash?
Specify procedures	In how much detail do we need to lay things out, so that everyone knows what to do?
Determine performance measures	What are those few key things that will determine whether we make it or not and how can we monitor them?

Example 5.3: Owner/managers' hopes and ambitions for the future

	Plan	Do not plan
Increase sales and establish a large customer base	69%	33%
Survive	45%	28%
Retire/sell out	33%	19%
Make money/ increase profits dramatically	46%	27%
Establish a good reputation	29%	10%

Source: BDO Stoy Hayward, 1999

Example 5.4: Strategic guidelines for new venture success and development

1 Focus on industries facing substantial technological or regulatory changes, especially those with recent exits by established competitors.

2 Seek industries whose smaller firms have relatively weak competitive positions.

3 Seek industries that are in early, high-growth stages of evolution.

4 Seek industries in which it is possible to create high barriers to subsequent entry.

5 Seek industries with heterogeneous products that are relatively unimportant to the customer's overall success.

6 Try to differentiate your products from those of your competitors in ways that are meaningful to your customers.

7 Focus such differentiation efforts on product quality, marketing approaches and customer service – and charge enough to cover the costs of doing so.

8 Seek to dominate the market segments in which you compete. If necessary, either segment the market differently or change the nature and focus of your differentiation efforts to increase your domination of the segments you serve.

9 Emphasise innovation, especially new product innovation that is built on existing organisational capabilities.

10 Try to secure natural organic growth through flexibility and opportunism that build on existing organisational strengths.

Source: Shepherd and Shanley (1998); Hofer and Sandberg (1987)

The case illustration from Derwent Valley Foods is a fine example of a successful venture that started life with a strategy that clearly defined the products to be offered, the customer groups to be targeted and the way in which the business chose to compete within its market. The rewards to the founder for thinking and acting strategically from the outset are a lesson to anyone aspiring after financial success.

To conclude this section, the following points distilled from contemporary research evidence are worth noting and paying attention to (see, for example, Beaver and Jennings, 2000):

- Entrepreneurial ventures and small enterprises are for the most part, managed far less formally than are large, established business organisations. Small firms with designs on rapid expansion and growth tend to follow the entre- preneurial mode of strategy formulation – characterised by bold moves and intuitive decisions.
- Small businesses that engage in contemporary strategic management practices tend to outperform those that do not. However, this does not mean that formal procedures are either necessary or desirable (although some organisational regularity is recommended). The process of strategic thinking and planning, rather than the plan itself, appears to be the key driver of business performance.
- Small firm practitioners appear to make little distinction between strategy formulation and strategy implementation.
- In many small companies, evaluation and control procedures are usually rather informal and reflect the owner/entrepreneur's preferences. Many small firms are often run on a cash basis and have minimum reporting procedures. For these and other reasons mentioned earlier, attempts to measure the strategic health of such enterprises using standard evaluation methods are often inadequate and frequently misleading (Porter, 1985, 1991; Beaver, 1997).
- The success of many new ventures is largely determined by the industry struc- ture, the owner/entrepreneur's skill as a strategist and venture manager and the avoidance of direct competitive retaliation, especially in the early days of business formation. A good example to illustrate this point is the early development of the now global and highly successful Hewlett-Packard.
- Successful small firms practise strategic management either consciously and visibly or unconsciously and invisibly (Beaver and Jennings, 1996; Jennings and Beaver, 1997).

CASE ILLUSTRATION 5.1

Strategic management and the smaller enterprise

Derwent Valley Foods

The founder of the exotic snack food specialist Phileas Fogg has pocketed more than £7 million just 10 years after starting up the business. The workforce of 300 also takes a slice of the £24 million that the food giant United Biscuits is paying for the business located at Consett in County Durham.

Roger McKechnie, who has a 30% stake in Derwent Valley Foods, Fogg's parent company, founded the business with three friends in 1982. They put up £47 000 between them. The backer 3i raised £235 000 for a 25% stake and government grants covered the rest of the £500 000 start-up costs.

McKechnie stated:

It was the only part of the £800 million food market where we could see a real opportunity.

United Biscuits, which sells KP snacks around the world, paid nearly 100 times the original investment and is also taking on £3 million of debt. It hopes to take Fogg's Shanghai nuts into China and its California corn chips into America. It will also be selling Phileas Fogg snacks in pubs and corner shops. McKechnie test marketed his products successfully in Australia, where KP has a strong distribution network.

Source: *The Financial Times*, 25 February 1993

Managing in a recession

We don't know that this is going to be a hard landing, but small firms should have plans ready even if they are not yet implementing them.

Source: Andrew Godfrey, Partner, Grant Thornton Accountants, June 1998

With the exception of two or three sectors that fall into the comfort zone, nobody will really be safe. There is an urgent need to develop defensive strategies but too many small firms appear to remain complacent about the effects of a hard landing.

Source: Price Waterhouse Coopers, *Economic Report*, October 1998

There are no substitutes for strategic thinking. Improving quality, price or service is meaningless without knowing what kind of adjustment is relevant in competitive terms. Entrepreneurship unguided by strategic perspective is more likely to fail than to succeed.

Source: Michael Porter, *The Economist*, 23 May 1987

During the period from September 1998 to June 1999, British economic growth, especially in many parts of the small business sector, slowed considerably to the extent that many industry and economic commentators classified it as a *recession*. In many government circles, the term 'recession' was strongly discouraged as it was believed to be alarmist and dangerous. Instead, reference to an 'economic slowdown' was preferred. (This was dismissed as naive and inaccurate by some very influential research – for example, Profit Impact on Marketing Studies (1999).) Whatever the required terminology, it was quite clear that many sectors of the economy experienced their worst trading period since the last 'official' recession under the Conservative government of 1991–93. Many sectors, often with large small firm populations, are only just starting to experience a return of confidence and an increase in demand for their products and services.

The role and applicability of strategy for the small enterprise is arguably of greater value when there are adverse economic conditions, as the operating context becomes more volatile and trading conditions deteriorate. As previously discussed, it is generally well accepted that sub-optimal performance and potential business failure are closely correlated with a lack of attention to business strategy. It follows, therefore, that those small firms facing a hostile commercial environment should fashion their competitive responses in accordance not only with any contingency plans that may have been developed but act in a positive and timely manner to underpin their chosen strategic position. Given that many small businesses experience a measure of disadvantage (Beaver and Harrison, 1994; Beaver and Jennings, 1996; Jennings and Beaver, 1997), owing not only to the size of the enterprise but also to their resource base and operating context, the need to embrace strategic management thinking and actions, especially in a recessionary environment, has never been more necessary.

Accordingly, this section is divided into four parts:

- The first considers the economic evidence underpinning the claims of recession and its impact on small firms.
- The second examines the research observations from the last recession on the reporting of small business financial performance.
- The third examines the characteristics and strategic responses of those enterprises that survived the last official recession, including the advice and assistance from a variety of sources that small businesses should consider in managing their affairs in a recession.
- The fourth part provides an interesting case illustration of the Sea-Band Company and its strategic approach to managing in a recessionary environment.

The economic evidence – extracts from selected economic surveys and forecasts from July 1998 to June 1999

British economic growth in many sectors was confirmed to be slowing and the recently published Lloyds TSB research covering 2000 medium-sized businesses showed fairly convincingly that the slowdown was gathering momentum. Furthermore, it was not just affecting exporters and the manufacturing sectors, usually thought of as the first to suffer; the problems are starting to filter through to the service sector.

The BDO Stoy Hayward survey of surveys (February 1999) suggested that the gloom was so widespread that many business specialists would not be surprised if many sectors of the economy were not in recession next year and possibly the year after. Its latest findings forecast a year-on-year GDP decline of nearly 1% by mid-1999.

A new index of companies in distress (the so-called 'Agony Index') compiled by the Mandis Group of Nottingham on the basis of profit warnings, job losses, downbeat trading statements and cuts in investment, shows that twice as many firms were experiencing serious problems (December 1998) as a year ago. The research covers approximately 100 000 companies from a wide range of industries and sectors. Surveys from Barclays Bank for its small business bulletin (March 1999) and National Westminster (February–March 1999) endorse these findings.

For some time, most sectors of the UK economy had experienced a slowdown in the growth of orders with retailing particularly badly hit by slower sales. On balance, only 18% of businesses reported an increase in orders over the period, against 29% 6 months ago. This, when combined with the intense domestic and foreign competition, meant that more companies were being forced to cut prices, producing an acute squeeze on profits.

For the first time since the six-monthly Business in Britain survey was launched in 1992, there had been a negative balance on prices – over the past six months 19% increased their prices, while 20% cut them. Consequently, just 3% reported higher profits, the lowest proportion since the previous recession. These depressing figures meant that business confidence had dipped to its lowest level since the last recession of 1991–93, with predictions that orders would slow further. Despite the slowdown, almost half of businesses were operating at capacity. The downbeat outlook meant that growth in investment and employment, which would help to alleviate constraints, had also slowed.

Initially these figures did not make for encouraging reading but, compared with the last downturn, businesses should not have suffered such a sharp decline and many would have been better prepared. It was predicted that many would emerge stronger and more competitive. Businesses – especially small firms and their banks, had learnt lessons from the last recession. As a result, many would be better placed to weather the storm and it is unlikely that there would be as many bankruptcies.

The businesses that set the pace initially and led Britain out of recession in the early 1990s were exporters. In order to discover how a business could successfully weather the storm of 1998–99, it is important to analyse why these exporters were in such a strong position. Manufacturers, badly hit in the first Thatcher recession of 1980–81, realised that to be competitive with a weak currency they needed to be more sophisticated in selecting their markets and that they would have to keep a very tight rein on costs. Unfortunately, this was not the policy adopted by many firms leading up to the early 1990s recession, when the tremendous boom meant that sales went sky high and there was not such a need to keep a watch on costs. There are some signs in 1998–99 those exporters were once again striving to improve their competitiveness.

The CBI research on exporting (Confederation of British Industry, 1999) has shown that more firms lost orders than gained them and that growth in exports was at its lowest since 1992. Only 32% of exporters increased their orders since January 1998, compared with 36% experiencing a fall. However, there is evidence that some firms were countering the effect of the strong pound. Over the next 6 months, 35% of exporters believe that conditions will marginally improve, against 25% that remain sceptical.

Many businesses, of all sizes and from all sectors, were becoming more competitive by concentrating on innovative products that sell on the basis of quality and service differentiation – and not relying on price as the major source of competitive advantage.

Many were forming stronger partnerships with overseas agents and distributors that can respond to local requirements and many trimmed shipping costs and profit margins to maintain sales. According to received economic wisdom, when the value of sterling does become more manageable, it is hoped that firms will become even more competitive.

Meanwhile, the clearing banks had planned for the coming slowdown in various ways: notably, working with their principal business customers to pre-empt problems that would otherwise have arisen 6 months down the line and perhaps be too advanced by that point. Over the past 2 years Lloyds TSB had seen a 15%

rise in the number of term loans taken out by small firm customers. This was regarded as a healthy sign because business owners were seen to be planning for the future rather than exhibiting the inevitable knee-jerk reaction of the unhealthy reliance on overdrafts and other short-term lending.

This policy of pre-empting funding problems, together with a movement towards longer-term planning, is defended by the banks on sound business reasons;

> As prudent and responsible lending should benefit both customer and lender in the long term when the upturn in business confidence appears.

Source: Lloyds TSB, February 1999

Observations on the reporting of small firms' financial performance

Observations during the last two recessions in the UK from a variety of research surveys have brought to light a curious phenomenon: the declared results and forecasts by small firms do not always square with the actual outcomes. It has been noticed that firms responding to research surveys appear typically optimistic, report better than actual profitability, do not easily reveal losses and generally demonstrate how the power of ignorance and self-deception can subvert reality and lead to misleading conclusions.

In an expanding market, proactive business strategies are likely to achieve positive results since, even with new competitors entering the market, sales are relatively easy to achieve and, with the minimum of controls, assist the net profit line. Thus the owner-manager only has to understand the sales function reasonably well to be in a fairly strong position to report on profits or the trend in profits.

In a contracting market, however, the reporting situation becomes more complicated. In the early days of demand stagnation, as soon as the level of future sales starts to become unpredictable, the owner's confidence about the currency of business information is undermined. As the decline in profits and the availability of cash to fund fixed and working capital become more invasive, the owner/entrepreneur responds by starting to cut down, or cut out, investment expenditure. Since there is no reliable method to predict future streams of income and profit from any such investment and of even more concern, there is no proactive marketing to squeeze profitable sales out of a declining market.

The one possible exception to this general rule is where price discounting is used to generate sales at lower gross margins. However, in this case since there is no reliable or up to date information about the contribution levels for different kinds of products and markets, the small firm practitioner is susceptible to the conclusion that increasing sales must again lead to continuing profits. It often comes as a shock when this is not the case.

In a prolonged recession, with the realisation that a reactive strategy no longer works and when sales have already started to fall away, profits can be eroded completely and losses quickly follow. This leads to a progressive deterioration of the capital base of the firm. Without tight controls, monthly cash flows rapidly become negative and the business becomes overdrawn. Relationships with the bank may well start to deteriorate as the temptation to operate at the maximum limit of the overdraft take effect. Sales tend to plateau early in the cycle and the business attempts to stabilise its cash position by cutting capacity to match sales. At this point the firm may be operating below its full-profit break even but just about at its cash break even, largely because the owner/entrepreneur has decided to reduce his or her own salary as well as cut out all forms of capital expenditure (not only is there no new cash expenditure on capital but also the impact of depreciation is eliminated). To an ill-informed owner/manager, the business appears to have weathered the storm but, to change metaphors, at this point it is merely bumping along the bottom.

As the previous section showed, there is considerable evidence that a substantial number of small firms in the UK were just surviving and hoping for an upturn in demand to lead them back to relative prosperity. Moreover, it is quite clear that there is nowhere for these businesses to go except upwards – in other words, to improve sales and performance. To admit otherwise would be tacitly to accept defeat, which no self-respecting entrepreneur would care to do. There is no category of unemployment called 'out of work entrepreneurs'. The socio-psychological pressures to ride out the storm are immense.

Thus, when small firm owners and practitioners are asked about the level of current performance and future prospects for the business, responses may well be governed not only by the lack of information about sales and profits but also by the psychological pressures to deny that things could get worse. Many small businesses will be tempted to report optimistically about their financial status and profit performance (current and future), since to do otherwise would force them to confront their own business mortality.

In summary, what then are the possible underlying causes of financial misrepresentation by owner-managers and entrepreneurs? They can be grouped into the following four areas.

A fixation with cash

There is a powerful cash nexus that drives many small firms, causing an imbalance in the owner-manager's perceived information about profit performance. Cash is clearly the lifeblood of the business, for without it there are no salaries, bills cannot get paid and no investment can be made in the long term.

It follows then that borrowing to achieve any of the above outcomes is unlikely to appeal to the owner with a strong cash fixation. The discomfort experienced by not having cash will be so strong in a recession that the owner will avoid borrowing (negative cash) in the face of uncertain repayment prospects. This perception and set of responses have their basis in the under-capitalisation of the business, which has been well documented throughout small business research.

A common motivation for starting a business is the need for personal achievement and the most explicit demonstration of this achievement is the conspicuous consumption achieved with the use of cash. There is little incentive to accumulate reserves for any contingency, especially in the case of an unincorporated business, which is assessed for taxation on profits before the drawings of the owner.

This fixation with cash means that many small businesses have little impetus to give due consideration to profit as a measure of performance.

Cash is collected and treated as an income stream that is used to pay suppliers, employees and other stakeholders and creditors. The balance is then available to the owners to distribute as they please. Not surprisingly, in this context the recording of profit has minimal relevance.

No proper understanding of the profit concept and no real perceived need for the recording and reporting of profit

The accounting concept of net profit has a very different meaning and relevance to the small firm practitioner compared with the large organisation's counterpart. As seen above, the former is primarily concerned with cash transactions than with net profit – but the concern is deeper than this. Profit is at best a notional concept devoid of any real meaning when it comes to calculating whether bills can be paid and whether sufficient moneys exist to fund future expenditures. This is because of the uncertainties that surround the timing of cash receipts from sales and the corresponding certainty of payroll and rent costs having to be met, which are by far the largest cost items in most firms. Other creditors too will not be deterred from making their claims on time.

The reasons are also conditioned by the nature and timing of costs. A first example is depreciation. Although recognised by the owner/manager as a cost, many firms do not regard the necessity to account for the using up of capital items over their useful life as a constraint on their thinking. This typically affects the outcomes of costing, estimating and pricing processes in many businesses that may be arbitrary at best. In a recession, there is every incentive not to include depreciation in a costing.

A second example concerns the cost of marketing and sales activities. In many small firms there are very few explicit marketing costs, the principal exceptions being travel, motoring, subsistence, some entertaining, printing and some advertising. The result is that marketing costs are typically understated.

The owner/manager or people who have other roles to perform undertake a great deal of the marketing. Moreover, the real costs of marketing may differ from the recorded costs, because many are hidden. If these were to be made explicit in the accounts, the real profitability of the business may be substantially worse than that currently perceived by the owner.

For many small business practitioners, net profit is not an accurate guide to the payment of income or corporation taxes. The adjustments that take place before firms and owners are assessed for taxation are frequently not revealed to small business practitioners by their accountants.

Thus the mystique that often accompanies the production of annual accounts tends to work against an understanding of the profit concept. In a recession, with losses more likely, the liability for paying tax is much reduced anyway. This tends to further reinforce the view that accurate, up-to-date recording of sales revenues and costs is not a priority for the business owner.

No concept of competitive performance

Small business practitioners tend to set financial performance standards according to internal considerations, such as how much the owner/manager(s) want as drawings and how well the business performed last year. The monitoring and recording of competitors' performance for many firms tend to be ignored.

This may be because information about competitors is not readily available but more likely it reflects the absence of strategic thinking. It is a sobering fact that, in a recent survey of small firms in the East Midlands (Beaver, 1997), only 34% of owner-managers in the research survey had a clear idea of why their customers bought from them. The absence of a strategy that sets goals and objectives driven from the market-place means that financial performance indicators and standards will be internally driven. In the absence of accurate reporting procedures, they are unlikely to be articulated frequently, with the result that their use to business practitioners is considerably reduced.

Short-term thinking and planning

This final cause of mis-reporting of financial performance by small firm owners and entrepreneurs is due to their propensity for a short-term, reactive style of thinking which dictates the management process in so many small businesses.

Reactive responses to market and other stimuli are the result partly of poorly developed business skills and partly of their lack of power in the markets for the resources necessary to attain true competitive advantage. It has been noted that disempowerment has a rational legacy of short-term thinking and lack of planning since, when the firm is subject to the vagaries of its market(s), there are no strong incentives to invest in the future. The *receding horizons* syndrome negates strategic planning as a philosophy – the belief that everything will come good at some unspecified time in the future and the ability to push back this time as one wishes. With such a philosophy, there is every likelihood that the long-term future will be regarded with relative disinterest. The result is a tendency to avoid long-term planning and the collection of data to inform the planning process. This in turn has the effect of devaluing the requirement for accurate performance indicators.

In conclusion, it can be seen from the above that the effect of a recession on small firms exacerbates the economic and psychological conditions that produce misreporting.

Small firms that survived the last recession exhibited many or all of the following characteristics

- They had a firm grip on their finances.
- They reduced the money that debtors owed by implementing an effective credit management system.
- They considered what purchases to make and deferred risky ones that were not necessary or negotiated better prices, extended credit or quicker deliveries to reduce stock.
- They concentrated on tight stock control, reviewing and identifying areas where efficiency and costs could be improved. Successful firms focused stock control efforts on high-price and high-volume items. They also minimised work in progress and finished goods stocks by making production processes as streamlined as possible.

● Sales and marketing activities were reviewed to increase efficiency and reduce costs where possible, including dropping marginal products and concentrating on the most non-price-sensitive products and services.

How to survive a recession – 15 ways to weather an economic downturn

1 *Business plan*. Examine the business forecasts carefully and return to the original plan to check and the assumptions made about sales volume and cash flow. Check that all the proposed expenditure is necessary.

2 *Cash flow*. This is the key area – the management of cash flow is the lifeblood of any business. Is the working capital sufficient for projected activity? Examine areas such as the purchases of new equipment, machinery and vehicles – and consider alternative approaches such as leasing to free up cash.

3 *The bank*. Review your relationship with the bank to ensure that things are on a sound footing. Banks have learnt much from the last recession and know that, if the firms that they lend to do not prosper, then neither will they. Recognise any problems at an early stage and inform the bank as soon as possible.

4 *Banking costs and charges*. Substantial savings can be made on banking charges, so it is advisable to check whether the cheapest methods are being used, such as automated payments or payments over the telephone and the Internet. Avoid unarranged overdrafts or exceeding agreed overdraft limits. Review insurance costs and other financial charges.

5 *Pricing policy*. Check to ensure that prices will be sustainable and whether the profit margin(s) will be sufficient if the volume of sales falls. If not then review the sales and pricing policy. Try and cull any sales where margins are already borderline.

6 *Overheads*. Scrutinise the costs that do not vary with output – areas to focus on include rent, rates and local taxes and utilities (the competition in the utilities sector in the UK at the time of writing has never been as intense, so it makes good sense to take full advantage). Turn off all unneeded lights. Look at plant, equipment and staff costs with the objective of cutting overheads. Consider making salaries less fixed and more dependent on performance – but be professional and sensitive.

7 *Competition*. Examine the nature, health and responses of identified competition. How are they faring? Valuable ideas and suggestions for dealing with tighter markets may well result.

8 *New customers*. Credit checks can be done quickly and are relatively inexpensive. Always check the credit status of a new customer and review the status of existing customers on a regular basis.

9 *Marketing*. This is a natural extension of the above point but worth thinking about in a strategic manner as marketing costs can be considerable. Attempt to improve the effectiveness of marketing and sales by reviewing the costs and margins of company products and services. Consider dropping unprofitable products and limit selling efforts to the most profitable ones.

10 *Credit limits*. Always attempt to establish how big orders will be and how often they will be placed. Set a credit limit for each customer and stick to it. For new customers, set a modest credit limit and only gradually increase it if they show that they pay on time. Never give unlimited credit.

11 *Terms of sale*. Terms of sale should always be stated on order acceptances, invoices and other documents that govern the trading relationship(s). Include a provision for adding interest to the outstanding amount to encourage payment on time. Be aware of the company's legal entitlements under the Late Payment of Commercial Debts Act (Chapter 7 provides more information on this topic).

12 *Overdue accounts*. Send out statements on a monthly basis and chase up overdue accounts on the telephone and by E-mail. Do not wait until the end of the month if you can send out invoices at the same time as you send out the goods. Be firm with slow payers and always send reminders by first-class post to promote a sense of urgency.

13 *Administration and records*. Always ensure that invoices are correctly addressed, relate to the goods delivered and include order numbers if they are required. Make frequent and regular checks to ensure that all details are up to date and accurate – in short, be as professional as you can.

14 *Suppliers and stock*. If your company is relying on two or three main suppliers, consider what would happen if alternatives had to found. Consider negotiating discounts for prompt payments or better terms to keep your cash for longer before paying bills. Review stock levels and talk to suppliers about the possibility of more frequent deliveries to keep stock levels low. Check to see whether old lines can be sold off and consider discounts for slow-moving items.

15 *Factoring*. Investigate the possibility of using a sales-linked finance organisation that has the systems and resources to improve cash flow and will cut the time devoted to credit control.

Finally, the key to ensuring that the business is prepared for a slowdown is to prioritise. Put cash flow first, profit second and sales third.

CASE ILLUSTRATION 5.2

Strategic recessionary management

Sea-Band

Anyone who suffers from travel sickness will probably owe a debt of gratitude to the Sea-Band Company, for this is the business that makes the elasticated wrist-bands that help combat nausea and make travel a lot more pleasant for thousands of people. The firm was started in the mid-1980s by Barry Jackson in Hinkley, Leicestershire, and seemed to prosper from its inception. Like many other entrepreneurs, who set up in business during the enterprise years of the Thatcher administration, Jackson began by expanding aggressively.

However, unlike many of his contemporaries that became casualties of the recession in the early 1990s, Jackson is still prospering. Sea-Band now enjoys annual sales of over £3 million and commands a strong British presence in chemists such as Boots and an 89-strong sales team covering 50 countries, including the USA, where virtually every drug chain and wholesaler carries its products. Sea-Band's survival stemmed from careful planning and taking measured advice at the first signs of an economic downturn. Jackson states that:

> Early on last time we realised that we were a marketing company and that was where our expertise lay.

Instead of attempting to carry on with business as usual, Jackson decided that he had to rationalise and jettison those non-core functions that distracted him from the focus of the business. He states:

> The business was not a debt-collector and the simplest way forward as a small company, was to give our debts to someone else.

The company took the factoring route to remove the time spent on credit control and chasing debtors:

> Factoring our debts helped us because we could then forget about them.

Factoring (essentially, the selling on of debts or invoices to a collection agency at an agreed rate) cost the business some profit but it secured cash flow. As a consequence, Jackson then felt free to concentrate his efforts on developing the company. He recognised that the way ahead lay in spreading the risks and for the business that meant moving into overseas markets so that the company could be free from over-reliance on the home market.

However, simply becoming an exporter was not of itself a sufficient answer. Sea-Band needed to sell efficiently in international and, ultimately, global markets. At the time, fax machines were relatively new but Jackson recognised that this facility would enable the company to sell overseas without the expense of having a sales team in place. Furthermore, faxing was cheap: it had low running costs and a modest capital outlay – but the benefits were immediate and substantial and enabled Jackson to develop a network of distributors and agents for the Sea-Band products. To quote Jackson:

> I liked the idea of going global at the time. Britain was important to us but it was a limited market, so I tried to spread as much as possible.

Unlike many entrepreneurs, Jackson was shrewd enough not to over-expand his operation or to over-reach himself by borrowing too much from the bank. He states:

> We kept lean in the early days and that stood us in good stead later on.

It meant that the company developed a strong relationship with its bank and relied on a modest overdraft rather than an unrealistic one that the bank could call in should the company falter.

By 1992 Sea-Band was in relatively good shape but, even though the economy had begun to grow again, Jackson still kept the company lean. It has eight direct workers, a relatively small sales network and no large overheads like factories. The result is that sales are up by 20% on last year, with much of the growth coming from its operations abroad. The continuing success of the business is due in no small part to careful forward planning, which Jackson states other owner-managers have also learnt is essential if they are to continue to do well and survive. Jackson says:

> The difference between the early 1990s and now is that firms are generally much more efficient as well as leaner. A lot of firms went to the wall during the late 1980s and early 1990s because of the recession but also because of poor management.

This time round, Jackson is confident that the current economic downturn will have less of an impact but he acknowledges that there will be casualties. One of the consequences, he says, will be higher unemployment as firms slim their work-forces to carry on trading or freeze them at current levels. Sea-Band is already feeling the adverse effects of the strong pound but the measures that Jackson has in place, combined with the experience he had trading through the last recession, should ensure that he survives a hard landing:

> We are not lowering prices, but we are improving the level of customer service by providing extra value.

Jackson monitors the financial trends very closely:

> We can jump on things pretty quickly in terms of our accounts so we can put something right in a maximum of six weeks, he says. Not everything is perfect but we are reasonably happy.

References and further reading

Aram, J. D. and Cowan, S. S. (1990) 'Strategy Planning for Increased Profit in the Small Business', *Long Range Planning*, December, 63–70.

Atkins, M. and Lowe, J. (1994) 'Stakeholders and the Strategy Formation Process in Small and Medium Sized Enterprises', *International Small Business Journal*, 12 (3), 12–24.

Banfield, P., Jennings, P. L. and Beaver, G. (1996) 'Competence-Based Training for Small Firms – An Expensive Failure?', *Long Range Planning*, February, 94–102.

Beaver, G. (1997) Management Styles and Performance in Midlands Small Firms: The Role and Contribution of Strategy, Nottingham Business School Working Paper, September.

Beaver, G. and Harrison, Y. (1994) 'TEC Support for Women Entrepreneurs: Help or Hindrance?', in 17th National ISBA Small Firms Policy and Research Conference, Sheffield, November.

Beaver, G. and Jennings, P. L. (1996) 'The Abuse of Entrepreneurial Power – An Explanation of Management Failure?', *Journal of Strategic Change*, 5 (3), May/June, 151–64.

Beaver, G. and Jennings, P. L. (2000) 'Small Business, Entrepreneurship and Enterprise Development', *Journal of Strategic Change*, 9 (7) (Special Issue), November, 397–403.

Beaver, G. and Ross, E. C. (1999) 'Recessionary Consequences on Small Business Management and Business Development: The Abandonment of Strategy?', *Journal of Strategic Change*, 8 (5), 251–61.

Beaver, G. and Ross, C. (2000) 'Enterprise in Recession: The Role and Context of Strategy', *International Journal of Entrepreneurship and Innovation*, 1 (1), February, 23–31.

Birley, S. (1989) 'Corporate Strategy and the Small Firm', in Asch, D. and Bowman, C. (eds), *Readings in Strategic Management*. Basingstoke: Macmillan, ch. 6.

Birley, S. and Westhead, P. (1990) 'Growth and Performance Contrasts between Types of Small Firms', *Strategic Management Journal*, 11, November/December, 535–57.

Carland, J. W., Hoy, F., Boulton, W. R. and Carland, J. A. C. (1984) 'Differentiating Entrepreneurs from Small Business Owners: A Conceptualisation', *Academy of Management Review*, 9 (2), 354–9.

Confederation of British Industry (1999) *Interim Report on the Export Readiness of British Industry*.

El-Namacki, M. S. S. (1990) 'Small Business – The Myth and the Reality', *Long Range Planning*, 23 (4), August, 78–87.

Hofer, C. W. and Sandberg, W. R. (1987) 'Improving New Venture Performance: Some Guidelines for Success', *American Journal of Small Business*, Summer, 12–23.

Jennings, P. L. and Beaver, G. (1996) 'Managerial Competence and Competitive Advantage in the Small Business: An Alternative Perspective', in 26th European Small Business Seminar, Vaasa, Finland.

Jennings, P. L. and Beaver G. (1997) 'The Performance and Competitive Advantage of Small Firms: A Management Perspective', *International Small Business Journal*, 15 (2), January–March, 63–75.

Porter, M. E. (1985) *Competitive Advantage – Creating and Sustaining Superior Performance*. New York: Free Press.

Porter, M. E. (1991) *The Competitive Advantage of Nations*. New York: Free Press.

Profit Impact on Marketing Studies (1999) Report presented to Warwick Business School Alumni Update Seminar, April.

SBA (1998) *Annual Report*. Small Business Administration (USA).

Shepherd, D. A. and Shanley, M. A. (1998) *New Venture Strategy*. London: Sage.

Storey, D. J. (1998, 1999) *The Ten Percenters*, 3rd and 4th Reports, *Fast Growing SMEs in Great Britain*. London: Deloitte & Touche.

Wheelen, T. L. and Hunger, J. D. (1998) *Strategic Management and Business Policy*, 6th edn. Reading, MA: Addison-Wesley.

Wickham, P. A. (1998) *Strategic Entrepreneurship*. London: Pitman.

6 Business planning

Objectives Business planning is clearly perceived by both government and the business support infrastructure that it helped to facilitate as an essential ingredient for the small business. Additionally, the role and importance of business planning appears to be the convention expected by the banks and other funding agencies if they are to advance the necessary finance for new venture creation and business development.

This chapter seeks to examine:

- the role, nature and composition of the business plan and the kind of information that it should include;

- the process and importance of business planning and its contribution to managerial decision-making;

- the process by which a plan can help facilitate the venture by providing the framework for analysis, guiding and promoting management action and communicating the potential of the enterprise to interested parties;

- the relationship between business planning and enterprise success and progression;

- the failures and shortcomings of business planning and what can be done to prevent them occurring;

- the evaluation of a business plan.

The importance and function of the business plan

A recent statement from the UK Cabinet Office (1996) serves as a useful introduction to the importance now attached to the role, function and expectations of the small business sector by government. The following statement also recognises the difficulties that the small firm and its management invariably experience in planning for its future and providing the required resources:

> Small firms have steadily increased their share of output and employment over the last twenty years. Their adaptability to change and their closeness to their customers give them a competitive edge in many markets. But smaller firms face particular obstacles. Smaller firms may be reliant on a small number of customers, they can face difficulties in raising finance and they may find it difficult to spare time from day-to-day management to the vital task of planning for the future.

By way of comparison, a similar, although more lengthy endorsement to the above is provided by the Australian Minister responsible for Small Firms in a publication from the Department of Industry, Technology and Commerce (1998):

> As the owner or manager of a business, you have responsibilities to yourself, your employees, shareholders, customers and suppliers to keep your business in a profitable and healthy state. Some of the responsibilities are immediate and can be described as short-term. You must manage your business to ensure solvency and liquidity today, tomorrow and next week. However, good management is about taking a longer-term view and this involves planning for the future development and growth of the business.
>
> It is not good enough to manage a business for the short-term only, because you are in business for the longer-term gains that you expect to make. Unfortunately, it is all too easy to fall into the trap of spending all your time managing day-to-day issues – fire-fighting as some call it – and leaving the long-term direction of the company to manage itself.
>
> If you are in business for the long term, you cannot afford to be technically superior and business-wise inferior. Planning for the future course of your business is a must. This publication will help you think about and plan for the future of your business through the construction of a business plan.

Political rhetoric and wishful thinking aside, the statement from the Minister goes on to provide one of the most succinct and accurate descriptions of a business plan and its value to the small firm:

> A business plan is much more than a necessary document to present to your bank manager. It is a detailed statement of the objectives and directions that you have set yourself and provides a balanced framework across all key functional areas of the business for the shorter-term day-to-day decisions that you have to make. Without a business plan, you really cannot say with any clarity, why you are in business, or where you are heading.
>
> Although you may well have a business plan locked away in your brain, experts agree that it is a very worthwhile exercise to formalise it and write it down. This will help you in your thinking about the business and will be an excellent form of communication which you can use to convince other people of what you are doing.
>
> Finally, a business plan is about the identification of your key sources of competitiveness. It will help you determine how best you can compete in the marketplace, with the ultimate aim of being a healthy, thriving and profitable business.

Defining the business plan

There are many writers and commentators on the subject of business plans and business planning, each with their own definitions and perceptions on the subject. An authoritative and comprehensive account is provided by Wickham (1998) who defines a *business plan* succinctly as an entrepreneurial tool. He reminds us that the activity of creating a formal plan consumes both time and resources and that, if it is to be undertaken and undertaken well, there must be an appreciation of the way in which the plan can actually be made to work as a tool for the business. He lists four mechanisms by which a business plan might aid the performance of a venture:

1 *As a tool for analysis.* A business plan contains information. Some of this information will be that used as the basis for articulating and refining the entrepreneur's vision, for generating the mission statement and for developing a strategy content and strategy process for the venture. The structure of the business plan provides the entrepreneur with an effective checklist of the information that must be gathered in order to be sure that the direction of the venture is both achievable and rewarding. Creating the plan guides and disciplines the entrepreneur in gathering this information.

2 *As a tool for synthesis.* Once data have been gathered and analysed in a formal way then the information generated must be used to provide a direction for the venture. The information must be integrated with and used to refine the entrepreneur's vision and used to support the development of a suitable mission and strategy. The planning exercise acts to synthesise the entrepreneur's vision with a definite plan of action in a unified way. This synthesis converts the vision into a strategy for the venture and then into actions appropriate to pursuing that strategy.

3 *As a tool for communication.* The business plan provides a vehicle for communicating the potential of the venture, the opportunities that it faces and the way in which it intends to exploit them in a way that is concise, efficient and effective. This may be of value in communicating with both internal and external stakeholders. The plan may draw internal people together and give them a focus for their activities. The business plan is particularly important as a tool for communicating with potential investors, gaining their interest and attracting them to the venture.

4 *As a call to action.* The business plan is a call to action. It provides a detailed list of the activities that must be undertaken, the tasks that must be performed and the outcomes that must be achieved if the entrepreneur is to convert his or her vision into a commercial reality.

The plan may also call on and deploy formal project management techniques in order to organise, prioritise and arrange tasks in a way which makes best use of scarce resources. Wickham also states that the four ways in which the business planning exercise contributes to the success of the venture do not operate in isolation. To be effective, they should underpin and support each other and the performance of the venture (see Figure 6.1).

Richardson and Jennings (1988) offer a simpler but no less convincing, explanation of what constitutes a business plan. They also take the view that a successful plan, i.e. one that achieves its outcomes and expectations, needs to be designed with both the planner (i.e. the entrepreneur/owner-manager) and the evaluator (i.e. the bank or resource-provider) perspectives in mind. In short, they state that a business plan:

- is many things depending on the specifics and operating context of the venture and has many desired aims and outcomes;
- is a set of related assumptions about what the future will contain, with outcomes often expressed in financial terms;
- integrates strategic, operational and administrative issues;

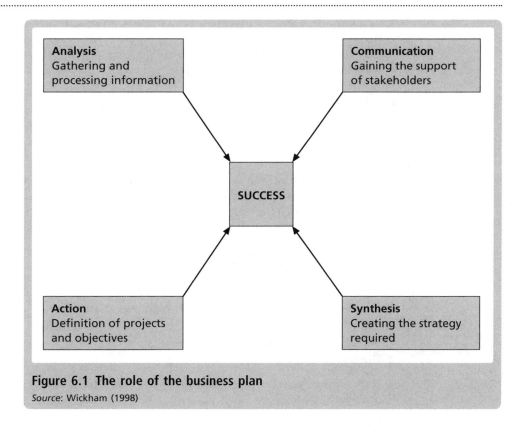

Figure 6.1 The role of the business plan
Source: Wickham (1998)

- is a mixture of quantitative and qualitative data and information;
- is an articulate bargaining strategy to obtain the necessary resources.

A cursory search of the literature reveals no agreed model or purpose of a business plan – save that it should contribute to the well-being of the business and assist the key players in becoming more effective in their management and decision-making. Burns' (1996) definition is as good as any – and more helpful than most – when he states that:

> The business plan entails taking a long-term view of the business and its environment. A good plan should emphasise the strengths and recognise the weaknesses of the proposed venture. Above all it should convey a sincerity of purpose and analysis which lends credibility both to itself and to the entrepreneur putting it forward.

The business planning process – developing a business plan

Essentially business planning involves an integrated process which begins with a strategic analysis of the business – whether as a new venture or as an existing enterprise seeking to expand or develop. This entails the formulation of objectives and aspirations, the current resources available and the present and potential environmental positions. This then progresses to the generation, evaluation and choice of strategic developments and possibilities.

In reality, the process involves some degree of reiteration as issues, preferences and outcomes are considered and reconsidered as the process unfurls. The business planning exercise is designed to challenge and test management assumptions and insight into the following questions:

- Where are we now?
- Where are we going?
- Where do we want to be?
- How do we get there?

A useful framework for a business plan has been developed by Richardson and Jennings (1988) which is detailed in Example 6.1. Frameworks such as this help the small business practitioner to begin the planning process and to structure their business plan in a logical (and reassuring) way and also serve as an introduction to a manner of thinking which for many potential or existing owner/managers is atypical.

Example 6.1: The framework for a business plan

Part 1: where have we been and where are we now?
- The background of the enterprise.
- Statement of past performance, markets served and products and services provided.
- Short description of the present plan that is proposed.

Part 2: where are we now and where do we want to be?
- Mission, vision, aims and aspirations of planners and principal stakeholders.
- Environmental analysis, competitor analysis, strengths, weaknesses, opportunities and threats (SWOT) analysis.
- Resource position audit.

This is essentially the *strategic analysis* phase which considers enterprise objectives in the context of present and potential stakeholder positions and aspirations, together with resource and contextual situations.

Part 3: where we want to be and how are we going to get there?
- The product/service and marketing strategies underlying the plan.
- The financial projections, including anticipated turnover, gearing, profitability (loss) liquidity (cash flow) and return on capital or equity.
- Contingency provisions for both shortfalls and take-off.

This is the *strategy generation, evaluation and choice* phase which is a well-documented, systematic and model-backed activity generating numerous potential enterprise scenarios and development opportunities that the key role-players must evaluate and select as the most appropriate.

Part 4: how are we going to get there – in more detail?

- The identification of key tasks and objectives for the performance and efficiency of the enterprise – including management attention to the credibility/resource merry-go-round (Birley, 1996).

- Financial arrangements and agreements.

- Implementation schedule – including attention and priorities to the key functional areas.

The last phase of *strategic implementation* provides the operational and administrative blueprint for activating the chosen strategies and identifies the key players responsible for each activity. In the business plan document, this section itemises the principal tasks and incorporates budgetary details and implementation schedules. The more sophisticated business plans may even document anticipated stakeholder reactions and management responses.

Source: adapted from Richardson and Jennings (1988)

It has been mentioned elsewhere in this text that small firms do not plan to fail, they simply fail to plan. The above process, while logical and strategic in complexion and design, does not suit a significant number of owner/manager/ entrepreneurs as the following reference to Bhide's (1994) work illustrates:

> However popular it may be in the corporate world, a comprehensive analytical approach to planning does not suit most start-ups. Entrepreneurs typically lack the time and money to interview a representative cross section of potential customers, let alone analyse substitutes, re-construct competitors cost structures, or project for alternative technology scenarios. In fact too much analysis can be harmful; by the time that an opportunity is investigated fully, it may no longer exist! A city map and restaurant guide on a CD may be a winner in January but worthless if delayed until December.
>
> A 1990 study of independent businesses that comprised 2994 start-ups, showed that founders who spent a long time in study, reflection and planning were no more likely to survive their first three years than people who seized opportunities without planning . . . Analysis can delay market entry until it is too late or kill ideas by identifying numerous problems.

However, he does add an important qualification to the above:

> All ventures merit some analysis and planning . . . successful entrepreneurs do not take risks blindly, rather they take a middle ground between planning paralysis and no planning at all . . . Astute entrepreneurs do analyse and strategise extensively . . . but they realise that new businesses cannot be launched like space shuttles with every detail of the mission planned in advance.

The following entrepreneurial codicil to the strategic business planning process is offered as an essential qualification to the formality advocated above by Richardson and Jennings:

1 Screen out opportunities quickly to weed out unpromising ventures.
2 Analyse ideas parsimoniously. Focus on a few important issues.
3 Integrate action and analysis. Do not wait for all the answers and be ready to change course.

What is clear and unequivocal from the evidence on business planning as a logical and strategic process, is that the standard checklist, one-size-fits-all approach does not work. Each business venture and its management is unique and therefore, the appropriate analytical priorities vary for each enterprise and its operating context. *Business planning then for the small and developing business is essentially a cyclical process with inter-related stages and activities.*

Most professionals and advisers to small firms generally agree that there are very real advantages in having a written business plan. These include:

- The act of recording and testing assumptions and ideas formally on paper is good business discipline. The use of a structured framework helps to ensure that the important ingredients responsible for delivering commercial success are covered. The consideration of the different and potentially conflicting aims and objectives of the planner and evaluator roles can enhance the probability of securing the required resources.
- The visible presentation of targets and objectives to be achieved over the life of the plan can be highly motivational for the key players concerned.
- The written document serves as a valuable management instrument that can be used to monitor the progress of the business and serve as an essential frame of reference in the case of disputes and disagreements which may arise.

In developing a business plan there are, by necessity, financial and non-financial considerations. The non-financial considerations are usually dealt with first as they provide the assumptions and parameters that govern the financial targets and issues. These considerations are again well covered in the course texts. Some of the major functional elements of a business plan are given in Example 6.2.

Example 6.2: The major functional elements of a business plan

Sustainable competitive advantage should result from attention to the following:

Marketing strategy:
- Positioning
- Target market
- Product range
- Product innovation
- Pricing approach
- Distribution and logistics
- Sales management
- Advertising and promotion

Production strategy:
- Capacity
- Production scheduling
- Process innovation
- Equipment requirements and planning
- Material requirements and suppliers
- Location and distribution
- Quality control
- Human resources management

Financial strategy:
- Financial history
- Required capital investment
- Profit and loss projections
- Cash flow projections
- Balance sheet projections
- Break-even analysis

Before concluding this section, it is as well to be reminded that some of the features of a good business plan are not simply the product of its structure and organisational formality – important though these things are: they are the result of detailed management investigation into the context and operating environment in which the business has to craft and sustain competitive advantage.

Notwithstanding the arguments of Bhide mentioned above, some of these questions are likely to include:

- Who are the important stakeholders? What is it that makes them important and what is the general approach to be taken?
- What are the principal organisational objectives? Many small businesses have several, often conflicting, objectives and it is necessary to identify those that are paramount to commercial survival and long-term viability. Objectives should possess certain characteristics if they are to be valuable and contribute towards enterprise development, e.g. measurability, consistency and realism.
- What are the strengths and weaknesses of the resource base of the firm? Which aspects of the business are fundamental in delivering competitive advantage in the chosen market segment/sector?
- Which environmental trends or events will produce threats or opportunities for the business? Can the business be defined or re-defined in a strategic way that facilitates a better sense of direction, or opportunity? The recent re-positioning of the World Wildlife Fund as a fund-raising business, rather than as a conservation organisation, is a good example of such a strategic opportunity (Medley, 1989).
- What is the nature of the existing or emerging competition and what are they doing, or not doing, that represents a threat or a business opportunity? What is the nature of their competitive advantage? A good example of this sort of question is the recent merger of ASDA with Wal-Mart of America which represents a substantial threat to some of the key players in the British retail sector.

The fundamental point for small business owner/controllers here is to make the questions incisive and pertinent to the venture and its operating context.

Evaluating a business plan

Professional organisations such as banks, management consultants, accountancy firms and the business support agencies frequently face situations where they have to judge or evaluate the business plans of small firms. Hussey (1996) states that:

> There are at least two aspects that need consideration here. The first is the quality of strategic thinking that goes into the plan: the second is the quality of the planning document – the plan – as a communication medium and an aid to implementation. Both are important and the simple matrix can be used as a way of exploring their significance. [See Figure 6.2].
>
> The preferred situation is when the strategy is sound and robust and the plan that describes this is clear, concise and well constructed. There can be few attempts at planning that do not strive for this condition as it gives the enterprise the best chance of deciding and implementing the right things. When the quality of the strategy is

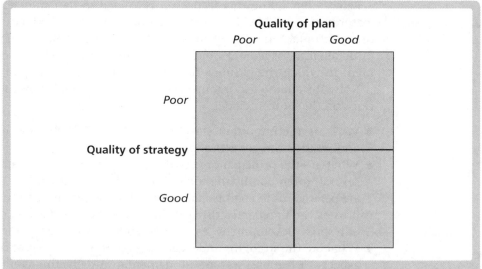

Figure 6.2 The relationship of the quality of plan to the quality of strategy
Source: Hussey (1996)

good but the plan is poor, there is a real danger that it will not be communicated effectively.

Perhaps the most dangerous situation is when the plan is good and therefore convincing but the underlying strategy is poor.

This can result in the wrong things being done with considerable zeal! The quality of the document may be such that the right questions are never asked about the appropriateness of the strategy. The document looks so good and reads so well that all parties assume that the strategy is sound.

The 'poor/poor' box in Figure 6.2 leads to a situation where little of the planning effort brings any real benefits to the firm – and some of the reasons why this occurs more commonly than is desirable are covered in the next section.

Example 6.3: The criteria frequently used by the commercial banks in evaluating business plans

CAMPARI	PARSA
Character	Person
Ability	Amount
Management	Repayment
Purpose	Security
Amount	Reward
Repayment	
Insurance	

Plans are written for different purposes and the particular purpose should be considered when the plan is evaluated. There is a wide spectrum of styles and formats that can be applied and there is certainly no one right way to compose a business plan. In summary, the evaluator needs to:

- understand the strategy;
- be convinced of its soundness in relation to industry structure, competition, the operating context and environment of the business;
- be convinced that it fits the competence and resources of the business;
- establish that it can be implemented;
- know the purpose for which the plan is written;
- establish that the plan caters for and delivers the evaluator's objectives.

Why business planning sometimes fails

To be effective and successful, however defined, business planning has to be adapted to the context and requirements of the enterprise. Planning is not a small firm panacea and no amount of strategising will compensate for an inadequate resource base or overcome the inevitable small business handicap of resource and positional disadvantage.

The planning pitfalls in the following list have been taken from contemporary research studies on business planning generally (Hussey, 1996, 1998) and small business planning in particular (Aram and Cowan, 1990; Richardson, 1991; Richardson and Hawkins, 1995):

- *The behaviour of the chief executive/principal owner-controller.* This is an obvious point but one which is frequently overlooked – and that is that planning will fail if the chief executive does not believe in it or does not understand it and accordingly shows a lack of interest in the process.
- *Lack of acceptance by management.* Perhaps the most serious obstacle to the adoption of planning is the subtle but occasionally open opposition of some key people that appears in the early stage of development. Equally dangerous is allowing some key people not to participate in the planning process. This will reduce its effectiveness and undermine its standing and value.
- *The lack of testing.* This is usually because management has failed to introduce adequate monitoring and control procedures. What so often happens is that the business produces a set of impressive documents which involve a hectic period of activity. The plans are then filed away and not used for the next year until the process starts again, if indeed it ever does.
- *The planners do not possess the appropriate skills and abilities.* The process of business planning is best facilitated by people who have the knowledge and competence in the use of planning techniques. This often involves commissioning a consultant either from the business support community or from a strategy/planning practice. Either way, it is often perceived as being expensive, inappropriate, overly academic and theoretical, too long term, or not really catering for the real needs of the business. Often the planning activity requires working with small firm practitioners in ambiguous and unstructured situations.

According to Hussey (1996), some managers pretend to know fully and completely when to plan when, in fact, the opposite is the case.

- *Confusion over strategic and operational planning together with too much detail and too much sophistication.* Again this seems an obvious point for the discerning student of enterprise and small business but one which seems to appear with depressing regularity. Simplicity should be the design keynote here, with assistance from a qualified professional or consultant to help facilitate the process and act as honest broker.
- *Plans are regarded as impractical, not useful, and unmeasureable.* Small business managers and owners accept plans when they are relevant and useful. Plans that are slow to demonstrate their value tend to get discarded or rejected. It is a cardinal sin of planning not to be able to measure the attainment or otherwise of goals, objectives and targets. Mintzberg (1994) stated quite emphatically that 'management implements only what it can measure'. Platitudes and broad generalities, such as 'improve efficiency', devalue the currency, value and worth of a plan because they cannot be measured.
- *The planning process is poorly managed and does not create involvement.* To be effective a plan must be implemented. Small business managers and practitioners that are expected to implement the recommendations and outcomes of a business plan but have had no involvement in its design or conclusions are unlikely to possess the necessary commitment to its implementation.

Business planning and enterprise success and performance – the contemporary research evidence

In considering the above, it is first necessary to mention that there are very real problems with the term 'success' and its various interpretations and perceptions in the small firm sector (see, for example, Chapters 3 and 5 in Scase and Goffee, 1987; Jennings and Beaver, 1997).

By its very nature, the small business community is characterised by its heterogeneity and this includes reference to the diverse range of ambitions and motives in business formation and management in many different sectors. Perhaps the best and most accurate way to judge success is to ask whether the particular goals of the enterprise have been achieved (Chapter 2 examines this theme in more detail).

For those who seek clear indications of the financial effectiveness of business planning, the evidence which emerges is mixed. Bracker and Pearson (1988), commenting on the use of planning in small, mature-firm contexts, found a clear correlation in the use of planning and enhanced business performance. Bryers (1991) examined much of the published work and concluded that earlier applications of business planning had been successful and resulted in superior performance but found that later results from research studies were more mixed. John Argenti (1990) and David Hussey (1998), who are arguably two of the leading business planning writers and consultants, both state that they do not know whether the process impacts directly on corporate performance but agree on its ability to improve the quality and nature of decision-making.

Aram and Cowan (1990), commenting from the position of planning consultants to small firms, express confidence in the ability of the business planning to improve organisational effectiveness and performance – provided that the planning process is undertaken effectively and professionally. They add that for the majority of small business owner/managers' planning is an atypical activity and therefore help and assistance should be sought from a qualified professional.

Schwenk and Shrader (1993) studied the effects of formal strategic planning on the financial performance of small firms and were able to provide support for the general assertion that business planning does have a significant and positive association with enhanced performance. Storey, in his considerations about the growth of small firms, makes the following comments:

> Formal planning procedures and their monitoring appears to be more characteristic of larger businesses. It may also be the case that faster growing firms are more likely to be devising and implementing formal planning procedures. The evidence is less clear whether this is a factor which encourages growth, or whether it is merely associated with a movement towards greater size and diversity.
>
> *Source*: Storey (1994, p. 148)

These comments suggest that the existing research on has failed to provide conclusive evidence of a direct relationship between small business planning and growth. However, is this really so surprising? It is noteworthy that many of the commentators and researchers distinguish between financial performance as one potential benefit and improved decision-making capabilities as another. Those who seek to answer the question, 'Does business planning improve performance?' suffer from the inability to establish what level of performance would have been achieved if planning had not been undertaken.

Finally, business planning may well be a proxy for a number of organisational activities and characteristics, such as management competence and involvement, style of leadership and employee participation. The issue is a complex one as the organisational activities suggested here are very difficult to measure and document accurately.

- *The problem highlighted in this review of planning is that business planning is not a technique or process with a clear definition and list of activities.*
- *Business planning can, and does, mean different things to different people. In some cases, business owners and managers may not recognise that they are engaging in the process, simply because it is not formalised.*

Concluding remarks

The essential value of a well-crafted business plan is that it enables small firms to plan formally and to plan long term (Joyce *et al.*, 1996; Jennings and Beaver, 1997).

Small firms need planning as an aid to innovation in business processes, to encourage the use of new technology and training to raise their performance and productivity. The act of business planning often instils the confidence to invest long term and to embrace new techniques and ideas which retain and enhance market share. But, perhaps above all, a business plan provides a framework for the assessment of overall performance, bearing in mind that assessment triggers the will to improve.

In the absence of a business plan, a venture may be profitable, but planning enables the comparison of outcomes with intentions. Such comparisons lead to the passing of a judgement on a business: its progress can be described as healthy and growing because the plan contains an ideal against which it is measured.

As Joyce *et al.* (1996) comment:

> Perhaps strategic planning reinforces the process by which aspirations go beyond the limits of present performance, inspiring the recruitment of extra employees whose energies and talents can be harnessed to the drive for increased turnover and profits?
>
> Thus if an entrepreneurial business may be defined as more oriented to growth and innovation than other small businesses, then this may explain why some people have argued that an entrepreneurial type of small business owner is more likely to use strategic planning than other small business owners This can all be summed up by saying that a modern small business needs to plan, not as a parody of corporate planning in big organisations, but as a way of spurring their own entrepreneurial motivation and their continuous interventions in and improvements of, business processes and products.

CASE ILLUSTRATION 6.1

Business failure through a lack of business planning

Maison Novelli

Jean-Christophe Novelli, one of the bright new hopes of the restaurant business, was at the pinnacle of his career and promised to deliver so much for the industry that was new and innovative. At 37 years old he had worked in some of the finest hotels in the UK and was in the process of opening his sixth restaurant in the heart of London's fashionable Mayfair district. With a staff of around 120, a reputation for exciting and creative cooking and the recent award of a Michelin star, he was popularly regarded as the new role model of restaurant success and achievement.

Novelli's enthusiasm and passion for his love of good cooking were contagious and his energy and determination to succeed were admirable. He rarely slept more than 5 hours a night and most times would go to sleep conceiving and composing new recipes for his restaurants. He received loyalty bordering on adulation from his staff and taught talented chefs to become great ones – paying them a pittance of £50–£75 a week in the first three restaurants, because that was all he could afford – and giving them small shareholdings in the business in lieu of bonuses. All the profits generated by the restaurants in the 3 years of business to that point had been re-invested into the company.

The plan was for some 40% of the company to be floated on the Alternative Investment Market (AIM) which would have valued the business somewhere in the region of £5.75 million. For a business just over 3 years old that was a considerable achievement. However, while Novelli was a gifted chef and motivator, his business acumen was at best questionable. By his own admission he had little thought for material things despite a poor childhood and a spartan upbringing.

The business began to experience difficulties when Novelli returned from a book-signing visit to the USA in June 1999. The bank had told him that the company was some £75 000 overdrawn – with no previously agreed overdraft facility, suppliers were owed about £50 000 and there was an outstanding staff wages account of £100 000. Novelli was given 3 days to find the money which, by the rapid sale of some of the restaurants and substantial offers of help from friends, he managed to do – but that was the beginning of the end. The outgoings from the company continued in excess of the revenues and four of the restaurants were closed during 1999 and the fifth in March 2000. At one point, Novelli was forced to approach his suppliers to pay his wages bill. The two remaining restaurants – the original *Maison Novelli* and the sister bistro *EC1*, went into voluntary liquidation at the end of June 2000, the restaurants having been sold a few weeks earlier to JJ Restaurants. Novelli is currently cooking in both of them.

The liquidator, Morison Stoneham, confirmed that according to the financial statement presented by the business to Companies House, Maison Novelli owed a total of some £205 487 and had assets of £13 000. The Customs and Excise and the Inland Revenue were owed respectively £14 000 and £24 743. The largest creditor claim was from J.-C.Novelli for £53 000. Some 63 other trade creditors are owed around £113 000.

Novelli's explanation of his business difficulties were refreshingly direct and straightforward:

> I blame it on poor planning and bad financial management that was all my fault. I should have stuck to the cooking and menu creation parts of the business and got somebody else to take care of all the other parts.

This is an explanation hard not to agree with – but, as this text discusses with some regularity throughout many of its chapters, much easier said than done.

References and further reading

Ackelsberg, R. and Arlow, P. (1985) 'Small Businesses Do Plan and it Pays Off', *Long Range Planning*, 18 (5), 61–7.

Aram, J. D. and Cowan, S. S. (1990) 'Strategic Planning for Increased Profit in the Small Business', *Long Range Planning*, 23 (4), 63–70.

Argenti, J. (1990) *Practical Corporate Planning*. London: Allen and Unwin.

Australian Department of Industry, Technology and Commerce (1998) *Preparing a Business Plan*. Canberra: Australian Government, AGPS.

Bhide, A. (1994) 'How Entrepreneurs Craft', *Harvard Business Review*, March/April, 150–61.

Birley, S. (1996) 'The Start-Up', in Burns, P. and Dewhurst, J. (eds), *Small Business and Entrepreneurship*. Basingstoke: Macmillan, ch. 2.

Bracker, J. S. and Pearson, N. (1988) 'Planning and Financial Performance among Small Firms in a Growth Industry', *Strategic Management Journal*, December, 591–603.

Bryers, L. L. (1991) *Strategic Management: Formulation and Implementation, Concepts and Cases*, 3rd edn. New York: HarperCollins.

Cabinet Office (1996) *Competitiveness – Creating the Enterprise Centre of Europe. A Summary*. London: HMSO.

Cosh, A. and Hughes, A. (1994) 'Size, Financial Structure and Profitability: UK Companies in the 1980s', in Hughes, A. and Storey, D. J. (eds), *Finance and the Small Firm*. London: Routledge.

Hussey, D. E. (ed.) (1996) *The Implementation Challenge*. Chichester: Wiley.

Hussey, D. E. (1998) *Strategic Management – From Theory to Implementation*, 4th edn. Oxford: Butterworth-Heinemann.

Jarvis, R., Kitching, J., Curran, J. and Lightfoot, G. (1995) 'Financial Management Strategies of Small Business Owners: The Case of Cash-Flow Management', in 18th ISBA National Small Firms Policy and Research Conference, Paisley, Scotland.

Jennings, P. L. and Beaver, G. (1997) 'The Performance and Competitive Advantage of Small Firms: A Management Perspective', *International Small Business Journal*, 15 (2), 63–75.

Joyce, P., Seaman, C. and Woods, A. (1996) 'The Strategic Management Styles of Small Businesses', in Blackburn, R. and Jennings, P. L. (eds), *Small Firms, Contributions to Economic Regeneration*. London: Paul Chapman, ch. 5.

Medley, G. J. (1989) 'Strategic Planning for the World Wildlife Fund', in Asch, D. and Bowman, C. (eds), *Readings in Strategic Management*. Basingstoke: Macmillan, 71–7.

Mintzberg, H. (1994) *The Rise and Fall of Strategic Planning*. Englewood Cliffs, NJ: Prentice Hall.

Richardson, W. (1991) 'Spreading Strategic Skills in the Small and Medium Size Enterprise', in Welford, R. (ed.), *Small Business and Enterprise Development*, Conference Proceedings. Bradford: European Research Press.

Richardson, W. and Hawkins, R. (1995) *Service and Business Planning for the New Enterprise*. London: MESOL.

Richardson, W. and Jennings, P. L. (1988) *Both Sides of the Business Plan*. Business Planning Centre, Sheffield Business School, Sheffield Hallam University.

Scase, R. and Goffee, R. (1987) *The Real World of the Small Business Owner*, 2nd edn. London: Croom Helm.

Schwenk, C. R. and Schrader, C. B. (1993) 'Effects of Formal Strategic Planning on Financial Performance in Small Firms: A Meta-Analysis', *Journal of Entrepreneurship, Theory and Practice*, 17 (3), 53–64.

Storey, D. J. (1994) *Understanding the Small Business Sector*. London: Routledge.

Wheelen, T. L. and Hunger, J. D. (2000) *Strategic Management and Business Policy*, 7th edn. New York: Addison-Wesley.

Wickham, P. (1998) *Strategic Entrepreneurship*. London: Pitman.

7

Financial considerations

Objectives A major issue for all small firms is the raising of the necessary finance to resource the start-up and subsequent growth and development of the business. In this chapter, financing is examined from both a theoretical and an empirical perspective.

In particular we will discuss:

● the general theory relating to the financing of the firm and its applicability to the small business;

● the key issues relating to the financing of small firms;

● the sources of external finance available for business formation and development, including an examination of debt finance (as provided by the banks) and equity finance (as provided by both formal and informal venture capitalists);

● the enterprise–banking relationship and its crucial role in formation and development of the business, plus an illustration of the necessary ground rules for managing the relationship;

● the government funding initiatives that are available to assist potential and existing small business practitioners in their search for finance;

● the latest legislation to provide the UK small business community with the legal right to charge interest on the late payment of commercial debts.

Introduction

Considerable progress has been made over the last 40 years or so with regard to improving our understanding of the financing decision. A seminal contribution was the analysis of capital structure to the value of the firm by Modigliani and Miller (1958). This marked the move away from the descriptive approaches to explaining the financing decision that had previously dominated the field to a much more rigorous and analytical approach. They challenged the then dominant assumption that there existed an optimal capital structure (i.e. a particular mix of debt and equity) that provided a lower cost of capital than any other given combination, which maximised the value of the firm.

Subsequent work by financial theorists has generated many viewpoints in explaining how firms choose their capital structures and whether indeed an optimal structure exists. In some theories, the existence of taxes makes debt relevant, while in others the relevance is due to *information asymmetry* – managers having information that investors do not have (Myers, 1984).

Although a detailed discussion on capital structure theory is beyond the scope of this chapter, it is a pertinent issue when considering how a small business should be financed. The critical finding is that there is no optimum capital structure per se for firms that will increase their value to investors. Nevertheless, there are a number of caveats regarding the use of debt finance as opposed to equity finance that are particularly relevant to the small business.

Capital structure and the small firm

It would be fair to say that there has been only a limited amount of research that has focused on small, growing entrepreneurial companies and the factors affecting the capital structure of these firms. Furthermore, theoretical and empirical capital structure research has, for the most part, ignored the small business sector. This is an important omission because financial policy and capital structure of small firms is a major area of policy concern and much of the work, particularly on the failure of small firms, has identified financial leverage as a major cause of decline (Keasey and Watson, 1987; Lowe *et al.*, 1991; Reid, 1993: Storey *et al.*, 1988).

Furthermore, virtually all the research done on capital structure focuses on quantitative analyses in explaining how capital structure is affected by a number of financial factors. There is a need for qualitative research, which examines the effect of management preferences, perceptions, beliefs and attitudes on the capital structure of firms – and small firms, in particular – if we are to understand capital structure practices (Norton, 1990, 1991a,b). Norton points out that this is especially important in small business research where the owner/manager plays a central role in the firm and there is usually little or no separation from ownership and control.

It is generally considered prudent to limit the amount of debt finance in a firm's capital structure where certain conditions prevail concerning taxes, levels of risk, nature of assets and financial slack. Clearly the advantage of tax relief on interest payments can only operate if a firm is in a non-loss-making situation. Therefore, unless the firm is achieving a sufficient income over the life of the debt to take advantage of interest shields, then the firm is likely to be disadvantaged by debt finance.

An additional factor to consider is that tax advantages might also be available to the business via, for example, capital allowances. Where there is a high level of business risk – and typically there is in a new small firm – debt finance should generally be minimised owing to the high costs of financial distress and bankruptcy.

For small firms whose value (and source of competitive advantage) is largely based on intangible assets – for example, many small businesses in the service sectors, the Internet and the professions – the costs of financial misfortune are likely to be higher. This is due to the lack of opportunity to leverage upon tangible assets and therefore debt finance should be used less – on average – than in those firms where tangible assets are an essential ingredient for doing business (for example, in manufacturing).

The final variable to be considered in relation to the use of debt finance concerns the amount of financial slack available for future growth and business development opportunities. If a business is too highly geared, it will not have the access to available competitive financing when it wishes to take such opportunities. For this reason, those firms with high growth strategies will (all things being equal) tend towards conservative capital structures (Brealey and Myers, 1988).

To summarise so far, the principal issue to note is that there is *no optimum capital structure that small firms should try to achieve*. That said, where firm value and competitive advantage is based on intangible assets such as its people, that from a theoretical perspective at least, debt finance should be used cautiously by such businesses.

The general conclusion from the work of Chittenden *et al.* (1998) in their research on capital structure decision-making in small firms is that the capital structure of a small firm at any time will be a function of the characteristics of the firm, its managers and the market-place.

From a public policy perspective the over-riding conclusion of this study is that in general, small business owners are averse to using external sources of finance, including bank debt and especially external sources of equity. Within this context, it would appear that this is a demand-side effect and that the largest providers of external finance to the small business community, i.e. the joint stock banks, are responding effectively to the needs of this important sector. However, there is general agreement that far too many small firms are under-capitalised and therefore the challenge to policy makers is to provide an environment in which owner/managers are able to retain sufficient profits in their businesses to fund the largest number of economically viable projects (Reid, 1996).

That said, the evidence from almost 30 years of research suggests that a large majority of small business owner/managers prefer to rely on internally generated funds and many would prefer to forgo growth opportunities rather than raising the external finance needed.

The financing decision

So far the discussion has said nothing about the inequality experienced by small firms in respect of their access to finance. It is certainly not the case that the small business community enjoys the same access to funding that their large business counterparts do. Examination of this issue has tended to focus predominantly on the supply side: the availability of capital.

An enduring theme has been the existence of a funding gap that results in small firms being discriminated against in their efforts to raise capital. There is, however, another aspect of this issue which until recently received much less attention. This concerns the demand side and the nature of decision-making regarding raising the finance required on the part of the small business owners, managers and entrepreneurs, mentioned briefly above. An examination of both these dimensions is necessary to enhance our understanding of the nature of financing and the small business.

Supply-side issues

Since 1931, when the MacMillan Committee reported (MacMillan, 1931), there has been continuing and vigorous discussion about the financing of small firms in the economy. The Committee found that there were problems for small firms in obtaining long-term capital in amounts of less than £200 000 – and this became known as the 'MacMillan Gap'. As Storey (1994) notes:

> Over the following sixty years, there have been a huge number of changes in the institutional framework for financing small firms and several learned committees (Bolton Report, 1971; Wilson, 1979), have examined this topic.
>
> On each occasion that the issue has been examined, the value of the 'gap' has fallen, in real terms. Nevertheless, it is still the case today that smaller firms find it difficult to obtain small sums of equity capital and feel penalised by an inability to obtain, or to obtain only at high rates of interest, loan capital.

The understanding of the term 'gap' is open to different interpretations by different commentators. For example, it has been attributed as being:

- the situation whereby small firms experience unwarranted prejudice from the capital market;
- the requirement by small firms to accept punitive interest rates or high levels of security;
- the higher risk that small firms represent relative to large and established firms;
- the situation where credit rationing discriminates unfairly against the small business, irrespective of the viability of the project or venture.

This finance gap then can take a number of forms but the common outcome is invariably the same – small firms generally experience greater problems than large ones in obtaining capital on favourable terms. Why then does this situation arise with such regularity?

With regard to debt finance, examining the nature of the transaction involved in business lending provides considerable insight on this issue. In respect of equity capital, there would appear to be certain demand-side characteristics that play an important role in explaining the apparent difficulty in raising the appropriate funding.

The nature and theory of business lending to the small business community

Storey (1994) identifies eight assumptions which underpin the majority of theoretical research in this area. These are:

- asymmetric information;
- agency issues;

- higher objective risk in lending to small firms;
- costly monitoring;
- competing banks;
- entrepreneurs vary in ability, honesty and motivation;
- entrepreneurs gain from increased project valuation;
- banks gain only from repayment.

Perhaps the most fundamental issue characterising the business lending transaction, discussed in some depth by Binks and Ennew (1996), concerns the presence of information asymmetries between the lender and the borrower. In essence, the lending transaction can be regarded as an agency problem whereby the principal (the bank) advances funds to the agent (the firm), which in return is expected to provide the bank with a stream of income that delivers a profit on the advance. The difficulty is that the transaction occurs under conditions of imperfect and asymmetric information (Keasey and Watson, 1993; Berger and Udell, 1993).

This is the problem that all lenders have in the evaluation of the proposal and the applicants and concerns the issue of adverse selection – how can the lender assure itself that it is not lending to a poor-quality proposal? In many instances the bank cannot accurately judge the actual abilities of the applicants or the qualities of the project. The subsequent monitoring of the firm's performance raises another difficulty – often referred to as moral hazard. Here there exists a monitoring problem because there is a risk that the small business will not perform as stipulated in the contract. Thus the lender seeks to obtain sufficient information to monitor the progress and behaviour of the firm, thereby assuring itself that its advance was a sound one and will achieve the success criteria that the applicants put forward.

Information asymmetry is present in all such transactions and the issue for the lender becomes one of how to manage it. (It is wrong to assume, as some writers in this area have theorised, that the problem can be eliminated – this is clearly naive and foolish as clearly the time and cost involved would be prohibitive – risk in all its forms can only be reduced.)

The lender has two principal mechanisms for dealing with the difficulties of information asymmetry in practice. One is to develop a close working relationship with the borrower and establish a good commercial understanding of the business and its operating environment; the other is to demand collateral as a condition of the loan advance.

In respect of the former, the value of getting to know a customer's business is being increasingly recognised by the banks who now for the most part recognise that selective lending to the small business community represents a profitable opportunity to be seized rather than an activity to be shunned. This will, according to Berger and Udell (1993), have a positive influence on both the quality and the quantity of information made available.

In respect of collateral, there are strong theoretical grounds for supporting this as an effective means of overcoming information asymmetry with respect to the problem of adverse selection. Essentially the argument is that those borrowers who perceive that their business proposals contain low risk are willing to demonstrate this to the bank by providing appropriate measures of security. This is an acceptable and rational mechanism where banks can lend to good projects and simultaneously contain their appraisal costs (Dempsey and Keasey, 1993).

Risky or doubtful applications for funding are unlikely to persuade small business practitioners to advance the required security for obvious reasons. The provision of collateral also alleviates the issue of moral hazard as it provides a significant incentive for the borrowers to ensure that their best efforts are focused on achieving the highest levels of business performance (Bester, 1987).

It should be noted, however, that there are situations where collateral will not be an effective mechanism. For example, it might not be forthcoming in the amount required by the lender, which may result in a viable project being rejected. A good example to note was the original business funding application from Anita Roddick in respect of The Body Shop to the loss, at least initially, of all parties concerned. This is a theme developed in more detail in Chapter 9, which discusses female entrepreneurship.

Also, it is not always the case that the borrower will be prepared to dilute the protection of limited liability status by providing suitable guarantees from personal assets. Where these types of problems occur, the bank must either forgo the opportunity to invest in a viable project or apply another mechanism to overcome the problem, hence the continuing development of relationship banking with small business owners and entrepreneurs.

The increasing competitive intensity in the banking environment and the direct criticism of existing practices have further increased the pressure on the banks to improve the quality of their lending services to small firms.

Demand-side issues

As mentioned above, there has been, until comparatively recently, a tendency to overlook the demand-side issues in small business finance and focus on the supply-side considerations. This approach is necessarily limited as it is constructed around the perception of the entrepreneur as an instrument of rational economic behaviour whose decisions are driven by profit maximisation and business optimisation. This of course is naive and inaccurate as the approach fails to recognise the often complex and prima facie irrational actions taken by small business owner/managers.

An obvious example here would be the common trait exhibited by many proprietors to maintain full control of their operation, perhaps to the detriment of business development and optimum profitability. This behaviour of *equity aversion* (Hutchinson, 1995) has its roots in the reluctance to delegate or relinquish control as a condition of growth capital and is widely reported in small business research (see, for example, Foley and Green, 1989). Consider the following, not uncommon, illustrations from this research:

● I own and control a successful business. Financially, I have few worries and I know my workforce. Why should I rock the boat? I don't need the money and I certainly don't need the stress and aggravation which would be involved in trying to expand the company.

- The traditional view that all small businesses want to grow and become multi-million successes is very much mistaken. Very few companies have the desire, let alone the ability, to achieve this level of success. Our research demonstrates quite conclusively that entrepreneurs and owner-managers have diverse ambitions that impact directly on business growth.

- We have encountered a number of owners who have stated that they are not motivated by money and will not borrow the necessary funds to expand the business beyond its current scope. They have deliberately chosen to restrict their businesses to what they feel is a manageable size.

Source: Foley and Green (1989)

Furthermore, the higher the debt/equity ratio, the greater the impact on the business of any financial downturn. Therefore, small business practitioners may well chose to operate their ventures with a lower debt/equity ratio in order to afford the business the best survival opportunity through a lower risk strategy on investment. Here, as in the illustrations above, the owner/entrepreneur has deliberately chosen to operate the firm below the theoretical maximised market value level – an irrational action if the neo-classical economic perspective of the firm is adopted.

The practice of risk avoidance strategies and the desire to retain full ownership and control have resulted in many small firm practitioners minimising the use of equity funding and relying more heavily on debt finance in the short and the long term, regardless of the strong theoretical arguments against this behaviour.

Where a small business owner/manager wishes to retain the flexibility to take business development opportunities as and when they arise, a very conservative level of gearing may be maintained to accommodate the necessary scope for raising the additional debt finance. If a small business practitioner is pursuing this sort of financing strategy, this may well have implications for the type and nature of market opportunities selected. The agency problem mentioned above is of particular relevance here.

Evidence provided by the research from the Wilson Committee in 1979 suggested that as many as 75% of small firms would resist any external participation in the equity of the company. More recently Binks *et al.* (1992) suggested that as many as 85% of small business owners would resist external equity participation because of concerns about the potential loss of control.

According to Keasey and Watson (1992b), bank debt represents some 31% of business liabilities and may be as important as directors' equity and trade credit in terms of sources of business finance. Hughes (1992) also notes that short-term debt has been much more important to small firms than either long-term debt or equity. Notwithstanding the research evidence presented above, the perception and use of debt and equity finance and its relevance to the small business sector are indeed ironic, irrespective of practitioner attitudes. Lister Vickery (1989) reminds us that:

Loan finance best suits a certain world. When a company receives a loan, both the amount of the repayments (principal and interest) and their timing is fixed in advance.

If the company is unable to pay the full amount on the due date, it is 'in default' and the financier may take immediate legal action. If a company performs better than expected and wishes to repay its loans in advance, there will usually be obstacles as though the financier were dissatisfied with his client's performance.

Equity finance on the other hand is well adapted to an uncertain world. Dividend payments are dependent on the realised earnings of the business and are fixed with regard to neither amount nor timing.

The business is not under any obligation to repay the initial investor, who recovers his investment by selling his shares to another investor, thereby realising a capital gain or loss, depending on the performance of the business.

Equity is thus essential to a business in order to allow it to continue to operate, despite uncertainty. Running a business with inadequate equity may be compared to driving a car with worn shock absorbers – not merely is it uncomfortable for the driver and wearing on the engine, it is also unsafe.

The sources of finance for small firms

The principal sources and options for small firms in raising finance are:

- owner(s)' capital – including directors' loans, family and friends – often referred to as internal equity;
- external equity and debt finance – venture capital providers including business angels, the banks and merchant banks, government schemes (local, national and European) such as the Small Firms Loan Guarantee Scheme (SFLGS), the Enterprise Investment Scheme (EIS) and the Venture Capital Trusts (VCTs);
- arrangements for leasing, hire purchase, debt factoring, trade credit, grants and soft loans.

Table 7.1 from the ESRC Centre for Business Research (CBR) at the University of Cambridge from 1995–97 indicates that bank finance was by far the most important source of funding for small firms. In 1998, the CBR study found that 41% of

Table 7.1 External sources of finance from a sample of 2520 small firms, 1995–97

Source	Percentage of respondents receiving some finance from source
Banks	68.7
Venture capital	5.2
Hire purchase/leasing	49.5
Factoring	13.4
Trade credit	5.3
Partners/working shareholders	14.4
Other private individuals	7.4
Other sources	6.3

Source: ESRC Centre for Business Research (1998)

their sample of 1520 SMEs and corresponding entrepreneurs had attempted to raise finance from external sources in the previous 3 years. This figure represents a considerable improvement on the Bolton Report of 1971:

> But it still represents some degree of introspection by small firms and entrepreneurs seeking finance.

Source: Deakins (1999)

Consideration will now be focused on the three main sources of external finance for small firms – the clearing banks, the venture capital providers (both formal and informal sources) and government sources of funding.

Small business and the banks

As Burns and Dewhurst (1989) remind us in their dedicated text on small business finance:

> It is almost impossible to overrate the importance of bank finance to small businesses. At present some 60% of all the funds needed by small businesses come from the banks. Although the pattern of borrowing by large businesses is changing, and there is some evidence that they are looking elsewhere in their search for funds, this is not true for small firms. If anything, the reverse is the case. Nowadays, small firms turn to their local branch manager, not only for short-term funds, but increasingly, for medium and long term funds. It is evident that the relationship that the proprietor has with his local branch manager is of crucial importance.

There is no doubt that in the UK, and indeed much of the developed world, banks represent the primary source of external financing for small firms, both past and present (Bank of England, 1998). The development of the banking system in the UK has had a profound effect on the nature of the relationship between the banks and their small firm clients. Unlike in many other countries, the British banks have a tradition of deposit protection services rather than industrial banking, (such as Germany) which has resulted in the more aloof association with their small firm customers and the resultant heavy criticisms that have occurred of late.

Essentially, it is the historical development and associated culture of the banking system that underpin the agency problem mentioned above and the accompanying emphasis on the provision of collateral as a primary condition in lending. As Binks and Ennew (1996) note:

> Criticism of the clearers has arisen from a wide variety of sources, much of it being anecdotal and poorly addressed. The most significant criticisms refer to their approach in lending, the extent to which there is short-termism in UK bank practice and customer perceptions of service quality.

This sustained and targeted criticism of the clearing banks for adopting a distant, risk-averse stance towards small firms, with an accompanying inability to focus on the income-generating potential of a venture when assessing the likelihood of repayment, has developed from a perspective of bank practices which is not in line with the commercial pressures faced by the UK banks today. For example, increased competition in the sector during the 1980s and economic pressures in the early and late 1990s as a consequence of recession on their property and small business portfolios have forced the banks to adopt policies of charging economic rates for many business service elements, which were in effect previously cross-subsidised by their more profitable activities (Gapper, 1993). Thus, in many ways, the banks are themselves victims of a much more demanding commercial environment, as are their small business customers. The combination of the nature and development of the UK banking system, the frequent unwillingness or inability of small firm owner/managers to relinquish control in return for equity capital and the problems in securing this type of funding create a tension in the relationships between banks and small businesses which is demanding for both parties.

At the Small Business Policy and Research Conference at Cranfield Business School in 1989 (at which all the major banks were well represented), it was decided by the organisers to ask the more senior bank delegates to give a presentation on their perceptions of the enterprise–banking relationship giving their suggestions for enhanced understanding and mutual benefit for both parties. Concluding his presentation, one of the bankers stated:

> Many small business representatives at this conference maintain that it is not possible to secure bank finance on reasonable terms, however, I can assure you that this is not the case for bank funding is always available for good business propositions.

One delegate then asked:

> Could you please tell us then what do you consider to be a good banking proposition and how do you identify it from the rest?

The banker replied:

> That's easy. It is one in which the bank would be prepared to lend money!

The above account, although amusing, is disconcertingly true.

Perhaps one of the most disturbing and emotionally charged complaints levelled by small firm owner/managers against the banks abusing their position is that of overcharging on their business accounts. Example 7.1 is fairly typical of the press reporting at the time.

CASE ILLUSTRATION 7.1

Banks overcharge small firms

Their banks, according to two investigations, are overcharging an increasing number of small and medium-sized firms. Anglia Business Associates, which specialises in reviewing accounts where banks appear to have overcharged customers, found mistakes in 82% of cases in a sample study. One customer was overcharged £75 000, another £38 000. The overcharging which totalled almost £200 000 has occurred in group accounts where multiple accounts were held by one firm at the same bank. Although the sample size was small, taken among firms in Norfolk and Suffolk, Mark Radin at Anglia believes his organisation has detected a worrying trend. He is especially critical of Barclays. He said:

There is a trend of overcharging emerging on Barclays' bank accounts with group arrangements.

In a larger survey of 16 000 small firms carried out by the Federation of Small Businesses, other banks were also accused of overcharging. The research discovered that almost all the firms polled thought they were victims of overcharging. David Hands of the Federation said:

> One in three businesses has appealed to their bank because they had been overcharged and 96% of them got their money back. It is not just Barclays, all the banks do it.

Both Anglia and the Federation are concerned that cases of overcharging are increasing. They say that money lost through overcharging can mean the difference between success and failure for firms if economic pressure increases in intensity. Radin said:

> Without a shadow of a doubt overcharging makes a difference, especially because we are looking at such large amounts. Stopping it would help smaller firms weather the storm.

The Forum of Private Business said that bank charges had been a key concern among its members for 10 years. It said that the answer was for owner-managers to take responsibility for checking accounts. Banks are aware that overcharging occurs, especially in group accounts, where interest is given on the net balance. Barclays said:

> Group accounts can get complex so owner/managers should make sure they keep the bank up to speed. If overcharging is found we will reimburse.

Source: The Sunday Times, 10 January 1999

In concluding this section, it is pertinent to quote again from Binks and Ennew (1996) who state:

> A key feature of the . . . relationship between banks and small firms is the importance of the customer in influencing its quality. A good banking relationship can help to ameliorate some of the problems of asymmetric information but only if customers are willing to participate and share information.
>
> The potential benefits of such participation are apparent . . . More participative customers are generally more satisfied, they perceive fewer constraints on their business, a better quality of service and a better banking relationship.

CASE ILLUSTRATION 7.2

The enterprise–banking relationship

Bank managers are alleged to enjoy declining loan requests to new and small business ventures, on the grounds that they represent a high risk, while at the same time lending irresponsibly to third-world governments and poorly managed organisations such as Polly Peck and the Maxwell Corporation. They are reputed to actively avoid seeing customers that they perceive as being marginal, while always managing to be engaged with an important client, and so the contradictions and anecdotal evidence continues.

Substantial recent evidence from the leading accounting firms, small business interest groups and the banks themselves has showed unmistakably that the single, number one hate among the business community is the level of charges made by the banks, which were regarded as excessive. As for bank managers' perception of the small business start-up, it is certainly true that they often have to seek further information and frequently turn down requests for loans on the basis that bank finance is not appropriate for the proposal concerned, or that the business cannot generate sufficient income to repay the loan installments.

The fact of the matter is that bank managers do like to help small firms because the only way that they will make money is to lend it – not indiscriminately – and because a satisfied small business customer is an excellent source of new business. The extent of the competition in the banking sector means quite simply that existing customers have to be retained and new ones courted.

The business plan – a mandatory document that demonstrates commitment and professionalism – must lend substance to the proposal. It must support the people involved, give credibility to the declared aims and objectives and set out answers to questions that a bank manager could only discover otherwise after a long interview. Presentation is also of vital importance but it does not compensate for a poorly constructed proposal and will do little to win the support of the bank.

Research evidence on the conduct of interviews for bank finance showed conclusively that it is essential for the applicant to be familiar – and happy – with the contents of the business plan and indeed any other information that is being offered in support of the proposal. Areas of agreement about the presentation of the business plan, the conduct of the interview and the management of the business account include the following.

- *The early months*. The purposes of the initial drawing of the business loan and overdraft facility are vital. New cars for the proprietor and his/her family will not impress the bank as much as they will the neighbours. A display of prudence at a time when funds are in short supply in the early days is far more likely to impress the manager and ensure their support.
- *Always come clean*. If problems emerge, whether foreseen or otherwise in the business plan, then it is best to inform the bank. Red-lining of overdrafts to disguise something fundamentally wrong fools nobody and will not encourage the manager to appreciate and support the difficulties that the business has to overcome.
- *The top line*. The bottom line is an expression that has become a cliché for modern life outside the financial world. What is important in forecasts, however, is the top line – the sales projection. If this turns out to be hopelessly adrift, the cash projection will collapse in ruins as well. Bank managers need to be comfortable with the figures, the assumptions behind them and the projected time lag between sales and the collection of the debts. If there is a simple, most important part of the whole business plan, then that is probably it. A good sales projection follows from the analysis of the market and the competition, the range of potential customers, the peculiarities of the operating context, etc. It is vital because it affects the profit and loss account,

the repayment of bank borrowing and, ultimately, the growth and development of the enterprise.

● *The business plan is a management instrument.* Business plans should not be regarded simply as a means of borrowing money from a bank. They should be used as a continuing source of reference and information for monitoring business activity. If small business practitioners and owner-managers engaged in the discipline of business monitoring and took the trouble to tell the bank manager when real life is diverging from the plan, it will demonstrate that the business is being run professionally – and do wonders for their credibility.

Venture (equity) capital and the small business

Equity capital is an essential ingredient in the long-term financing of small business growth and development. This involves the small firm practitioner offering an ownership stake in the enterprise in return for the necessary venture capital required for expansion. In practice, after family and friends, this funding can be obtained from two sources:

● the formal equity market, which results in a capital injection for the business from a venture capital firm;
● the informal equity market, which involves a private individual – or a syndicate of individuals (often referred to as *business angels*), again providing capital for business development in exchange for an ownership stake.

Irrespective of the source of equity capital, the point needs to be appreciated that, in both cases, the owner/entrepreneur(s) involved will have relinquished some element of ownership and control for the additional finance required.

As has been shown in this and other parts of the text, this invariably represents a significant psychological barrier for many small business practitioners and is thought by many to be a principal differentiating factor between a small business with its *patrimonial* view of control and an entrepreneurial venture with its *strategic* perspective and concerns for business performance.

Government and small businesses financing

Most governments have a policy towards encouraging the growth and development of their respective small business sectors for obvious reasons. Whether the support is focused at local, national or European level, the motivation is driven by a belief that the small firm is handicapped by some form of disadvantage – whether positional or resource based – and that the market mechanism has failed to address the capital needs of small businesses.

The picture of government funding initiatives directed at the small firm community is a complex one and subject to the political vagaries prevalent at the time. Governments of all complexions and from most developed countries have differed in their emphasis, targeting, commitment and approach to financing small businesses, with assistance for new business start-ups being preferred or not, for help for the existing stock of firms and their desire for growth and expansion.

Most governments then have sought to stimulate small business and enterprise development by creating and supporting financing schemes that should alleviate the present market deficiencies. In the UK as in much of the European Union (EU), funding initiatives have been conceived and introduced to provide for both equity and debt finance provision. Both have experienced varying rates of success and longevity dependent on the level of both political consistency and commitment (some schemes have been notoriously short term) and the design of the particular initiative in catering for the real – as opposed to the perceived – needs of the small firm sector.

In the UK as an example, the Small Firms Loan Guarantee Scheme (SFLGS) was introduced in 1981 to address the perceived gap in the provision of loan finance for small enterprises. This involves the government underwriting, or guaranteeing, a percentage of a loan made to a small firm by a bank to fund a viable project, which would otherwise not normally qualify for debt finance on commercial terms. The percentage has varied over the life of the scheme from 70% to 85%.

Another government initiative introduced to cater for the lack of appropriate equity finance – the Business Expansion Scheme – provided tax advantages for individuals to invest in qualified unquoted companies. It was designed to stimulate small equity investments in businesses seeking to expand but, in reality, became a vehicle for tax avoidance for the wealthy. As Storey (1994) notes, it is highly questionable that it came anywhere near to achieving its objectives of injecting equity into those small enterprises that really needed it and, besides, the administration of the scheme became so complex that even the Inland Revenue had trouble understanding and operating it. Other commentators such as Mason and Harrison (1994) suggest that there were indeed a number of very real benefits to the scheme, such as raising the profile of the small firm as representing the appropriate investment vehicle for private investors.

The late payment of debt and the response from parts of the small business sector

In November 1998, Britain's small firm community gained the legal right to claim interest on the late payment of commercial debts. The statutory right to claim interest on late payment was one of the Labour Government's key pledges when it came to power and a personal campaign for Barbara Roche, then the minister responsible for small business affairs.

However, the small business community has long been divided over the effectiveness of the legislation and there is evidence that the new provisions may remain largely unused. According to research from the National Westminster Bank and Barclays Bank (October 2000), only one in 10 firms polled in the surveys have made any plans for the late payment legislation. To add further weight to these findings, Barclays Bank has published research which suggested that less than a quarter of the small firms in the survey were planning to enforce the Late Payment of Commercial Debts (Interest) Act.

A statement from a Barclays spokesman summarises the concerns of many:

> It is not a question of the legislation not working. It is just not the full solution. Many of the consequences surrounding enforcement have either been ignored, or not fully thought through.

The main problem is that recourse to legislation could damage the delicate relations that exist between small firms and their customers or suppliers. A comment from a member of the Federation of Small Businesses illustrates the point:

> Legislation will lead to businesses not wanting to disturb the relationships they have with customers.

As the statutory right to interest is not compulsory, the Federation suggests that firms may opt instead for a suggestion in their negotiations that they could enforce the law if agreements were not kept. This way, customers and suppliers are more likely to continue the trust-based relationships they now have with small businesses, rather than introduce a heavy legal aspect to their commercial dealings. This point was endorsed by a National Westminster spokesman who agreed that the relationship issue is likely to deter owner-managers from using the legislation:

> The chance is that if a small firm says to a customer that payment is overdue and that interest will be claimed, then the potential damage to an ongoing relationship will out-weigh the value of the interest on the debt.

The rate of interest will be calculated at the Bank of England's prevailing base rate and will be tiny, especially on the smallest debts. Another problem the late payment legislation may create is if big companies use it to force small firms to pay them on time, precipitating a situation where small businesses do not enforce the law but big companies do, therefore backfiring against small firms.

This would be a reversal of the present position, in which small firms have been the worst affected by late payment. There have been several cases in recent years where one bad debt has been enough to cripple an otherwise successful venture. It is a fine irony that, high interest rates and excessive bank charges notwithstanding, all the evidence from contemporary financial research into the small business sector has highlighted late payment as one of the key problems. Many small firms simply do not have the resources to bounce payments around to compensate for late settlement.

Under the first phase of the law's timetable, small firms – defined as those with fewer than 50 employees – will be entitled to claim interest from (large) organisations in both the private and public sectors on debts incurred under contracts agreed when the new act passed into law. From November 2000, small firms have the right to claim interest from other small businesses and, by November 2002, all businesses (irrespective of size or sector) will be able to claim interest on late payments. The new legislation should bring benefits at the outset, not least because it will focus attention once more on the late payment issue and encourage small enterprises to take a firmer line with their customers. A statement from Barclays contends that:

> The late-payment act in general sets out to improve the payment culture in this country. Legislation can only be good for the British economy and the small business sector.

This legislation has brought a focus to the problem. A statutory right to interest may not be the tool that a lot of smaller firms will use but it is making them think that there are customers who have problems paying bills.

If this is correct, then a further benefit that the legislation may bring is to help focus small firms on maximizing cash flow as a principal financial objective. As the commercial pressures continue for many small businesses, the statutory right to claim interest may find favour with many firms.

However, this presupposes that businesses know about the Act. The research from National Westminster reveals that two-thirds of companies are indeed aware of the new measures but that awareness is much higher among larger organisations. Among firms with sales turnover between £1 million and £5 million, 74% know about the legislation, compared with a 96% awareness among firms with sales of between £5 million and £20 million and 100% awareness among firms with sales of more than £20 million.

The most alarming element of the National Westminster research is that, of those firms that have already begun to review their policy on payments, only 11% have spoken to customers and suppliers about the changes. It would appear that there is a long way to go before an anti-late-payment culture takes root. Whether or not small firms use their right to enforce interest payments on late payments, the banks certainly seem united in their policy, which is to encourage small businesses to tighten up their payment procedures and to adopt a more professional approach to credit management.

New provisions for the late payment of debt: an overview

The issue of the late payment of commercial debt has been cited as a major problem affecting small firms and has precipitated much debate. In the UK, this has led to the establishment of the Better Payment Practice Group in conjunction with the legislation mentioned above, to enforce a statutory right to interest on late payments.

A number of surveys have highlighted the extent of the late payment problem and suggested possible causes for it but there has been relatively little theoretical and/or empirical work on understanding the payment behaviours of firms. An exception is the work of Howorth and Wilson (1998), who developed 13 small firm case studies where the management and financing of trade credit was examined. Their analysis showed that, while late payment affected all the firms in their sample, some of them managed it far better than others did.

At the extremes there were two distinct types of firms. Those who found late payment to be the greatest problem were juggling various forms of short-term finance to fund their working capital. Their credit management procedures were ad hoc and unsystematic but there was no evidence that they were at the mercy of dominant suppliers. The firms that managed late payment had systematic credit management procedures in place and a good knowledge of when to expect payment from each of their customers. Longer-term sources of finance provided them with the stability to plan ahead and there was sufficient flexibility in their financial structure to cope with minor problems.

The principal findings from this study are given below and introduce some interesting management and policy implications to conclude this chapter:

- Firms who pay late regard it as a legitimate source of finance.
- Those firms using longer-term sources of finance were less affected by late payment.
- Firms with systematic debt collection have a reduced late payment problem.
- Small firms who suffer least from late payment adopt some or all of the following good credit management practices:
  - *pre-sale* – find out about customers' purchasing and payment habits formally, e.g. credit references, or informally, e.g. sales force or industry grapevine;
  - establish payment terms prior to sale;
  - *post-sale* – prompt and accurate invoices;
  - check before payment is due that the invoice has been received and that there are no problems with either the goods or the invoice and, at the same time, confirm the expected payment date;
  - if payment becomes overdue, take swift and decisive action, with records of actions and promises.

CASE ILLUSTRATION 7.3

Red tape and procedure as a barrier to government grants

There is considerable evidence from the Small Business Service to suggest that there are a variety of sources of grants available for enterprise development. However, securing a grant for business formation and/or expansion is for the most part a bureaucratic and procedural rigmarole that leaves many applicants frustrated and angry.

Small business advisors and consultants have regularly reported on the considerable difficulties and complexities facing entrepreneurs and owner-managers in their search for funding. Application procedures for many grants require the completion of forms approaching 30 pages in length and insist on the provision of complex financial forecasts that realistically cannot be accurately verified. Some grant applications can take from 12 to 15 months for a decision to be reached.

It is estimated that there is more than £100 million of grant funding available although the accuracy of this figure cannot be guaranteed as government cannot confirm the precise figures because grants are not centrally monitored. Grant Thornton, the accountancy firm that specialises in advising owner-managers, has commented that applying for one of the 1900 grants available for business and enterprise is often much more trouble than it is worth. The head of its advisory services stated:

> The grant system is such a nightmare to deal with that it is often not worth the bother. The bureaucracy involved often makes it very difficult for companies to get the quick decision that they often need. There are grants, for example, that are available in certain regions but they can often be micro-regions, so that what is available in one part of town is not obtainable in the other.

119

Managing this bureaucracy is essential if money is to be forthcoming and there are business advisors that specialise in securing grant funding. Most seem to agree that understanding the technique and procedure is probably more important than persuasive communication of the business concept. Equally, some industries are favoured, such as engineering, biotechnology and high technology, and are more likely to succeed than others. There is considerable evidence to suggest that many firms turn to their local Business Links for advice about grant funding but that many of the advisors struggle to keep up with the vast array of grants available.

Grants available for business (selected)

Name	Purpose	Amount
Smart Awards	Development of technology	£2500–450 000
Regional Selective Assistance	Job creation in assisted areas	5–15% of project costs
Enterprise Grant Scheme	To enable projects in grant areas	Maximum £75 000
European Commission	Research and development	Up to 50% of project cost
Regional Development Agencies	Conversion of rural buildings	25% of cost
Shell Live Wire	To help start-ups	£2000–£10 000

Source: Small Business Service, January 2001

References and further reading

Bank of England (1996) *Finance for Small Firms: A Third Report*. London.

Bank of England (1998) *Quarterly Report on Small Business Statistics*. London: Business Finance Division.

Berger, A. N. and Udell, G. F. (1993) 'From Lender to Investor', *The Financial Times*, 23 March.

Bester, H. (1987) 'The Role of Collateral in Credit Markets with Imperfect Information', *European Economic Review*, 31 (4), 887–99.

Binks, M. R. (1991) 'Small Businesses and their Banks in the Year 2000', in Curran, J. and Blackburn, R. A. (eds), *Paths of Enterprise: The Future of the Small Business*. London: Routledge.

Binks, M. R. and Ennew, C. T. (1996) 'Growing Firms and the Credit Constraint', *Small Business Economics*, 8, 17–25.

Binks, M. R., Ennew, C. T. and Reed, G. (1992) *Small Business and their Banks*. Knutsford: Forum for Private Business.

Bolton Report (1971) *Report of the Committee of Enquiry on Small Firms*, Cmnd 4811. London: HMSO.

Brealey, R. A. and Myers, S. C. (1988) *Principles of Corporate Finance*. New York: McGraw-Hill.

Burns, P. and Dewhurst, J. (1989) *Small Business – Planning, Finance and Control*, (2nd edn). London: Macmillan.

Chittenden, F., Michaelas, N. and Poutziouris, P. (1998) 'A Model of Capital Structure Decision Making in Small Firms', *Journal of Small Business and Enterprise Development*, 5 (3), Autumn, 246–60.

Deakins, D. (1999) *Entrepreneurship and Small Firms*, 2nd edn. Maidenhead: McGraw-Hill.

Dempsey, M. and Keasey, K. (1993) 'Small Firms and the Provision of Bank Finance', *Journal of Accounting and Business Research*, 23, 291–9.

ESRC Centre for Business Research (1996) *The State of British Enterprise – Up-Date*. Department of Applied Economics, University of Cambridge.

ESRC Centre for Business Research (1998) *The State of British Enterprise – Up-Date*. Department of Applied Economics, The University of Cambridge.

Foley, P. and Green, H. (1989) *Small Business Success*. London: Paul Chapman (Small Business Research Trust).

Gapper, J. (1993) 'The Equation That Did Not Add Up', *Financial Times*, 2 February, p. 15.

Howorth, C. and Wilson, N. (1998) 'Late Payment and the Small Firm: An Examination of Case Studies', *Journal of Small Business and Enterprise Development*, 5 (4), Winter, 307–15.

Hughes, A. (1992) 'The Problems of Finance for Small Firms', Working Paper 15, Small Business Research Centre, University of Cambridge.

Hutchinson, R. W. (1995) 'The Capital Structure and Investment Decisions of the Small Owner-Managed Firm: Some Exploratory Issues', *Journal of Small Business Economics*, 7, 231–9.

Keasey, K. and Watson, R. (1987) 'Non-Financial Symptoms and the Prediction of Small Company Failure', *Journal of Business Finance and Accounting*, 14, 30–40.

Keasey, K. and Watson, R. (1992a) 'Banks and Small Firms: Is Conflict Inevitable?', *National Westminster Bank Quarterly Review*, May, 30–40.

Keasey, K. and Watson, R. (1992b) 'Investment and Financing Decisions and the Performance of Small Firms', National Westminster Bank Report, London.

Keasey, K. and Watson, R. (1993) *Small Firms Management*. Oxford: Blackwell.

Lowe, J., Tibbits, G. E. and McKenna, J. (1991) 'Small Firm Growth and Failure: Public Policy Issues and Practical Problems', in Renfrew, K. M. and McCosker, R. C. (eds), *The Growing Small Business*, Proceedings of the 5th National Small Business Conference, 175–90.

MacMillan, H. (1931) *Report of the Committee of Finance and Industry*, Cmnd 3987. London: HMSO.

Mason, C. M. and Harrison, R. T. (1993) 'Strategies for Expanding the Informal Venture Capital Market', *International Small Business Journal*, 11 (4), 23–38.

Mason, C. M. and Harrison, R. T. (1994) 'Informal Venture Capital in the UK', in Hughes, A. and Storey, D. J. (eds), *Finance and the Small Firm*. London: Routledge.

Modigliani, F. and Miller, M. (1958) 'The Cost of Capital, Corporate Finance and the Theory of Investment', *American Economic Review*, June, 291–7.

Myers, S. C. (1984) 'The Capital Structure Puzzle', *Journal of Finance*, 39, 575–92.

Norton, E. (1990) 'Similarities and Differences in Small and Large Corporation Beliefs About Capital Structure Policy', *Small Business Economics*, 2, 229–45.

Norton, E. (1991a) 'Capital Structure and Small Public Firms', *Journal of Business Venturing*, 6, 287–303.

Norton, E. (1991b) 'Capital Structure and Small Growth Firms', *Journal of Small Business Finance*, 1 (2), 161–78.

Reid, G. C. (1993) *Small Business Enterprise: An Economic Analysis.* London: Routledge.

Reid, G. C. (1996) 'Financial Structure and the Growing Small Firm: Theoretical Underpinning and Current Evidence', *Small Business Economics*, 8 (1), 1–7.

Storey, D. J. (1994) *Understanding the Small Business Sector.* London: Routledge.

Storey, D. J., Watson, R. and Wynarczyk, P. (1988) 'Fast Growth Small Businesses: A Study of 40 Small Firms in North-East England', Research Paper 67, Department of Employment, London.

Vickery, L. (1989) 'Equity Financing in Small Firms', in Burns, P. and Dewhurst, J. (eds), *Small Business and Entrepreneurship*, 1st edn. London: Macmillan, ch. 8.

Wilson, H. (1979) *The Financing of Small Firms, Report of the Committee to Review the Functioning of Financial Institutions*, Cmnd 7503. London: HMSO.

8

Enterprise growth and development

Objectives This chapter focuses on the frequently misunderstood but vitally important subject of enterprise growth and business development. Growth, particularly as it affects the smaller firm in the economy, is a complex and difficult arena, not least because of the heterogeneity of the sector and the variety of motivations and ambitions influencing and underpinning small business creation and expansion. The potential for growth is a defining feature of the entrepreneurial venture.

This chapter seeks to examine:

- the principal small business growth theories and their strengths and weaknesses;

- the importance of understanding the process and complexity of small firm growth and its role and appreciation in the formulation of policy towards the sector;

- the characteristics of small firms, other than size, which distinguish and influence decision-making in relation to business growth and competitive advantage;

- contemporary research on business growth and its implications for entrepreneurs, owners and managers in their search for profitability and success, with examples taken from the McKinsey research on hypergrowth companies and the Warwick Business School research on the Ten Percenters;

- a case example of successful business development through innovative strategic thinking and positioning.

Introduction

It is clear from the substantial research evidence that the majority of small firms do not grow to any appreciable size, being classified predominantly as *lifestyle businesses* (Burns and Dewhurst, 1996). The majority of small businesses which survive continue as *small businesses* and display no apparent aspirations to grow or develop beyond a certain size and complexion, compatible with the owner/controller's motivations, capabilities and expectations (Beaver, 1984; Gray, 1992; Storey; 1994; Freel, 1999). The opening paragraph by Freel (1999) summarises the position succinctly and well:

> There is a basic distinction between the person or entrepreneur who wishes to go into self-employment to pursue their own interests (and perhaps enters self-employment because there is no or little alternative) and the person or entrepreneur that enters small

business ownership because they have desires to develop their businesses, to achieve growth, expand employment and grow into a medium-sized or large firm. The former type of small business owner has very different managerial objectives from the latter. The objectives of the first will be concerned with survival and maintenance of lifestyle, whereas those of the second type will be concerned with growth and expansion with the entrepreneur (perhaps) eventually owning several companies.

This chapter seeks to examine those small firms which plan to achieve enterprise growth and development with particular attention on those factors that influence the growth process, recognising fully that business development is invariably a complex and difficult process. The group of small businesses that wish to attain some measure of growth are of particular importance and interest for a number of reasons.

The first is that they may well provide new employment opportunities within the small firm sector, even though as Storey (1994) reminds us:

> They only constitute a small proportion of all small firms – they may be of interest to public policy makers whose task is to maximise the creation of employment opportunities for all.

Fast-growth firms are a source of both economic growth and renewal, especially important to those areas and sectors that have suffered the worst of the consequences of corporate downsizing, rationalisation, outsourcing and the damaging effects of acquisition and merger activity (Hussey, 2000). The significance of this new employment generation can be appreciated further if Storey's (1994) evidence is taken into account (emphasis added):

> Out of every 100 small firms, the fastest growing *four* firms will create half the jobs in the group over a decade.

This is endorsed by other studies, undertaken at different times and in different sectors and regions. For example, Gallagher and Miller (1991) state that:

> It is the high flying firms that create the jobs . . . the difference between the high flyers and the sinkers in terms of job creation was considerable. In the South East [of England], while the high flyers made up only 18% of all firms, they nevertheless accounted for 92% of the jobs created . . . Similar evidence was found in Scotland.

Second, fast-growing firms are of very real interest to the providers of finance, irrespective of whether they require equity or loan capital, since, if they can be identified, they are likely to demand a wide range of financial services and products.

Third, fast-growth firms are a potential source of revenue to those providing advisory and professional services such as accounting, financial and management consultancy and recruitment, not least because non-growth firms will only require modest assistance.

Those small firms wanting to achieve growth and enterprise development will obviously be affected by, *inter alia*, different opportunity sets, sector specific chances and developments, managerial competences and abilities and the resources available to the business. Growth rates among any small firm population will vary and some commentators have attempted to segment firms into different growth categories. An example is the new venture classification produced by Hisrich and Peters (1998) who attempt to locate firms into one of four categories:

- life-style small firms;
- marginal small firms;
- successful small-growth firms;
- high-growth firms.

They state that the growth of a new entrepreneurial venture is a function of both management and market factors, a subject that will be discussed later in this chapter. The small business literature contains many such attempts at classifying firms and some are more useful than others. For example, the research on high-growth firms variously describes such businesses as 'gazelles', 'entrepreneurial ventures' and 'high-flyers' while the authors refer to the process of 'picking, creating or selecting winners' (see, for example, Beaver and Jennings, 1995).

Freel (1999) identifies the principal concern of venture capitalists, financiers and policy-makers in the search and identification of these enterprises.

> There has been much speculation about whether such entrepreneurial firms can be identified ex ante, that is, before they achieve growth, rather than ex post, after they have demonstrated growth. This presents a problem for researchers and policy makers and for investors such as venture capitalists who will want to identify high growth and high performer firms. It is a classical adverse selection problem created by uncertainty and limited (if not asymmetric) information.
>
> Despite the inherent built-in difficulties of identifying such growth firms, this has not stopped policy makers from establishing agencies such as the Business Links to support existing small and medium-sized firms that have the potential for growth.

In order to better understand small business growth (or lack of it) and the role of entrepreneurial behaviour, strategic thinking and decision-making in that process, this chapter takes Storey's (1994) position as its starting point. Storey suggests that there are three key influences on the growth rate of a small independent firm:

- the background and access to resources of the entrepreneur(s);
- the (nature of) the firm itself;
- the strategic decisions taken by the firm once it is trading.

These influences will be discussed in turn below and related to other parts of the text where necessary.

Small business entrepreneurs, owners and owner-managers

Chapter 3 examines the above small business practitioners' profiles and motivations in some detail and it is therefore only necessary to briefly identify those issues that relate to enterprise growth and development. It has been recognised throughout the small business literature that people enter the sector for a variety of reasons. Hakim (1989) identifies two consistently acknowledged reasons: independence and the possibility of greater financial reward than from alternative salaried employment. However, her research showed that some 55% of small enterprises had no ambitions to grow at all, with a further 35% planning slow *steady* growth, leaving only 10% of small business owners seeking fast growth. This has been endorsed by a number of studies confirming that the majority of owners (as distinct from entrepreneurs) do not have business growth as a primary objective, preferring instead to pursue other motives (Storey, 1994). It is important to note that, as Birley (1989) states:

> This is not an irrational act indicative of poor managerial ability, for although this may produce a company with a very strange profile to an outsider, it is one which is in fact pursuing a strategy that is internally consistent.
>
> The objectives of the firm and those of the owner become one and the same. The pressures that determine these objectives will encompass personal lifestyle and family considerations as well as commercial ones. The entrepreneur often starts his own business with the declared intention of becoming independent and once established may have a clear intention of maintaining his independence by keeping day to day operational control. To achieve this, his strategic goal becomes one of no growth or minimum growth consistent with survival.

(For an expansion of this theme see Chapter 5 on strategic management issues.)

The issues most prominent in the small business literature in relation to the influence of the characteristics of the owner/entrepreneur on small business growth include the following:

- gender;
- motivation;
- education;
- ethnicity;
- age;
- family history.

Interestingly there appears to be no conclusive evidence indicating that any particular aspect of the above characteristics is positively correlated with small business growth.

In their prominent and authoritative article on growth, Stanworth and Curran (1986) propose a social action view of the small firm that focuses on understanding the internal social logic of the enterprise. One of their central conclusions is that there is:

> No one single entrepreneurial role and thus by implication, no single pattern of business growth.

Stanworth and Curran stress that small firm growth is a complex social and psychological process and not a simple economic one that occurs normally unless it is specifically actioned and initiated by the key players.

The key to understanding the frequent lack of growth lies essentially in the motivational and social attitudes of the owner-manager/entrepreneur – the dominant figure in the enterprise. Small business owners are predominantly people with strong needs for autonomy and independence, limited managerial skills and abilities and are often socially marginal, i.e. people that feel that somehow the often modest employment roles they achieve in society are discrepant with their true talents and ambitions. Such people may well be reluctant as business owners to allow their enterprises to grow beyond a certain size since the requirements of growth might well threaten their autonomy and independence, expose their lack of managerial skills and expose them to further reminders of their social marginality.

Much of the above is endorsed by, *inter alia*, Scase and Goffee (1987), Gray (1992), Beaver and Jennings (1996) and Banfield *et al.* (1996).

Small business characteristics

Of the choices available to owners and entrepreneurs as to the legal form of the business covered in Chapter 2, the studies undertaken in the UK consistently point to more rapid growth being experienced by limited liability companies than by either partnerships or sole-proprietor status.

Freedman and Goodwin (1992, 1994) have examined the choice of legal form in detail. Their conclusion from surveys of entrepreneurs and business advisors is that the principal benefit from corporate status is the protection afforded by limited liability followed by the enhanced credibility which the firm enjoys with both its bank and its customers. This can of course be diluted, as many owner/entrepreneurs are required to provide personal guarantees as a condition for bank finance and the benefits of incorporation are not really appropriate (or beneficial) for the majority of micro-enterprises.

Nevertheless, there is considerable research evidence to suggest that, other things being equal, limited companies are generally associated with faster growth and business development. However, the establishment of a causal relationship is a difficult one, for, as Storey (1994) points out:

> We cannot reject the hypothesis that current legal status is a consequence rather than a cause of growth . . . It will also be recalled that limited companies had a higher failure rate than either sole proprietorships or partnerships. Hence it would be unwise to assume that the incorporated form is necessarily conducive to good management.

Of the studies that are reviewed by Storey (1994) in an attempt to determine the effect of business size as a growth variable, he concludes that the general pattern is clearly for young firms to achieve more significant growth than older firms. This is possibly explained by the need for new businesses to grow quickly to achieve a minimum efficient scale:

> The fact that once this is achieved businesses subsequently grow less rapidly can be explained either by a lack of motivation by the individuals to continue to grow the business once they have achieved a satisfactory level of income from the firm, or by a low minimum efficient scale, particularly in service sector businesses, or by the diseconomies that emerge from the need to employ and manage others.

Stage models of business growth

Much of the early theoretical work on business growth and development attempted to 'conceptualise the metamorphosis of Penrose's caterpillar' (Freel, 1999), in terms of stage, or life cycle, models of firm growth. Indeed, the concept of stage or sequential models of business development is prominent in the strategic management literature and have been widely discussed in relation to small business growth.

These models envisage that the firm passes through a number of stages (usually five), with an inevitable and gradual movement along a known growth trajectory. At each stage the business passes through a number of changes in organisational structure and design, management practices and style, choices of strategy and so on, so that the business at the final stage of the process is truly distinct from the stage 1 firm from which it derived. These stages have been given a variety of names and classifications, and are typically:

- *Birth, formation or existence*. Here the firm is directly managed by the owner personally; a simple organic structure.
- *Survival*. This involves a more complex structure with some delegated tasks, supervised by the owners.
- *Growth, or take-off*. Functional management has appeared and the owner is concerned with maintaining profitability and whether future growth and business development are a personal aim.
- *Maturity or consolidation*. Here the firm acquires a more divisional management structure, with or without the original owner/entrepreneur.
- *Resource maturity, divestment or rejuvenation*. Internal systems and complexity reveal a business concerned about obtaining the maximum return on its investments and/or requiring re-organisation and rationalisation in order to re-invigorate the firm, its product portfolio and/or its management processes.

The most commonly cited stage models of business growth are those developed by Greiner (1972) and Churchill and Lewis (1983), both of which are very well described and reviewed by Freel (1999). As to their applicability and relevance to small firm growth, Freel acknowledges that there are fundamental flaws associated with the rigidity of such models and from the literature. Notably, Storey (1994) and Burns and Harrison (1996) cite four of the most serious criticisms:

1 Most small businesses, as noted above and elsewhere in the text, experience little or no growth and therefore never reach stages 3, 4 and 5 described in the models. This is mild by comparison with some of the criticisms articulated by Gray (1993) who states that the models are riddled with unsupported assumptions and should be discredited because of their obvious weaknesses:

> These models incorporate neo-classical economic assumptions which ignore the reality of small business management and the fact that only a tiny proportion of small firms ever grow to a size where internal functional divisions and professional top management teams are in any way feasible. Even as models for entrepreneurial development they appear to be too static and unreal. It is assumed that a management learning process occurs but by and large, these models do not provide an explanation of why the firm was founded in the first place and what relation there is between the founding motivations and objectives and subsequent developments.

2 The models do not allow for a backward movement along the continuum, or for the skipping of stages depending on the operating context of the firm and

its opportunity set. Freel (1999) states that it is surely conceivable that many firms will reach take-off, only to find themselves plunged back into a struggle for survival owing to unexpected changes in markets, technology or consumer preferences. Furthermore, the requirement for the firm to complete each stage before moving forward to the next one seems both simplistic and limiting. A good example to illustrate this last point is the case illustration of Powderject plc in Chapter 12 in the discussion of innovation and high technology.

3 Because of their theoretical construction and underlying assumptions, the models do not permit firms to exhibit characteristics from one or more stage, to become hybrids. As Freel correctly states:

> As brief illustrations from Greiner we can conjecture a situation where the top management style is participative (Phase 5), whilst the organisation structure is informal (Phase 1); from Churchill and Lewis a situation such that formal systems are either maturing (Stage 4) or extensive (Stage 5) and yet the major strategy is survival (a new franchise may be one such example).

4 The labels and classifications of the various stages and phases are too limiting and/or inaccurate and do not reflect the operational and strategic realities and capabilities of the firm in relation its chosen markets and sectors. For example, it is entirely reasonable to expect that a firm which has secured a favourable funding package, from say a venture capitalist, will be actively assisted to pursue rapid growth over a relatively short time, not least because of the extra management skills, capabilities and vision that such a deal would attract.

The discussion of the McKinsey research on hypergrowth companies that follows illustrates the last point and others besides very well. It is difficult not to agree with Freel (1999), when he states that:

> It is quite conceivable that some firms will lurch from crisis to crisis and that these crises will not be of leadership, autonomy, control and red tape, but of market stagnation, market saturation, technology, finance or skills . . . The frameworks suggested are overly rigid. The inevitability of each stage and crisis is implausible. To assume that firms move from one stage to another along a narrow path, shaped only by periods of regularly recurring crises, ignores the variability and complexity of small firm growth.

Gray (1993, 1998), although highly critical of the rigid assumptions that underpin stage models, does acknowledge that, if they are used with some selectivity, they are capable of shedding some light on aspects of the small business growth process. However, he emphasises that the business objectives, motivations and expectations of the entrepreneur/owner(s) and key actors in enterprise development are a major determinant shaping the complexion of business growth. His research and conclusions concur with the findings of Storey (1994) that there is only a minority of small business practitioners for whom sustained growth and enterprise development is a substantive issue. This is further endorsed by the work of Bennett (1989), Beaver and Jennings (1995) and Jennings and Beaver (1997) who advocate that strategic thinking and planning is a fundamental necessity for those small firms looking to expand.

What is certain is that the growth process is different for every enterprise and the practitioners that set up and manage them and that each has specific critical success factors that are peculiar to the business and its operating environment. The encouragement of enterprise growth is an important agenda and one that is vital to the continued health of a vibrant, mixed economy. The small firm practitioners that take a firm from inception to a successful, profitable and independent venture are to be congratulated for, as Beaver and Jennings (1995) state:

> There is nothing automatic about the birth and development of a winning small firm. It has to be planned and managed from the top against a seemingly endless array of internal and external constraints. The complexity and dynamism of the business environment demands attention to a combination of factors, which is tempered by astute, competent management if the venture is to prosper.

Contemporary research on business growth

Hypergrowth

There is a clear distinction between regular business growth and development and hypergrowth with the challenge it brings to business. The most successful hypergrowth companies use efficient performance evaluation systems to create tangible links between business objectives, individual roles and incentives. The material in this section has been compiled from the *McKinsey & Company Report on Hypergrowth Companies*, by Wiebe Draijer, Jochen Messemer, Grieg Schneider, Somu Subramaniam and Luis Ubinas of the Amsterdam Office, October 1999.

To support managers in hypergrowth organisations, the best practice from some of the most successful companies needs to be appreciated. Specific lessons from managers who have not only survived hypergrowth but who have built some of the most successful companies in the economy today.

Accordingly, the McKinsey team interviewed over 30 independent companies and divisions of larger corporations that have gone through hypergrowth (i.e. growth of 50% or better for 2 years or more) in diverse industries as multimedia, telecommunications and pharmaceuticals. All of these cases involve organic growth, as opposed to growth through acquisitions. One of the principal findings was that hypergrowth requires substantial re-organisation of a business. Whereas many companies can sustain high growth for extended periods of time, without needing to adapt their business systems, hypergrowth overwhelms management processes and forces companies to find new ways of operating.

Three significant challenges emerged from the research:

- The first is to switch from the start-up phase to one where opportunities must be prioritised without losing the spirit of business development.
- The second is more difficult because it is involves behavioural change. It is the requirement for managers to delegate control. The start-up phase forces a company's senior management to give all they can and to be involved in every decision. As the business accelerates, it becomes impossible to command the full array of tasks. They must delegate to experts in the management ranks rather than held at the top. Letting go is particularly hard to do and many

leaders resist delegating control for too long. They want to be kept involved and informed and often do not trust new employees with their business. This clouds decision-making and leads to unclear role descriptions for those beneath the top.

- The third is the need to implement fast but structured processes. While all companies must balance control with the freedom to act, hypergrowth companies must develop processes that maintain small-company flexibility in increasingly large organisations.

Although the companies that were included in McKinsey's research vary in size, industry, number of employees and several other dimensions, their judgement of how to succeed in hypergrowth is remarkably consistent. The key factors for success are:

- fast and effective decision-making;
- maintaining maximum flexibility;
- the use of strong incentives.

The speed of the decision-making process was a major differentiator between the successful and the unsuccessful hypergrowth companies. Successful companies clearly distinguish between the routine, day-to-day decision-making and the atypical/major choices and decisions. The routine decisions are achieved by delegating to the lowest possible level and clearly communicating to all parties involved where the final decision lies.

The atypical decisions, in contrast, require input from senior executives but this can be achieved by bringing key decision-makers together and providing them with the relevant information, thus enabling timely decisions that all can accept. Trusting intuition over analysis-paralysis is crucial. Quick and efficient communication of decisions to all levels constitutes the second factor that differentiates the successful from the less successful organisations. In thriving businesses, the decision-making processes were highly visible. Lower levels knew not only what the decisions were but also who made them and how they came about. At the same time, the communication processes were critical. Co-location of management and employees was found to be important in many cases, allowing senior executives to be seen to be endorsing decisions and gathering immediate input and feedback.

Effective implementation of decisions was often accomplished by integrating the key functions within the organisation into an integrated process. This process – often involving key customers – was the most important in the introduction of new products. Typically, these activities were led by one member of the senior management group to facilitate the necessary interaction between the various functions. To maintain the flexibility to succeed in a hypergrowth environment, nearly all the companies in the research stressed the importance of having the right people, working in teams and being supported by an organisation with open control systems.

It takes a certain type of person to thrive in a hypergrowth environment (a similar theme echoed and endorsed in the Powderject case) and successful companies do what it takes to recruit them. Because there is limited time for training, the companies in the research mainly hired personnel with either great experience in managing hypergrowth, or with specific industry experience. Key managers were typically recruited from outside as well, as very few hypergrowth companies believed they had all the talent and experience among their own employees. Some of the better companies in the research stressed that growth is conditional on the people that can be recruited.

Cross-functional teams were clearly highlighted as a second major drive for the required flexibility as they allowed management to merge, split and reassemble certain skills in the team, in response to changing needs. Simple milestones were typically used to monitor progress and were highly tailored – for example, time to market for product development; innovation targets for R&D, etc. These milestones are easily and widely communicated and are limited in number. Employees are held accountable for reaching them and are given wide flexibility and control to make it happen.

The glue that holds hypergrowth companies together is an incentive-based compensation system and the most successful players thrive on what might be termed hypergrowth people. Attracting and retaining such people requires giving them ample control and compensating them so they can capture the required momentum while sharing the risk and accepting the consequences of under-performance.

Hypergrowth companies use efficient performance evaluation systems to create tangible links between business objectives, individual roles and incentives. Often, simple and aggressive goals were set and the targets never reduced. All of those interviewed stressed the importance of a risk-based incentive system. To attract the best people, substantial rewards were attainable within each of the best companies. Although different schemes were being used, there appeared to be no substitute for stock options to provide the necessary reward and to align incentives. The best of these companies also included potential downsides, so that performance levels could be visibly differentiated.

The former owners of the better companies generally accepted the transition to a minority shareholding to allow the company to pursue its aggressive growth path and allow more key personnel to benefit from successful growth and business development. The research team from McKinsey was impressed by the predicament of the companies in their survey. The companies were doubling in size every year, in both sales turnover and the numbers of people employed, which the team note demands a drastically different approach than when faced with just high growth. Even though the principal findings may come across as simplistic and obvious, the importance of these direct approaches to decision-making, maintaining flexibility and recruiting and developing the right people as a source of their continued successful hypergrowth was fervently underscored by the better performing organisations.

The Ten Percenters

Successful entrepreneurs are often depicted as autocratic operators. They are the individuals that reject management textbooks and work on intuition and instinct. Is it possible for successful companies to be run in such a fashion? The answer appears to be yes and perhaps this way of operating may be the reason under-pinning their success.

That is one of the principal conclusions from a long-term study conducted by David Storey at the Centre for Small and Medium Sized Enterprises at Warwick Business School. The research examined middle-market companies with turn-overs from £5–100 million that have achieved 30% a year sales growth or better over a 5-year period, beginning in either 1990 or 1991.

These 700 firms amounted to 10% of the UK's small and medium-sized companies, hence the title of the study, 'The Ten Percenters'. The performance of the same firms was then tracked over a later 5-year period, beginning in either 1992 or 1993, to establish whether and why their growth trend had changed direction.

One of the most striking findings of the study was that many successful entrepreneurs have their own unique style of management. Arguably, they succeed by being badly managed and while an almost equal number of firms were well managed – as defined by the management texts – they were no more successful. However, one thing that the Ten Percenters have in common is their ability to identify and exploit a particular market niche.

Many of the fastest-growing companies Storey identified were in unfashionable industries such as food manufacturing. Their skill had been to locate a profitable niche even if the industry as a whole had not been expanding. Crucially, almost three-quarters of the sample were in specific niches and very few competed directly with large enterprises. For example, some of the most successful firms were in the travel industry, noted for its fierce competitive rivalry and low margins. However, the firms in the study had identified niches that were not serviced by the large operators. The travel agents that qualified as Ten Percenters had all chosen to specialise by geography or by offering customised leisure or business travel. However, the outstanding performers of the Ten Percenters report, those firms that had maintained a 30% growth over the two study periods, were in restaurants, hotels and catering, retail, electrical equipment, and computer and related services.

Outsourcing, the growth of supermarkets' own-label ranges that require suppliers and preferred supplier relationships plus specific local circumstances that entrepreneurs could take advantage of such as housing demand were also found to be niche-creating opportunities. Something as ordinary as pet food provides an example of how social change has created a new niche market. The reports quote a successful retailer – L. F. Jolleye – that exploited the growth in demand for pet foods of all types. The company has applied retail values more commonly associated with fashion to its industry, arranging the shop interiors to be both attractive and accessible and selecting staff for their ability to talk to customers in an informed and friendly manner.

The company, which has sales of £18 million, has opened shops in retail parks next to supermarkets thereby taking advantage of parking facilities. Managers are responsible for all store activities and each week they submit their figures to head office, which responds by sending back group figures enabling them to compare their performance with other stores in the chain. While there are no formal meetings, line of communication are open enough to allow office managers to talk to all the store managers at least once a week. While there may be no stated objectives or appraisals, it is clear that in such a transparent system, with sales information so readily collated and shared, nobody is going to be much in doubt about what they should be doing.

However, not all the respondents are managed in such a manner. A number believe that continued growth will push them towards greater formalisation. Bridge the World, a travel agency, is such an example. The company was founded in 1981 to provide long-haul travel to people who wanted more than just bargain flights. It offers tailor-made holidays, where the customer can specify any travel package and the sales staff will arrange it. The company employs graduates who have travelled extensively to perform this complex logistical task. The Gulf War in 1991 enabled the company to negotiate discounts with the big airlines and it now has sales of £38 million. Bridge the World is aiming to become a big player in its market, for which it needs to prepare its staff. It is determined to build systems that will sustain such growth and the responses to the survey questions about formal management practice are very positive, with the company having clearly stated objectives and job descriptions. Formal appraisals are regularly undertaken and staff performance is measured against key indicators. All sales staff without exception have training in customer service, assertiveness and sales techniques. Also, unlike many of the Ten Percenters, Bridge the World also conducts extensive market research, encourages systematic customer feedback and has recently employed a consultancy to help increase net margins.

Not all of the firms in the research were continuously successful – although by the standards of most businesses they still performed very well. One-quarter of the Ten Percenters in 1996 had dropped out of the £5–100 million category by 1998. Of these, 9% had been acquired, 4% had experienced a decline in turnover below the qualifying threshold, 5% were untraceable (probably out of business) and 7% were excluded because up-to-date financial records were not available. By contrast, 29% were very successful, growing sales by more than 30% or more each year between 1990/91 and 1995/96 – and 1992/93 and 1997/98. Just under half of the firms (46%) were classified as decelerators in the research, having showed a slowdown in growth. They had grown between 1990/91 and 1995/96 at 30% per annum but had not been able to sustain this performance from 1992/93 to 1997/98. However, more than a third grew sales by more than 20% and nearly a third saw their sales increase by between 10% and 20%.

The evidence suggests that professional managers and qualified personnel are not responsible for managing growth throughout most of the firms in the survey. In one of the reports, Storey found that no more than one in six Ten Percenters gave a consistently high priority to training. Where it did occur, training tended to be a response to growth, rather than a cause of it. However, there are some notable differences where training was given a high priority, but training by itself does not necessarily lead to business growth.

References and further reading

Banfield, P., Jennings, P. L. and Beaver, G. (1996) 'Competence Training for Small Firms – An Expensive Failure?', *Long Range Planning*, 29 (1), 94–102.

Beaver, G. (1984) 'The Entrepreneurial Ceiling: An Examination of the Small Business Management Process', in 7th National Small Firms Policy and Research Conference (UKEMRA), Nottingham Business School, September.

Beaver, G. and Jennings, P. L. (1995) 'Picking Winners: The Art of Identifying Successful Small Firms', in Hussey, D. E. (ed.), *Rethinking Strategic Management – Ways to Improve Competitive Performance*. Chichester: Wiley.

Beaver, G. and Jennings, P. L. (1996) 'The Abuse of Entrepreneurial Power: An Explanation of Management Failure?', *Journal of Strategic Change*, 5 (2) 89–105.

Bennett, M. (1989) *Managing Growth*. Harlow: Longman.

Birley, S. (1989) 'Corporate Strategy and the Small Firm', in Asch, D. and Bowman, C. (eds), *Readings in Strategic Management*. Basingstoke: Macmillan, ch. 6.

Burns, P. and Dewhurst, J. (1996) *Small Business and Entrepreneurship*, 2nd edn. Basingstoke: Macmillan.

Burns, P. and Harrison, J. (1996) 'Growth', in Burns, P. and Dewhurst, J. (eds), *Small Business and Entrepreneurship*, 2nd edn. Basingsloke: Macmillan, ch. 3.

Churchill, N. and Lewis, V. (1983) 'The Five Stages of Business Growth', *Harvard Business Review*, May/June, 30–50.

Deloitte & Touche (1997–99) 'The Ten Percenters: Fast Growing Small and Medium Enterprises in Great Britain', reports and findings.

Freedman, J. and Goodwin, M. (1992) 'Legal Form, Tax and the Micro-Business', in Caley, K., Chell, E., Chittenden, F. and Mason, C. (eds), *Small Enterprise Development: Policy and Practice in Action*. London: Paul Chapman.

Freedman, J. and Goodwin, M. (1994) 'Incorporating the Micro-Business: Perceptions and Misconceptions', in Hughes, A. and Storey, D. J. (eds), *Finance and The Small Firm*. London: Routledge.

Freel, M. (1999) 'Entrepreneurial and Growth Firms', in Deakins, D., *Entrepreneurship and Small Firms*, 2nd edn. Maidenhead: McGraw-Hill, ch. 9.

Gallagher, C. C. and Miller, P. (1991) 'New Fast Growing Companies Create Jobs', *Long Range Planning*, 24 (1), 96–101.

Gray, C. (1992) 'Growth Orientation and the Small Firm', in *Small Enterprise Development, Policy and Practice in Action*. London: Paul Chapman.

Gray, C. (1993) 'Stages of Growth and Entrepreneurial Career Motivation', in Chittenden, F., Robertson, M. and Watkins, D. (eds), *Small Firms, Recession and Recovery*. London: Paul Chapman.

Gray, C. (1998) *Enterprise and Culture*. London: Routledge.

Greiner, L. E. (1972) 'Evolution and Revolution as Organisations Grow', *Harvard Business Review*, July/August, 37–46.

Hakim, C. (1989) 'Identifying Fast Growth Small Firms', *Employment Gazette*, 97 (1) 29–41.

Hisrich, R. D. and Peters, M. P. (1998) *Entrepreneurship*, 4th edn. Boston, MA: McGraw Hill.

Hussey, D. E. (2000) 'Mergers and Acquisitions: The Fastest way to Destroy Value?', *Strategic Change*, 9 (5), 265–67.

Jennings, P. L. and Beaver, G. (1997) 'The Performance and Competitive Advantage of Small Firms: A Management Perspective', *International Small Business Journal*, 15 (2), 63–75.

Scase, R. and Goffee, R. (1987) *The Real World of the Small Business Owner*, 2nd edn. Beckenham: Croom Helm.

Stanworth, J. and Curran, J. (1986) 'Growth and the Small Firm', in *The Survival of the Small Firm*, Vol. 2, *Employment, Growth, Technology and Politics*. Aldershot: Gower.

Storey, D. J. (1994) *Understanding the Small Business Sector*. London: Routledge.

Storey, D. J., Keasey, K., Watson, R. and Wynarczyk, P. (1987) *The Performance of Small Firms*. London: Croom Helm.

9 Female entrepreneurship

Objectives
The role of women in the economy has been growing in importance for many years. Increasingly, women are taking the decision to start their own business either after a career break or by making the transition from salaried employment to self-employment. However, this group of women, although economically significant, remains largely invisible, both in terms of the available published research on entrepreneurship and in terms of the business support infrastructure available to assist potential female entrepreneurs (Beaver and Harrison, 1994; Cohen, 1997; Carr, 1998).

This chapter seeks to examine:

● the profile and characteristics of the female entrepreneur;

● the development of alternative perspectives for understanding the role and motivations of women seeking to enter the small business sector;

● the impact of the enterprise climate and the wider cultural and business conditions associated with traditional gender roles and their effect on female entrepreneurship and comparisons with male entrepreneurship;

● the role of the business support infrastructure in encouraging, promoting and facilitating female entrepreneurship and what improvements can be effected to enhance their effectiveness and behaviour;

● a brief case history of successful female business development.

Women and the small business sector

The Bolton Report of 1971 undoubtedly kick-started the current day fascination and preoccupation with people (popularly referred to as entrepreneurs) who start and manage their own businesses. It has been stated that the small firm sector post-Bolton has been the subject of one of the most sustained and consistent areas of academic research and reporting (Curran and Blackburn, 1991; Scase, 1998). Indeed, it is hard to think of an MBA programme in the UK, North America and much of Western Europe that does not offer an elective or a major specialisation on small business, new venture creation or entrepreneurship. Entrepreneurs are commonly perceived as the self-made business professionals of the moment, creating their own wealth rather than inheriting it. All aspects of the media frequently report on the popular entrepreneurial personalities such as Richard Branson and Anita Roddick who are regarded as the role models which aspiring business people should seek to emulate.

Furthermore, as discussed in Chapters 1 and 3, the act of entrepreneurship is now portrayed as an economic necessity within a modern economy, promoting structural balance, economic growth, employment choice and national and personal prosperity (Beaver and Jennings, 1995). This perception of the contribution of entrepreneurial activity has helped accelerate a growth in small business start-ups, which according to the latest figures from Barclays Bank (2000) are at an all-time high in certain service sectors and especially by women. The contribution of women to the economic health and performance of the small business community and the economy generally has been very well articulated by Lady Howe (1988) in a speech to the Business in the Community Initiative, who stated:

> We need to find out what more needs to be done to help women realise their full potential as contributors to our economic life. We need to do this because not to do so is to continue to waste an enormous asset which can enrich and stimulate our business by tapping new talent. We need to do it more now than ever because future population trends show that business success and industry are going to have to rely increasingly on women in the 1990s and beyond.

Deakins (1999) also notes that the national picture in the UK small business sector is for women to be catching up with the activity rates of men as some of the traditional barriers (for entering entrepreneurship) come down but still lag a long way behind those of men.

The fact is that women entrepreneurs have become a significant economic force and yet, despite their increasing number, there is still a relative dearth of in-depth qualitative literature on the subject. This has resulted in a lack of theoretical understanding of the experiences of such women: their motivations, problems, successes and aspirations (Moore, 1990; Cohen, 1997; Carr, 1998; Rae, 1999). While there is an ever-increasing literature on entrepreneurship, much of the research has a distinctly male bias, not only in terms of the examples and cases cited but also ideologically (Goffee and Scase, 1985; Lee-Gosselin and Grise, 1990; Stevenson, 1990). Many writers on the subject have noted that, even where female samples have been selected, the recorded behaviour is frequently interpreted in terms of male models and constructs and set against male standards. This serves to reinforce the stereotypes and misconceptions about women in business. Indeed, the term entrepreneur conveys meanings and associations which are often at variance with the perceptions and experiences of many women (Beaver and Harrison, 1994; Holmquist, 1997; Cohen, 1997; Carr, 1998).

Research by Cohen (1997) provides an illustration of the above in the interview summaries cited in her work:

● 'I don't feel as though I am an entrepreneur at all because I don't make a lot of money.'

(co-director of a training and consultancy firm)

● 'I would be very flattered if anyone called me an entrepreneur but I don't think that I am the same sort of calibre.'

(owner/manager, travel business)

- 'An entrepreneur gets on with it and follows through all his ideas and I am only doing recruitment . . . I don't know if I could be an entrepreneur . . . I am just a dedicated person.'

(recruitment consultant)

These brief but typical illustrations confirm that the women Cohen studied understood the term 'entrepreneur' in diverse ways, ranging from an emphasis on financial success to innovation and risk-taking. However, what they all shared was an almost total lack of identification with the concept. Although many of the respondents in the sample perceived the entrepreneur as an interesting and intriguing character, 'he' had very little resonance for them.

Arguably women have invariably been involved in entrepreneurship and small business through their role as co-entrepreneur though this has not always been acknowledged or given, until recently, its proper recognition and value (Scase and Goffee, 1987). As co-entrepreneurs, women have provided a range of valuable and frequently unpaid services for their husbands' businesses. These services include the performance of business tasks, such as accounting and secretarial roles, as well as the responsibility for domestic support and provision. Such assistance has contributed significantly to the economic viability of new businesses, particularly during the difficult start-up period.

In the UK in 1980, women in self-employment on their own account constituted only 4% of the total female paid labour force, making up 20% of the self-employed and employer sector (Goffee and Scase, 1985). Although data on the exact level of female entrepreneurship are difficult to find, as much of the available information is not broken by gender, what there is indicates that, from the low starting point in 1980, increasing numbers of women are starting their own businesses. Between 1981 and 1987, a 70% increase in the number of self-employed women was recorded, compared with a corresponding increase of 30% for men (Stephens, 1989). In the USA during the 1980s, the number of self-employed women increased five times faster than the number of self-employed men – and three times faster than the number of female employees. Research undertaken in the 1990s indicates that women start almost half of all new businesses in the USA and, as mentioned briefly above, there are similar trends evident in the UK. In 1990, more than 3.5 million women in the USA owned their own business, generating a revenue stream exceeding $40 billion a year (Rossman, 1990). Indeed, it has been estimated that, by 2005, 40% of all businesses in the USA will be owned and managed by women.

As has been shown in previous chapters (notably, in Chapters 2 and 6), the process of establishing a new venture is a critical and demanding time for any potential business entrant – and the prevailing culture and volatile business environments of many economies may make this process overly difficult. The survival rate for new firms in economies such as the UK's is low, with just 40% of new enterprises surviving beyond the first 3 years (Gavron et al., 1998). This has led to calls throughout the last two decades for the creation of an enterprise culture that supports, promotes and values entrepreneurial activity and provides the required support for new business practitioners. It would seem that the current emphasis is placed on the quality of new ventures through the provision of suitable advice and information that is crucial to their long-term survival and profitability (Gavron *et al.*, 1998). All new businesses are vulnerable and fragile entities and all must successfully negotiate the resource/credibility-merry-go-round (Birley, 1996). However, female entrepreneurs face additional gender-related problems which can have a profound impact on the success and viability of their businesses. According to Stephens (1989) and Cohen (1997), these include difficulties obtaining finance, a lack of managerial experience and a range of domestic pressures and expectations.

The female entrepreneur/owner-manager

The comparatively recent but significant entrance by women into self-employment has meant that female enterprises are characterised by three principal characteristics:

● recent origin;
● small scale;
● service-related in nature.

The recent growth in female businesses can be related to the contemporary increase in the female labour force. Although women have been looking for work outside the home in increasing numbers for the last 40 years or so, there has been a considerable rise in the size of the female labour force in much of the Western world over the past decade. In the UK, the number of women looking for work grew from 9.55 million in 1988 to almost 13.5 million in 2000, with the projection that the increase shows no sign of slowing down. Studies in the USA by Hisrich (1986) and Hisrich and Brush (1985) revealed that only 31% of all women owned/managed businesses had been in existence for more than 5 years. However, there is consistent research evidence from a range of studies to suggest that female enterprises enjoy a better survival rate than their male counterparts (Brush, 1992; Rosa *et al.*, 1994; Cohen, 1997).

The service-related nature of many female businesses is not surprising given the traditional presence of women in sectors such as retailing, public relations, educational services and catering. The result, according to Hisrich (1998), is often smaller firms with lower net earnings. According to Hisrich and Peters (1998) and Brush (1992) – see Table 9.1 below – some 90% of female entrepreneurs start service-related businesses. However, recent evidence suggests that women are now entering into traditionally male-dominated areas such as high technology, construction and finance (Reidy, 1997; Carr, 1998).

The third characteristic of female owner/managed firms is their relatively small size. However, this must be placed in the national economic context of the small business sector under consideration. For example, in the UK, the sector is composed largely of micro–businesses. However, there is evidence to suggest that, when placed alongside comparable male firms, female enterprises tend to be smaller in size, having a lower sales volume and generating less income (Johnson and Storey, 1993; Beaver and Harrison, 1994).

It is difficult to be prescriptive in suggesting definitive reasons for female self-employment but it does appear that both push and pull factors are at work. *Push* factors would include events such as redundancy or continued unemployment, while *pull* factors could embrace a need for achievement, independence or personal fulfilment (Borooah *et al.*, 1997). Women are often pushed into entrepreneurship because of the lack of opportunities in the labour market and the presence of the glass ceiling. It can also be the method by which many women avoid the low pay and poor conditions of many traditional female occupations (Scase and Goffee, 1985).

The overall picture from the research evidence indicates that women tend to enter the small business sector from a more precarious labour market position than men and associated with a significantly lower level of financial reward (Borooah *et al.*, 1997). The flip side of this factor, though, is that running a small business makes it easier for many women to undertake their home and work responsibilities.

These motivations are reflected in the typology of female entrepreneurs developed by Goffee and Scase (1985, 1987). Deakins (1999) is rather dismissive of their typology, stating that their approach was useful but that it is rather outdated as a method of classifying types of female entrepreneur. Also, he states that the concept of entrepreneurial ideals advanced by Goffee and Scase is rather ill defined. Deakins' assertions, though, would be more convincing if he gave reasons for the rejection of their framework and suggested a modern replacement typology which would be of assistance in understanding female entrepreneurship.

A typology of female entrepreneurs

The typology developed by Cromie and Hayes (1988) is examined in order to contribute to our understanding of this important issue. Their research set out to explore the contention put forward by Goffee and Scase that it is inappropriate and naive to speak of the female entrepreneur – rather there are different types of female business ownership.

Cromie and Hayes' work reinforced the suggestion that it is incorrect and unhelpful to talk about the female entrepreneur, just as it is inaccurate to refer to the generic small business. Rather, female entrepreneurship is characterised by a significant amount of diversity among women proprietors. A key distinguishing factor that emerged from this research was the presence (or absence) of children, as opposed to marriage per se. This led to the construction of a three-fold classification, (in comparison with Goffee and Scase, who suggested four types) as follows:

● type 1 – *innovators*;
● type 2 – *dualists*;
● type 3 – *returners*.

Innovators

This classification is very similar to the innovators in the Goffee and Scase typology. They share common motives with many male entrepreneurs such as a desire for autonomy (independence), the need for achievement, dissatisfaction with either job or career and a strong financial ambition. Their knowledge of business and employment history is also very similar to that of male entrepreneurs. They are very well educated, possess managerial experience, run firms with growth and employment potential and are likely to be found in manufacturing and services. The business represents an important focal point in their lives, so much so that they frequently reject traditional female roles and enjoy personal satisfaction and success through development of their business. Invariably, this type of female entrepreneur does not have children.

Dualists

This group is characterised by women who have made significant career progress in traditional female occupations such as nursing or teaching and who have children. A principal motivation for these women is to successfully combine home and work responsibilities, and therefore there is a strong perception that business ownership is more likely to accommodate these needs than a conventional organisational career as it affords the necessary flexibility.

Compared with the innovator, this type is much more likely to be found in the traditional services sector. However, like the innovator, the desire for independence and the need for achievement are key motivations for business establishment and dualists frequently possess some managerial skills and good educational qualifications. Unlike the previous category, childcare responsibilities are a key factor in business creation.

Dualists are not strongly driven to advance further in their careers but they are reluctant to relinquish the benefits of paid employment. From their perspective, self-employment allows them to fulfil both career and domestic roles simultaneously. This choice highlights a significant difference between male and female entrepreneurs and is well documented in several studies (Watkins and Watkins, 1984; Goffee and Scase, 1987; Rosa *et al.*, 1994; Cohen, 1997 – to cite but a few).

Returners

Women in this group have usually interrupted their careers to have and raise their children. These women usually return to work at a suitable time in their children's development and are frequently unimpressed or dissatisfied with the type and quality of jobs available. Not surprisingly, business establishment may offer a better alternative for occupational advancement. Returners tend to lack employment experience and possess limited managerial and technical skills. Low levels of educational attainment are also a common trait of this group. The overall profile of returners reflects the traditional cycle of female employment common to many women, i.e. an absence of developmental careers and the paramount role of domestic responsibilities and childcare over paid employment.

Comparing Cromie and Hayes' typology with that of Goffee and Scase, there are obviously many similarities between the innovators in both studies, with both having a strong resemblance to male entrepreneurs. Further similarities are also evident between Goffee and Scase's domestics category and Cromie and Hayes' returners. Equally, the conventionals from the Goffee and Scase typology could also be grouped with the dualists. However, a significant difference between the two classifications is that the conventionals are working-class women driven by the need to earn money, whereas the dualists have successful careers but reach a point where they want to spend more time with their children. From their perspective, self-employment is the best vehicle to allow them to achieve this. (There is no category in the Cromie and Hayes typology which can be matched with the radicals in the Goffee and Scase classification.)

Other than the unsubstantiated comments from Deakins mentioned above, the typologies of both Scase and Goffee and Cromie and Hayes have attracted criticisms from other writers and researchers, most notably Allen and Truman (1988, 1993) and Carter and Cannon (1992). Allen and Truman take issue with the concept of women's attachment to entrepreneurial ideals as this presupposes a choice that in reality is not available to a large number of women. Also, they argue that implicit in the notion of attachment to conventional gender roles is the assumption that the experience of women to domestic subordination is uniform, thus failing to account for the tremendous diversity of women as a social group.

Carter and Cannon (1992) question the way in which these classifications represent small business ownership and indeed the small business owners themselves, as static and unchanging. They comment that:

> The sector is inherently turbulent. New ventures are started, grow, decline, face changes and develop. This ferment calls for many and varying behaviours and attitudes among entrepreneurs.

Their theoretical framework, based on a comprehensive study of 60 business owners in London, Nottingham and Glasgow, takes as its starting point the notions of heterogeneity and change. They identified five types of women entrepreneurs, namely:

- *Drifters*. These were typically young women, opting for self-employment as a response to unemployment.
- *Young achievers*. These were aspiring, generally well-educated women that used training as a way of making up for their limited business experience.
- *Achievers*. These were similar to the category above in terms of attitudes and values, but the achievers were somewhat older and possessed considerable relevant work experience. While some achievers had children, others had no intention of having a family.
- *Returners*. In contrast to the achievers, this group was seen as those women that selected self-employment as the route back into occupational activity after a career break. Although their businesses tended to be organised around domestic and childcare responsibilities, it was found that most of these women were very keen to see their enterprise grow and develop.

- *Traditionalists*. This group were typically older women (45 years plus) who had principally worked in family-owned and managed businesses. Coming from backgrounds where self-employment was the norm, such women had limited if any, experience of salaried employment.

In offering the above classification, Cannon and Carter emphasise the flexibility of these categories together with the accompanying dynamism and variety that constitute small business ownership and management.

To conclude this section, although work in this area still remains relatively sparse and fragmented, there are a growing number of studies into the lives and experiences of women entrepreneurs. Although it is beyond the scope of this text to provide a review of such work, the overall picture that emerges is characterised by both diversity and commonality, fundamental to which is the notion of gender as a key determinant in the experience of women entrepreneurs. There are other important themes, such as the role of social and professional networks, the consideration of what constitutes success for women in business and the performance and function of training initiatives and support agencies – more of which will discussed later.

A comparison of male and female entrepreneurs

As previously stated, research into female entrepreneurship and small business management is comparatively recent. Despite the burgeoning literature on small firms and entrepreneurship, only a small proportion concentrates on issues of gender and business performance. Johnson and Storey (1993) note that:

> Despite the obvious numerical importance in the small business sector of firms which are owned and controlled by women and despite the growing interest in the role of women in the labour market more generally, there has been surprisingly little research into women and self-employment/small business ownership. There has been even less work, which has compared the characteristics and background of male and female business owners and/or the characteristics of their businesses.

Given the above, it would be useful to examine and compare the characteristics and experiences of male and female business proprietorship.

As a starting point, Table 9.1, taken from Hisrich and Peters (1998), which details their understanding (based on a résumé of research findings) of the principal differences between male and female entrepreneurship, will serve as a useful reference from which to consider the additional evidence and critique that follows.

The research evidence suggests that men tend to be younger than women when starting up in business although in recent years the age of women entering self-employment has been decreasing. This probably reflects the increasing numbers of women selecting self-employment and the recently recorded higher trend of women in lower age groups choosing to run their own business (Borooah *et al.*, 1997).

The age distribution of female entrepreneurs tends to be bi-modal, with significant concentrations in the 25–35 and 55–60 age groups, compared with

Table 9.1 A comparison between male and female entrepreneurs

Characteristic	Male entrepreneurs	Female entrepreneurs
Motivation	• Achievement – strive to make things happen • Personal independence – self-image as it relates to status through their previous role in the company • Job satisfaction arising from the desire to be in control	• Achievement – the accomplishment of a goal • Independence – to do it alone
Departure point[a]	• Dissatisfaction with present job sideline in college, sideline to present job, or outgrowth of present job • Discharge or layoff • Opportunity for acquistion	• Job frustration • Interest in and recognition of opportunity in the area • Change in personal circumstances
Sources of funds	• Personal assets and savings • Bank financing • Investors • Loans from friends and family	• Personal assets and savings • Personal loans
Occupational background	• Experience in line of work • Recognised specialist, or one who has gained a high level of achievement in the field • Competent in a variety of business functions	• Experience in area of business • Middle management or similar level of experience in the field • Service-related occupational background
Personality characteristics	• Opinionated and persuasive • Goal oriented • Innovative and idealistic • High level of self-confidence • Enthusiastic and energetic • Must be own boss	• Flexible and tolerant • Goal oriented • Creative and idealistic • Medium level of self-confidence • Enthusiastic and energetic • Ability to deal with the social and economic environment
Background	• Age when starting venture: 25–35 • Father was self-employed • College educated – degree in business or technical area (usually engineering) • First-born child	• Age when starting venture: usually, 35–45 • Father was self-employed • College educated – degree in liberal arts or similar • First-born child
Support groups	• Friends and professional colleagues • Business associates • Family and networks	• Close friends • Spouse
Type of business	• Manufacturing or construction	• Service – related – educational, consulting or public relations

Note: [a] Activities occurring when the venture is started.
Source: Hisrich and Peters (1998)

men whose age distribution tends to be evenly dispersed around a mean age of 39 years old (Johnson and Storey, 1993). The bi-modal nature of the female age profile is reflected in the Cromie and Hayes typology, with the returners more likely to be found in the older age group and the innovators more likely to be located in the younger age band.

In terms of educational attainment, the research findings indicate that men are more likely to hold some form of professional qualification (Johnson and Storey, 1993). Where men and women both hold formal qualifications, the evidence suggests that women are more likely to hold an arts degree, while men have a science- or technically related degree such as engineering or technology. However, this situation is changing as more women are studying for business- and engineering-related qualifications and vocational degrees generally (Brush, 1992; Borooah *et al.*, 1997).

Marital status appears to be the demographic characteristic with the largest variance separating male and female entrepreneurs. Contemporary research suggests that the majority of men entering the small business sector are married. However, it would appear that there are as many female proprietors that are divorced, single or widowed as there are married (Goffee and Scase, 1985; Johnson and Storey, 1993; Cohen, 1997).

While marriage can provide the emotional support and encouragement for business start-up and expansion, for the female entrepreneur managing the balance between the demands of a business and family expectations can be extremely difficult. This is compounded by the evidence from many research studies that show that the male proprietor rarely contributes (or only minimally contributes) towards the running of the home and family. This is a significant difference between male and female owned/managed firms, as there is considerable evidence to show that many male-owned businesses could not survive without the (frequently unpaid) contribution of wives, both at home and in the business (Goffee and Scase, 1985; Cohen, 1997; Leach and Bogod, 1999).

The different impact of marital status is reflected in the motivations for entering self-employment. For many women, the strongest motive for business establishment is to combine the roles and responsibilities of business and family life. In contrast, for men it seems that the principal ambition is to be their own boss and enjoy an independent lifestyle (Borooah *et al.*, 1997).

As shown above in the illustration from Hisrich and Peters, there tend to be strong similarities between male and female entrepreneurs, with both inclined to be goal-oriented, energetic and independent. However, there is one important characteristic where they do differ significantly – that of self-confidence. The evidence suggests that women sometimes have the tendency to discredit their own abilities, to have lower expectations of themselves and to attribute business success to factors other than their own competence and abilities (Reidy, 1997; Cohen, 1997; Carr, 1998). Such differences in personal characteristics and traits cannot be dismissed, given that one of the principal aims of creating and promoting an enterprise culture is to encourage and develop certain characteristics and personality attributes, such as self-reliance, that encourage the creation and development of new enterprises. This is not to suggest that men do not suffer from a lack of confidence or self-esteem but that the research evidence suggests that women are more likely to experience these difficulties than men. In their concluding remarks, Johnson and Storey (1993) in their review of male and female entrepreneurs and their businesses state:

> This chapter has illustrated that the differences between businesses run by men and women are fairly marginal in most respects, with very few differences being significant in statistical terms. However, it does appear to be the case that women founders of business are on average older than their male counterparts, are less well qualified and that female founders are less likely than men to obtain start-up finance from the commercial banks. The businesses run by women are smaller on average, in terms of the numbers employed but not in terms of financial turnover and are less profitable than male-run businesses.

The final part of this chapter will examine what initiatives can be conceived, designed and implemented to address some of the disadvantages and shortcomings experienced by women proprietors, of the sort highlighted above.

The encouragement and promotion of female entrepreneurship – initiatives and recommendations for start-up, growth and development

Attention is now focused on considering what can be done for female entrepreneurs in the wider context of the enterprise culture. This includes changes in the behaviour and response of the business support infrastructure to accommodate the needs and requirements of potential and existing women entrepreneurs. However, caution needs to be exercised in attempting to isolate and correct the effects of gender as an independent variable in comparative studies of small firm performance. The difficulties here should not be underestimated, for, as several respected and well-managed studies and investigations have shown, the overall evidence is inconclusive (Kalleberg and Leicht, 1991; Johnson and Storey, 1993; Rosa *et al.*, 1994; Cohen, 1997). As a consequence, Cohen has suggested that:

> Given the existence of both perceived and real additional obstacles for women it may be inferred that the lack of concrete evidence linking underperformance with women entrepreneurs suggests that gender is a significant influence on the ability to overcome barriers to the creation of successful businesses.
>
> It is clear however, that the lack of consideration for women has ensured that the decision-making processes of funding agencies and policy makers have been informed almost entirely by the analyses of the experiences and actions of male entrepreneurs and does not take into account the experiences of women.

What then could or should be done by the business support infrastructure to promote and support female entrepreneurship? Predictably, this is not an easy question to answer for the numbers of considerations are frequently mutually exclusive and/or conflicting.

The following represent some of the principal issues and research findings that need to be understood and accommodated if the role and contribution of women in enterprise creation and development are to be enhanced.

- Small firms in general tend to employ more women and women entrepreneurs are much more likely than men to employ other women in their business (Johnson and Storey, 1993; Curran *et al.*, 1991). Encouraging women proprietors to enter the small business sector therefore has a beneficial multiplier effect.

- As with so much of the literature on small firms, there is a danger of classifying women as a homogenous grouping when, in reality, heterogeneity is the case. This would serve to distort the situation and must be resisted. The degree to which any problem or difficulty acts as a real barrier to business start-up or development should be determined situationally. Support agencies must, therefore, simultaneously address a wide range of issues which will individually impact on different entrepreneurs to a greater or lesser extent but which will, collectively, ease the additional burden imposed on all female entrepreneurs.

- Greater representation of women in the formulation and implementation of enterprise policy would enhance the profile and significance of female owner/managed small firms. This should also contribute towards the refinement and clarity of understanding of the special needs and characteristics of the female proprietor and enterprise.

- Building on the point above, consideration could be given to the construction and delivery of training and development initiatives specifically focused on the particular needs of the female enterprise together with facilitating suitable business networks.

- The research evidence consistently identifies that women entrepreneurs suffer discrimination from important stakeholder groups presenting them with an unfair and unjustified commercial disadvantage. For example, Goffee and Scase (1985) and Storey (1994) both comment on the need to re-educate decision-makers in financial institutions to change their attitudes towards women applicants in their requests for funding.

In her work, Carr (1995, 1998) draws attention to the diversity of criteria and approvals required, when a business plan or request for finance is presented for consideration. She states that:

> Subjective factors drawn upon when judging female entrepreneurs include opinions, interpretations, evaluations of 'objective' aspects and stereotypical ideas about sex roles. The perceptions that bank managers have about applicants should not be underestimated. Entrepreneurial characteristics such as ambition, perseverance, resolution and commercial acumen are not usually attributed to women. The result is that women are not perceived as entrepreneurs.

It is clear from much of the research evidence that what will cause a bank manager to endorse or reject an application for funding is determined as much by feelings and perceptions of the applicant, as the quality of the business proposal as evidenced by the business plan. Many commentators have noted that women are not taken as seriously as men are (Koper, 1993). Indeed some, notably Carter and Cannon (1992), have stated that this problem is so bad that the only real solution may be the provision of women-only financial institutions, with women lending staff, dealing with women applicants. Carr draws the same conclusion but falls short of suggesting the same radical solution as Carter and Cannon. She states (Carr, 1998):

The cultural and perceptual disadvantage experienced by women entering entrepreneurship manifests itself in the form of procedures and criteria which are used to judge business proposals based on an androcentric paradigm.

In conclusion, several prominent research studies (many of which have been cited in this chapter), have identified three principal ingredients that significantly enhance the chances of success (however measured) for women entrepreneurs. These are training, networking and increased professionalisation. It would appear that, in developing an improved business climate for women entrepreneurs, the enterprise support infrastructure should focus some of its limited resources on activities that address these key areas.

CASE ILLUSTRATION 9.1

Female entrepreneurship

Anita Roddick and The Body Shop plc

The presentation of a business plan can be just as important as the facts and figures contained in it. That was the lesson that Anita Roddick learnt when she approached her bank manager for the start-up capital to open her first Body Shop. She came up with the name after finding her premises between two funeral parlours in Brighton. It was a move that prompted a legal threat from her neighbours, who claimed that the name was a tasteless stunt.

At the end of October 2000 the manufacturer and retailer of bodycare products reported half-year profits up 4% to £9.4 million on sales of £271 million, up from £262 million. The company now has a market value of £222 million, operates more than 1,600 outlets in 47 countries, and makes 400 products. The numbers are a far cry from that small shop that Roddick opened in 1976. The storey of her rise to fame and her subsequent hiccups has been told many times. Not so well known are the details of how she touted around her first business plan and the prejudice she suffered because of her casual appearance and the fact that she was a woman. Roddick states:

> The most difficult thing was raising money for the first shop. I knew that I had a good idea and a reasonable business plan and I thought naively that this was all that was important. I went to see my bank manager in my T-shirt, with my two small children in tow.
>
> I thought that my enthusiasm and energy would convince the bank manager to believe in me but he turned me down, which really set me back. My husband, Gordon, told me to have another go but this time dress up like a bloke in pin stripes and leave the kids behind. He came too. After taking his advice, I was able to walk out of the bank with a £4000 loan.

Roddick had grown up in Littlehampton, Sussex, the daughter of Italian immigrants. 'We never fitted in' she states. Her father, who ran his own café, died when she was 10. Roddick had to help her mother who always told her that she would succeed. She did well at school and was desperate to see the world. Before embarking on that, she joined a teacher training course at the University of Bath but fondly remembers being asked to leave school for writing a swear word on the blackboard to illustrate a linguistic point. She worked on a kibbutz, travelled, married Gordon and ran a bed-and-breakfast hotel before starting Body Shop. Roddick had always wanted to start her own business and when, in 1976, Gordon took several months off, to make a trip from Argentina to New York, she decided that it was time to realise her ambition.

She herself had travelled extensively. Having run out of shampoo in one remote place, she experimented with rubbing extracts from fruit and vegetables on her hair:

> In its raw state, almost anything that is harvested out of the ground can polish, clean and protect your body. It was not only economic necessity that inspired the birth of Body Shop. Women, when they want to earn a livelihood, usually earn it through what they are interested in or what they are knowledgeable about. My travels exposed me to the body rituals of women all over the world.
>
> Also, the frugality that my mother exercised during the War made me question many retail conventions. Why waste a container, when you can refill it? Why buy more of something than you can use? We refilled, re-used and recycled everything.

Roddick began with one shop. She paid a friend £25 to design the Body Shop logo and painted the store green to cover the damp mouldy walls. She started by selling 25 hand-mixed products that she produced in various sizes to make the range seem larger at 200 items. She dreamt up some marketing gimmicks that included sprinkling scent on the pavement close to the shop to entice customers. She took a £4000 investment from Ian McGlinn, a friend, and within 6 months had opened a second shop. Another friend wanted to open one in Bognor Regis and a haphazard network of franchises evolved, all taken by women. Body Shop soon had stores in London and started opening others on the Continent. Gordon came up with the idea of self-financing more new stores, which sparked the growth of a more organised franchised network.

By 1984, Body Shop was making a profit of £1 million on sales of £5 million. Two years later, it floated on the stock market and 4 years after that it made profits of £14 million on sales of £56 million. However, in 1999, profits plunged 91%, falling from £38 million to £3.4 million, after the company bought back many of its franchises and embarked on a big restructuring programme. Roddick says that the business in Britain is hierarchical with 'generals' at the top who stifle creative thinking. She states that:

> There is a real timidity towards energy and passion in this country. You can't make yourself have passion. Curiosity, optimism, a great idea, self-esteem and networking are important in starting a business.

Source: Adapted from Steiner, R. (1999) *My First Break: How Entrepreneurs Get Started.*
London: Sunday Times. Also featured in *The Sunday Times*, 24 October 1999

Example 9.1: Venus and Mars in small business

Research conducted by the National Foundation of Women Business Owners in Australia (2000) indicates that there are significant differences in how man and women view and operate their businesses. The report shows that women are more likely than their male peers to rely on fellow business owners for information and advice. It also found that 80% of women feel that a 24 hour business help-line is important compared with only 63% of the men surveyed. The report suggests that women are more price sensitive than men and tend to use a lot of the same brands as they do at home. It also shows that women are significantly less likely to take risks with the business than men are.

For some time, large international companies have used such research findings when formulating their marketing strategies. For example, the US-based Wells Fargo bank established its very successful Women's Loans Program, the goal of which is to lend $10 billion over 10 years to women business proprietors.

In Australia, the Commonwealth Office of the Status of Women reports that women constitute 35% of Australia's 1.3 million small business operators. The growth rate of female entrepreneurs from 1995 and 1997 was three times that of men. Perhaps more significantly, women's earnings are continuing to grow faster than those for men so it is no surprise that corporate Australia is identifying women entrepreneurs as a lucrative target market.

An example is Westpac, which has set up a dedicated Woman in Business unit. Westpac claims that the unit was a response to a survey that revealed that 40% of women in Australia felt discriminated against by their bank on the basis of gender. The company also reports that many women claim little knowledge of managing or obtaining finance.

Ernst and Young has also conducted a survey of women entrepreneurs (2000) and some of the key findings were as follows:

- While both sexes cited an opportunity for independence as the principal reason for going into business, women cited family reasons as an important secondary motivation.
- Men are more likely to develop business plans than women are but women are more likely to stick to their plans when they produce one.
- Women have more modest expectations of their capacity to grow their business.
- Male entrepreneurs are more likely to export than women.
- Both sexes stated that problems with staff and business partners were among the most difficult issues facing their businesses.

Source: *Dynamic Small Business Magazine*, October/November 2000 (Sydney, Australia)

References and further reading

Allen, S. and Truman, C. (1988) 'Women's Work and Success in Women's Business', in 11th National Small Firms Policy and Research Conference, Cardiff, November.

Allen, S. and Truman, C. (eds) (1993) *Women in Business: Perspectives on Women Entrepreneurs*. London: Routledge.

Barclays Bank (2000) *Economic Survey, The UK Small Business Sector*, October 1999. London.

Beaver, G. and Harrison, Y. (1994) 'TEC Support for Women Entrepreneurs: Help or Hindrance?', in 17th National Small Firms Policy and Research Conference, Sheffield, November.

Beaver, G. and Jennings, P. L. (1995) 'Picking Winners: The Art of Identifying Successful Small Firms', in Hussey, D. E. (ed.), *Rethinking Strategic Management*. Chichester: Wiley.

Birley, S. (1989) 'Female Entrepreneurs: Are They Really Any Different?', *Journal of Small Business Management*, 2 (2), 32–46.

Birley, S. (1996) 'The Start Up', in Burns, P. and Dewhurst, J., *Small Business and Entrepreneurship*, 2nd edn. Basingstoke: Macmillan, ch. 2.

Borooah, V. K., Collins, G., Hart, M. and MacNabb, A. (1997) 'Women and Self Employment: An Analysis of Constraints and Opportunities in Northern Ireland', in Deakins, D., Jennings, P. L. and Mason, C. (eds), *Small Firms: Entrepreneurship in the Nineties*. London: Paul Chapman.

Brush, C. B. (1992) 'Research on Women Business Owners: Past Trends, a New Perspective and Future Directions', *Entrepreneurship Theory and Practice*, 16 (4), 5–30.

Carr, P. (1995) 'Riding the Juggernaut: Selectivity and Entrepreneurship in Ireland', *Irish Journal of Sociology*, 5 (2), 67–88.

Carr, P. (1998) 'The Cultural Production of Enterprise: Understanding Selectivity as Cultural Policy', *Economic and Social Review*, 29 (2), 27–49.

Carter, S. and Cannon, T. (1992) *Women as Entrepreneurs*. London: Academic.

Chell, E., Haworth, J. and Brearley, S. (1991) *The Entrepreneurial Personality: Concepts, Cases and Categories*. London: Routledge.

Cohen, L. (1997) 'Women in Transition: From Employment to Self-Employment', unpublished PhD thesis, Sheffield Business School, Sheffield Hallam University.

Cromie, S. and Hayes, J. (1988) 'Towards a Typology of Female Entrepreneurs', *Sociological Review*, 36 (1), 87–113.

Cromie, S. and O'Donoghue, J. (1992) 'Assessing Entrepreneurial Inclinations', *International Small Business Journal*, 10 (2), 66–71.

Curran, J. and Blackburn, R. (1991) *Paths of Enterprise: The Future of Small Business*. London: Routledge.

Curran, J., Blackburn, R. A. and Woods, A. (1991) *Profiles of Small Businesses in the Service Sector* (ESRC Centre for Research on Small Service Sector Enterprises, Kingston Polytechnic).

Deakins, D. (1999) *Entrepreneurship and Small Firms*, 2nd edn. Maidenhead: McGraw-Hill.

Gavron, R., Cowling, M., Holtham, G. and Westhall, A. (1998) *The Entrepreneurial Society*. London: Institute for Public Policy Research.

Goffee, R. and Scase, R. (1985) *Women in Charge: The Experience of Female Entrepreneurs*. London: Allen and Unwin.

Goffee, R. and Scase, R. (1987) 'Patterns of Business Proprietorship among Women in Britain', in *Entrepreneurship in Britain*. London: Croom Helm, 60–82.

Hisrich, R. D. (1986) 'The Woman Entrepreneur: Characteristics, Skills, Problems and Prescriptions for Success', in *The Art and Science of Enterpreneurship*. Cambridge, MA: Ballinger, pp. 61–84.

Hisrich, R. D. and Brush, C. B. (1985) 'Women and Minority Entrepreneurs: A Comparative Analysis', in Proceedings from the 1985 Conference on Entrepreneurship, pp. 566–87.

Hisrich, R. D. and Peters, M. P. (1998) *Entrepreneurship*, 4th edn. Boston, MA: Irwin McGraw-Hill.

Holmquist, C. (1997) 'Guest Editorial: The Other Side of the Coin – Women's Entrepreneurship as a Complement or an Alternative?', *Entrepreneurship and Regional Development*, 9 (3) (Women's Entrepreneurship Special Issue), 179–82.

Howe, E. (1988) 'Introductory Address', in Business in the Community Initiative on Women's Economic Development, Preston, November.

Johnson, S. and Storey, D. J. (1993) 'Male and Female Entrepreneurs and Their Businesses: A Comparative Study', in Allen, S. and Truman, C. (eds), *Women in Business: Perspectives on Women Entrepreneurs*. London: Routledge.

Kalleberg, A. L. and Leicht, K. T. (1991) 'Gender and Organisational Performance: Determinants of Small Business Survival and Success', *Academy of Management Journal*, 34 (1), 136–61.

Koper, G. (1993) 'Women Entrepreneurs and the Granting of Business Credit', in Truman, C. and Allen, S. (eds), *Women in Business: Perspectives on Women Entrepreneurs*. London: Routledge.

Leach, P. and Bogod, T. (1999) *The BDO Stoy Hayward Guide to the Family Business*, 3rd edn. London: Kogan Page.

Lee-Gosselin, H. and Grise, J. (1990) 'Are Women Owner-Managers Challenging Our Definitions of Entrepreneurship? An In-Depth Survey', *Journal of Business Ethics* (9), 423–33.

Marlowe, S. and Strange, A. (1994) 'Female Entrepreneurs – Success by Whose Standards?', in Tanton, M. (ed.), *Women in Management: A Developing Presence*. London: Routledge.

Moore, D. (1990) 'An Examination of Present Research on the Female Entrepreneur – Suggested Research Strategies for the 1990s', *Journal of Business Ethics*, 9 (9), 275–81.

Rae, D. (1999) *The Entrepreneurial Spirit: Learning to Unlock Value*. Dublin: Blackhall.

Reidy, M. (1997) 'Female Entrepreneurs and Self-Esteem', in ISBA, National Small Firms Policy and Research Conference, Belfast, November.

Rosa, P., Hamilton, D., Carter, S. and Burns, H. (1994) 'The Impact of Gender on Small Business Management: Preliminary Findings of a British Study', *International Small Business Journal*, 12 (3), 25–32.

Rossman, M. L. (1990) *The International Businesswoman of the 1990s: A Guide to Success in the Global Marketplace*. New York: Basic Books.

Scase, R. (1998) 'The Role of Small Business in the Economic Transformation in Eastern Europe', *International Small Business Journal*, 16 (1), 13–21.

Scase, R. and Goffee, R. (1985) *The Real World of the Small Business Owner*. London: Croom Helm.

Stephens, M. (1989) 'She's the Boss', *Employment Gazette*, 97 (10), 529–33.

Stevenson, L. (1990) 'Some Methodological Problems Associated with Researching Women Enterpreneurs', *Journal of Business Ethics* (9), 439–46.

Storey, D. J. (1994) *Understanding the Small Business Sector*. London: Routledge.

Watkins, D. and Watkins, J. (1984) 'The Female Entrepreneur: Her Background and Determinants of Business Choice, Some British Data', *International Small Business Journal*, 2 (4), 21–31.

10 Electronic business (E-business)

Caroline Ross
The University of Warwick

Objectives This chapter considers the rise and development of electronic business (E-business). It discusses the benefits and opportunities that it offers and examines some of the current ways in which it is used with special attention given to small firms. The main aim of the chapter is to provide a relatively non-technical introduction to the fundamental E-business issues that modern enterprises need to understand if they are to fashion and sustain competitive advantage.

In particular, the following issues are examined:

- definitions and understandings of E-business and its impact and acceptance in firms both large and small;

- an examination of some pre-Internet technology applications and how Internet technology has developed in recent years;

- some of the opportunities for cost savings created by adopting E-business;

- the risks of not adopting E-business.

Introduction

> We believe the next Internet revolution is about to begin – customers are saying I want my email and I want it anywhere. We have heard about convergence for a long time but now it's going to happen. In five to ten years, TV, telephone and music machines will all be one and the same technology. They'll all be inter-operable and on the same broadband pipe. It's going to create a tremendous wave of innovation.
>
> Barry Schuler, President of interactive services group at America Online

The statement above serves to remind us how dynamic and rule-breaking the technology surrounding E-business is and the tremendous pace of technological change that is to be expected on the home and work front. As more companies become aware of the strategic implications of electronic business, its use is increasing daily. Internetindicators.com have forecast that, in the United States alone, E-business will grow to over $707 billion by 2003, with growth in the United Kingdom expected to follow a similar trend.

There has been considerable hype around the subject with many claims that E-business is set to revolutionise the business world. The degree of change that will occur has yet to be seen but it does seem certain that its acceptance by companies and the public in general is increasing with great speed and is here to stay. For many small firms wishing to stay ahead of the game and fashion competitive advantage and profitable business development, it would appear to be imperative to learn about what would be involved in adopting the new technology. There are lessons to be learned about small firms that ignored the tide of technological change and tried to fight against disruptive technologies. According to Christensen (1997) a disruptive technology is one that can displace an entrenched technology not because it performs better but rather because it delivers an overall better value. Obvious examples of disruptive technologies include the development of railways, cars, radio, television, the telephone, aeroplanes and microprocessors. All of them in turn challenged existing businesses to change and adapt to markets which were expanding, bringing goods and information at increasing rates of speed and decreasing costs.

The following letter is copied to show how fear and reluctance to embrace change are typically associated with disruptive technologies. The letter is cited in many books and articles and is merely a legend, spread by both the Internet and traditional means. It is evidence also of how easy it is to publish on the Internet, which is with time being accepted as legitimate by a receptive and trusting audience. It is also a reflection of a type of fear that many small business entrepreneurs share – the reasons may be different but the disruption caused to them will no doubt be far reaching:

To: President Andrew Jackson

The canal system of this country is being threatened by the spread of a new form of transportation known as 'railroads.' The federal government must preserve the canals for the following reasons:

1 If canal boats are supplanted by 'railroads,' serious unemployment will result. Captains, cooks, drivers, hostlers, repairmen, and lock tenders will be left without means of livelihood, not to mention the numerous farmers now employed in growing hay for horses.
2 Boat builders would suffer and towline, whip and harness makers would be left destitute.
3 Canal boats are absolutely essential to the defence of the United States. In the event of the expected trouble with England, the Erie Canal would be the only means by which we could ever move the supplies so vital to waging modern war.

As you may well know Mr. President, 'railroad' carriages are pulled at the enormous speed of fifteen miles per hour by 'engines' which, in addition to endangering life and limb of passengers roar and snort their way through the countryside, setting fire to crops, scaring livestock and frightening our women and children. The Almighty certainly never intended that people should travel at such breakneck speed. For the above-mentioned reasons the government should create an Interstate Commerce Commission to protect the American people from the evils of 'railroads' and to preserve the canals for posterity.

Respectfully yours,

Martin Van Buren
Governor of New York
January 31, 1829

This plea as we all know was to no avail and so it will be with objections to E-business. The pace of change has been swift and acceptance equally so. According to Glover *et al.* (2001) it took radio more than 35 years and television 15 years to reach 60 million people. The Internet reached over 90 million people in just 3 years and Internet traffic doubles every 100 days.

What is E-business?

According to Compaq electronic business is *the electronic connection of business operations to customers, suppliers and partners.*

E-business is fundamentally about re-building commerce around the Internet and related communications technologies to fashion a streamlined and responsive firm. Whether it be wiring the sales force or integrating real-time communications links with suppliers and vendors, connecting different parts of the organisation and sharing knowledge are the principal goals. It is leveraging information – the often latent information spread around an organisation as data – to use and deploy it to achieve and sustain competitive advantage. Once these data are available, powerful simulation and modelling techniques make it possible to maximise resource allocation and increase profits.

E-business is very powerful in that it removes traditional boundaries. The most notable of these are time and geography. Business can be conducted more quickly using the Internet to communicate information. This is true whether the communication is with the supplier or customer in a nearby town or with a business on the other side of the world. It also facilitates the creation of new virtual communities of suppliers and customers. Most important, however, is the fact that E-business uses information technology and electronic communication networks such as the Internet to transform vital business strategies and processes.

The definition above of E-business emphasises the increasing use of electronic mechanisms to help companies perform better. This may include facilitating collaboration and data sharing among employees, as well as providing improved customer support. Transactions such as this can take place within a company, between companies, between companies and individuals and between individuals.

The Internet and information technology in general are being used increasingly to help business process re-engineering on a large scale. The reason is that the technologies available can help companies improve their current business processes. Traditional methods and E-business are not mutually exclusive and can be integrated with care to provide better value and satisfaction to companies and their customers.

Often there is confusion over the terms E-business and E-commerce and they are frequently used interchangeably – however, there is a significant difference. E-business is the generic term and includes E-commerce. E-commerce can be defined as follows:

E-commerce means conducting business electronically to provide goods, information and services using Internet technologies.

Generally, E-commerce is seen to focus on online trading, that is the buying and selling of goods and services over the Internet. This holds good whether the transaction is between business and business (B2B) or between businesses and consumers (B2C). E-business, however, operates on a wider scale and has the capacity to enable organisations and their partners to co-operate with regard to strategy, process, organisation and technology. For firms who have an E-business strategy in place, it will not only include E-commerce but also encompass business done throughout the entire value chain. This includes transactions with suppliers of raw materials, manufacturers and customers. It should, in effect, transform the operational activities of many small and medium-sized firms.

The fortunes of some companies who have wholeheartedly adopted E-business in the past few years have been disastrous while, for many others, it is seen as the dawning of a new era of business process. According to Regan (2001) there seems now to be less of a reluctance to venture into the world of E-commerce and more of an acceptance that it has woven its way into the fabric of business and personal lives. Consumers are increasingly using the Internet to source products and an unusual example of E-commerce is that which occurred when an order came into www.lookfantastic.com, a small company that sells professional beauty and hair products. The company processes some 3000 orders per week through its warehouse facility. One of its customers placed an order from the South Pole and, in order to discharge it, the US armed forces and the Royal Mail were both used to deliver the product to the customer by helicopter within a week of the order being placed. This is an interesting example of good service but is it good business? Dilemmas such as this will face many companies as they make choices on markets, competitive positions and the strategies needed to attain them.

In summary, E-business will force users to try to understand customer needs better, review delivery methods and timing and examine their objectives with regard to cooperating and integrating with external partners. Although use of the Internet is fuelling the boom in E-business, the idea of using electronic networks to link computers within and between organisations has been widely used since the 1980s.

Pre-Internet technology

Chen (2001) defines electronic network exchange of data as 'the transfer of structured data by agreed message standards from one computer system to another by electronic means'. However, E-business is not merely the use of the Internet for trading but includes taking full advantage of other E-business facets to help integrate systems such as accounting and operations.

In the UK electronic data interchange (EDI) is being used by many firms but because of the high cost involved is used mainly by larger ones. However, it is commonly used by small firms in the automotive components industry who are suppliers to and partners of the vehicle manufacturers. The process may work in the following way:

1 Manufacturer needs additional materials.
2 Manufacturer's system, just-in-time, generates a purchase order.
3 An order is E-mailed to the small firm supplier by the manufacturer.
4 The small firm supplier confirms order and delivery capability.
5 The small firm sends notice to warehouse to ship the goods.
6 The small firm sends electronic invoice.
7 Manufacturer receives electronic invoice and confirms goods received.
8 Manufacturer transfers payment.
9 The small firm receives notification that funds have been deposited.
10 The small firm notifies customer that payment has been received and thanks customer.

The main advantages of EDI are improved inventory management, reduced transaction time and reduced cost. The above system at steps 8 and 9 highlights electronic funds transfer (EFT) which is the transfer of funds which has been initiated through an electronic terminal, telephone or computer and is yet another facet of electronic business.

E-business technology

The Internet is often described as a worldwide communication technology that is virtual in that it has no physical home. British Telecom has estimated that the value of electronic business will increase 1000 times in the next 5 years. In Britain around three-quarters of small firms are as yet not trading on the Internet and almost a third of these firms have no plans to trade online in the foreseeable future. This is perhaps a worrying fact because, in countries such as France and Germany, recent consumer research has shown that time spent on the Web is increasing to such an extent that it has outstripped the time that people spend reading magazines. This would suggest that unless firms have a presence on the Web they are likely to lose business.

In order to highlight how the technology available could be used by even the smallest of firms, Example 10.1 is a brief scenario of how a self-employed person could utilize the new technology. Although the example highlights British Telecom technology offerings, there are other options available in the marketplace such as Cable and Wireless Internet Life, which could be considered.

Example 10.1: The high-technology self-employed individual

Martin is a heating, ventilation and air conditioning engineer. He enjoys being his own boss and is keen to make use of the opportunities which new technology can offer. British Telecom has introduced Asymmetric Digital Subscriber Lines (ADSL) which Martin has started to subscribe to. ADSL offers users a permanent connection to the Internet which uses broadband access; this means that he is able to use the telephone for voice calls at the same time as he is using the Internet.

In the mornings before setting out for his first call of the day Martin checks his diary, which can be accessed from any Net-compatible device. During the day Martin uses his WAP mobile phone to dial his Web service and check his appointments, enter new ones and send and receive E-mails and voice messages. This type of diary is much better for Martin who in the past was frequently guilty of losing his diary – to the anger of his waiting customers.

One of the main reasons why Martin decided to take advantage of technology is that his supplier of parts could send a video to his inbox. The video not only showed the spare part that was ordered but also the way in which the part should be installed. This is a great help in that it saves Martin a lot of time. He no longer needs to read long, complicated instruction leaflets or telephone the manufacturer for details if something is unclear.

Martin's parts supplier is not local. In fact he is located hundreds of miles away. However, he does offer the best prices and has an excellent record for technical support. The reason Martin had changed from his local supplier was that the new supplier had used target-marketing techniques to approach him using the Internet. The promotion had outlined the major benefits that the supplier offered and Martin decided to give them a try. To date he has been delighted with the service offered.

Another service from BT that Martin is considering is its Click for business service, which provides Internet access, domain name registration, E-mail accounts, Web space and a professional Web-design service. In his leisure time Martin enjoys using his interactive television, he uses it to send E-mails, do his grocery shopping, his banking, make changes to his investment portfolio as well as play games. All in all, the Internet and the technology available have helped Martin in his business, and he now makes more money as well as being better organised. Martin feels that the subscription fee for ASDL is money well spent.

The example given above reflects a few of the many changes available with the help of new technology. With a little more thought regarding how to make use of E-business, many small firms could benefit from the way in which their business is conducted. It is therefore especially important that small firms examine their operational and administrative processes to ensure that opportunities for improvement afforded by the Internet can be effected. It is useful here to refer back to some statistics given in Chapter 3 about self-employed professionals (SEPs). The research evidence suggests that only around a quarter of SEPs surveyed have a Web site.

Adcock *et al.* (2001), summarised some of the ways in which the technology can be implemented and stated that the use of E-commerce by an organisation is often made more beneficial if the technology is used in the most beneficial way. An example of this is where a small firm can use an Intranet. An Intranet means that the company uses Internet technology within the business and can link this via firewalls to the public Internet. A firewall allows Internet access for employees but allows outsiders access to only limited non-confidential information on the Internet. This is more likely to be used by larger firms but is not exclusive to them. One example, albeit of a large company, is Hewlett Packard. The company has an Intranet that has more than 100 private news groups for employees. It can be accessed by more than 125 000 users and the aim is to encourage employees to discuss opportunities for new products and product improvements.

Where a firm wants to use E-commerce but only with a few trusted suppliers or large customers, an Extranet can be set up. An Extranet is an extended Intranet but it only allows privileged users access to the company system. To help improve the effectiveness and efficiency of transactions within the supply chain, firms can use a dedicated Extranet. An example of how one company makes use of an Extranet is Uniphar plc. The company is a wholesaler of pharmaceutical products to many pharmacies throughout Ireland. Uniphar uses an Extranet to give access to recent product and medical information to pharmacies. It also has current issues forums with regard to pharmaceuticals and provides the facility to identify the availability of pharmacy locums.

If a company has an Extranet it provides the means by which staff from the organisation and staff from its suppliers can work on a joint project with a greater degree of openness. The project may be to develop a new product and the Extranet helps the collaborative process with regard to product specifications and production methods. This is more likely to be put into place by larger firms who use small firms as dedicated suppliers. The following is an example of the kind of application that the technology is being used for within the buying arena.

In industrial settings when a machine was designed it was understood that the process of sourcing all of the required parts to build the machine would take quite a while. Some parts would have to be purchased and others manufactured. This whole process was difficult to organise and usually took a long time. With the increasing use of the Web, engineers in companies have an enormous amount of information available to them. It is possible now to request quotes electronically, place orders and receive the necessary parts in a fraction of the time that was previously required. This alone has the potential to help firms reduce costs dramatically as well as help source suppliers of particular products.

A site currently being developed by Ybag.com to target small firms hopes to enable buyers to type in a request for the products or services that they require and then wait for a reply from prospective suppliers. The providers of the Internet site will make money by charging suppliers every time they offer a quote. A variation on this is the Internet site Mondus.com that offers a similar service to companies but charges only when a transaction has been completed. Another site, Bizz2Biz.com, is set to become important to manufacturing companies in that it will provide networking trading links and firms will be able to buy or sell products and services worldwide.

Other technology that can be used is video conferencing. Video conferencing enables people who are many miles apart in distance to converse with each other as if face to face. Small firms may find that this allows for massive savings in travel costs if a valued client or customer is located at some distance.

The major form of communication using the Internet is the E-mail. This has become very widely used both in homes and in business and has replaced the use of the telephone and letters in many instances. E-mail can save both time and money. At best a letter is not delivered until the day after it has been sent and, even if a reply is written and posted back the same day, the total time taken is 3 days. An E-mail arrives seconds after it has been sent; if the person responds immediately or later the same day then the information exchange can take place quickly, even on occasion within a few minutes. This type of communication can be very efficient but a study by Which?Online found that only one in 20 Internet users said that electronic messages were their favourite way to communicate. The reason for the declining popularity of E-mail was found to be linked to information overload when workers are bombarded every day with an excess of messages. This drop in popularity has been quite dramatic, the number naming E-mail as their preferred means of communicating falling by more than two-thirds since 2000 when the figure was one in seven. Small firm owners and managers need to be mindful of this issue to avoid problems.

In sum, it can be seen how Internet technologies have spread: Intranets within organisations and Extranets with partners, the use of video conferencing, mobile phones and E-mail, each becoming more readily available to the more receptive small business. The principal attributes of E-commerce and E-business that are driving change include the following:

- *Simplicity*. It is relatively easy for firms to become E-enabled.
- *Speed*. E-commerce enables the rapid exchange of information between buyer and seller.
- *Change*. E-business will encourage the adoption of supply chain integration.

Opportunities afforded by E-business

Access to new markets

Perhaps one of the most visible advantages that E-business can offer is the opportunity to reach new markets and thus increase sales and profitability. Many small firms have found that they have transformed their business by developing Web sites. A Web site is like a shop window: it enables customers using the Internet to access the small firm's Web page and view what is on offer. A good Web site is a very powerful tool as it can make even the smallest of businesses noticeable and visible. The features of a good Web site are as follows (Adcock *et al.*, 2001):

1 registered with search engines and therefore easy to access;
2 looks good and is easy to use;
3 good integration with all company systems;
4 easy to update by company staff;
5 produces company records which can be audited;
6 can interact with visitors to the site;
7 can be controlled and maintained by owner not developer;
8 incorporates security features for financial transactions;
9 has an interactive form for transactions to encourage visitors to purchase;
10 does not take too long to load pictures and items when in use.

Some of the key issues that should be considered when introducing a Web site for global reach include researching why it should be undertaken in the first place. One of the main reasons may be that it offers economies of scale, in that if the small firm operates in one country, the cost of entering a second will probably require less investment than the first and similarly for the third and fourth. The registration of a domain name is another factor which small firms should take into account. According to Murphy (2001) only 17% of companies have registered their domain name. However, one of the main considerations when making decisions regarding expansion policies for the small firm and the Internet is to examine which countries have high user penetration. Murphy states that in Sweden, Norway and Iceland penetration is over 50% of the population and just below 50% in Denmark. However, the population in these countries is relatively low. In China, however, although there is only 1% penetration, this would equate to 28 million users, which is more than the Scandinavian countries added together. According to US market analysts Jupiter, by 2003 India is projected to have 70 million users, China 80 million and Japan almost 60 million. At present Jupiter rated Japan top on 50 million, followed by Germany 44 million, the UK with 36 million and Canada and China each with 28 million.

For a small firm to develop globally, penetration statistics are only one factor to consider. Another aspect is the choice and implementation of business strategy. The strategy must take into account how the Internet is accessed. For example, in the UK access is mostly by personal computer, with a growing awareness of digital television access, whereas in Japan it is the I-mode mobile Internet service. Other considerations would be whether or not a local company partner is required and whether there is the possibility of channel conflict, with other distributors being alienated, as well as which language to use. There are usually numerous cultural issues and considerations that contribute to the complexity of process.

In many instances small firms are finding that they cannot compete with the benefits that the Internet brings to customers. According to research carried out by the Institute of the Motor Industry (2001) many smaller independently owned dealerships are being affected by car manufacturers exploring new ways to sell cars – including the Internet. More people are using the Internet to purchase cars: recent figures show that the number of people who buy online is expected to rise from 3% to 22% by 2005. Overheads, such as large showrooms and the commission-related salaries of salesmen, do not have to be met by car sales Web sites and they can therefore offer vehicles at reduced prices. The Web site of GB Cars (UK) Brokerage promises to beat any Internet or dealership quote on any Vauxhall vehicle and offers customers price reductions of up to 27% on most new car makes and models. This example from car dealerships could be equally applicable to many other industries and markets where small firms are located.

Cost savings on marketing

E-business transactions are generally completed faster, cheaper and more accurately than most traditional dealings and therefore there is more scope to make savings online. With regard to sales opportunities, as mentioned above, global sales become a possibility and the number of potential customers can increase phenomenally. Another major benefit of E-business for marketing is that, by providing product information, technical support and order information online, sales personnel can be freed from these tasks and can therefore pursue higher-value activities that generate new sales.

Traditionally business is undertaken during the day in most industries but an E-business can be open 24 hours a day, 365 days a year, and can be accessed from anyone connected to the Internet. This then enables profitable business to be conducted any time and can facilitate fast and flexible responses to market opportunities as they arise.

The research undertaken by the Internet Advertising Bureau (2001) has found that banner advertisements and sponsorships are the most popular means of Internet promotion and account for 58% and 29% respectively of all advertising revenue. Forrester Research (2001) estimates that online advertising spend will reach $22 billion in the United States with a similar trend forecast for the United Kingdom by 2004.

One of the major ways that marketing costs can be reduced is by using the electronic information that accompanies E-business. This can afford great savings on marketing research and can be used to monitor customer behaviour and other marketing information, which can be used to help with the selection and targeting of customers and forecasting.

Reduced supply chain costs

Many small firms are becoming increasingly aware that they can reduce costs by automating their supply chains using the Internet. A recent survey from the Chartered Institute of Purchasing and Supply (2001) among UK purchasing managers found that the number purchasing goods or services on the Internet is set to very nearly double within 2 years. Clearly buying online could have a major impact on many smaller manufacturers' profitability and efficiency. In another survey of more than 300 manufacturers of all sizes and across all sectors (NTC Research, 2001), only 2% reported they were using the Internet to a significant extent, although a further 38% said they used it a little.

The research also showed that nearly a third of UK manufacturers expected to go online in the next year and only a quarter conversely said they did not intend to start using the Internet in the same period. Closer examination of the results, though, reveals large variations in the extent to which companies in different sectors have taken up the E-commerce challenge and, perhaps more importantly, it shows big differences between sectors as to how many companies expect to go online in the near future.

The research confirms that the Internet is used much more for business-to-business E-commerce than for direct contact with consumers. While 42% of manufacturers reported using the Internet to sell to other businesses, business-to-consumer use was only 25%. Perhaps the reasons for this have more to do with business-to-consumer transactions representing typically only 20% of the supply chain and consequently there is more scope for making savings in company-to-company buying and selling transactions.

It would therefore appear that those sectors that have a history of involvement with cutting-edge technologies are not surprisingly more likely to adopt E-commerce. At the other end of the scale, timber and paper products companies and the food, drink and tobacco sectors are less technically advanced. Furthermore, the culture in different sectors is likely to vary from those in which the management and workforce welcomes change or, at least, are less likely to be resistant to new technology to those who are totally opposed to change.

Finally, the nature of supply chains in different sectors will tend to affect the likelihood of E-commerce presenting obvious advantages. In a highly mechanised industry such as vehicle production, or in the case of the automotive component supply of the small firms within it, the supply chains tend to be highly efficient and finely tuned in line with just-in-time or lean principles. The automotive supply chain involves a relatively small number of specialised partners supplying specific items. It is already highly automated and the move to an Internet-based system is not a major decision.

The food and drink sector, by contrast, typically involves a large number of small producers who are historically not organised in a highly technological environment and typically would involve many more small businesses. (There are of course several notable exceptions.) However, for many in this sector the adoption of E-commerce may appear to be expensive, difficult to embrace and lacking in any obvious short-term advantages. It has to be recognised that, for many small firms, in being slow to adopt E-commerce they are merely being cautious and mindful of their limited resources. Many are unsure of the advantages and benefits E-commerce will deliver.

Risks of not adopting E-business

In the past capital and skilled labour were the traditional factors of production; however, in many industries and markets they are no longer the principal drivers of competitive advantage. A growing factor in determining corporate posture and market status is the ability to control and manipulate information. Industrial and consumer customers are now able to source information on the Internet, which gives them considerable leverage. The increasing use of the Internet to access information on products, price, availability and choice enables potential customers to make comparisons and ultimately decide which is the best provider of the product or service required. Small firms instead of perceiving this as a threat could also use it as an opportunity to source raw materials at lower costs, enhance their product mix and obtain a better service from their suppliers.

Another danger in ignoring the Internet is that small firms would forgo the opportunity to capitalise on an aspect of buyer behaviour that is increasing in popularity – that of product customisation. This is where customers describe the products or services they require and ask those who can supply it to submit details of price and service available. This presents a threat to those small businesses that previously had been content to offer only fixed product lines and a standard service. Continued viability and commercial success in many markets depends on the supply of goods and services to a precise specification in very short lead times.

Conclusion

The managing director of handbag.com, Dominic Riley (2001), summarised the opportunities offered by the Internet well when he said:

Customers are changing their behaviour, spending more time on the Internet and less on television and other activities. This will drive corporate focus and investment but to capitalise the Internet industry needs to demonstrate integrity, honesty and effective organisation.

It remains to be seen what the future will hold for E-business but it is certainly something that small businesses ignore at their peril. From the recent study undertaken by TSS Research (2001) it was found that the growth in online business was predicted to at least double over the next 10 years with those questioned expecting reduced costs, increased sales and healthy profits. It is to be hoped for those small firms embracing E-business to fashion their competitive posture that such predictions hold true.

References and further reading

Adcock, D., Halborg, A. and Ross, E. C. (2001) *Marketing Principles and Practice*, 4th edn. Harlow: Pearson Education.

Bayler, M. and Stoughton, D. (2001) 'Delivery and Authority are the New Essentials', *Revolution*, 9 May.

Chen, S. (2001) *Strategic Management of E-Business*. Chichester: Wiley.

Christensen, C. M. (1997) 'The Innovator's Dilemma: When New Technologies Cause Great Firms to Fail', *Harvard Business Review*.

Corbitt, T. (2000) 'Virtual Realities', *Insider CIMA*, December.

Glover, S. M., Liddle, S. W. and Prawitt, D. F. (2001) *E-business Principles and Strategies for Accountants*. London: Prentice-Hall.

Lorek, L. (2001) 'Clicks-and-Mortar Deliver E-Profitability', *Interactive Week*, 28 May.

Murphy, D. (2001) 'Managing Global Content', *Marketing Business*, June.

Nottage, A. (2001) 'Vital Statistics', *Revolution*, 30 May.

Regan, K. (2001) 'Signs of an E-Commerce Comeback', *E-Commerce Times*, 25 May.

Rushe, D. (2000) 'Internet Giant Prepares for Shake Out of Dinosaurs', *The Sunday Times*, 6 February.

Simmons, L. (2001) 'Corporate Evangelists Offer Internet Redemption', *Revolution*, 9 May.

Smith, S. (2001) 'Web War Threat to Car Showrooms', *Coventry Evening Telegraph*, 12 June.

11 Enterprise culture: understanding a misunderstood concept

Patricia Carr
Brunel University

Objectives This chapter seeks to examine:

- the origins and development of the enterprise culture, particularly in the British context;

- the role that the state plays in the creation of enterprise culture;

- the impact of the enterprise culture on business life and society in general over the past two decades in the United Kingdom;

- the contribution that the enterprises culture has made to enhancing the profile of entrepreneurship and small business.

Introduction

The term 'enterprise culture' has emerged in political and academic discussion during the 1970s in both the UK and America, gaining a similar relevance and momentum in the rest of Europe at a later time. Nevertheless, despite the increased importance of this entity and its continued position at the forefront of political debate, it is a slippery concept that many writers have great difficulty in defining with any common precision. The confusion and ambiguity surrounding our understanding of this term has led commentators such as Burrows (1991a, p. 5) to suggest that enterprise culture:

> possesses only a small residual explanatory status in accounts of the materiality of the restructuring of western economies.

From this perspective enterprise culture is presented as a simple justificatory discourse for the enormous changes and industrial shifts which countries such as the UK have experienced in recent years. Although certainly it is problematic to attribute contemporary economic restructuring solely to attempts to create an enterprise culture on the part of government, it is equally problematic to conceive of these attempts in simple justification terms (Carr, 2000a).

Should the vagueness that has characterised accounts of the enterprise culture concept constitute any real surprise? It probably should not, particularly given that it was not accurately defined in policy terms when the British Conservative Party came to power in 1979. This lack of definition has not significantly diminished despite 20 years of attempts to create and fashion it. The ambiguity surrounding this concept has been further entrenched by the reluctance on the part of management researchers to develop an understanding of enterprise culture judging by the small amount of research on this concept (Blackburn *et al.*, 1992). Difficulties attached to attempts to secure a commonality of understanding in something like enterprise culture have often meant it has been sidelined in favour of the more accessible concept of small business, with the latter being privileged as an analytical category (Carr, 2000a).

However, given the fact that enterprise culture has been in existence for two decades and that the current British government has committed itself to making Britain 'a country of enterprise' (Gavron *et al.*, 1998), it is important that this ambiguity and lack of clarity which has conventionally surrounded this concept are confronted.

Enterprise culture: the beginning

The first attempts to create an enterprise culture centred on the promotion of a culture for enterprise largely through the implementation of a range of external structural changes (Morris, 1991). It was hoped that such changes would allow Britain to pose an effective and successful economic challenge to countries such as Germany, Japan and the USA. These structural changes focused on a retreat from government intervention and the re-instatement of the market mechanism as the fundamental determinant of the economy and included the following structural changes in enterprise culture (Carr, 2000a):

- dismantling the welfare state;
- reducing the power of trade unions;
- deregulation;
- marketisation;
- privatisation;
- cuts in taxation;
- reducing the role of the state and enlarging that of the individual;
- reducing the public sector borrowing requirement;
- introducing firm monetary and fiscal discipline, thus bringing inflation under control;
- promoting self-employment.

Nevertheless, important though structural change was in the original attempts to establish an enterprise culture (and continues to be so to this day), a recognition emerged that the success of a market order was heavily dependent on the individuals who populate it. Advocates of enterprise and entrepreneurship such as Margaret Thatcher emphasised the need for a moral revolution as much as an economic one. From this perspective it is believed that economic challenges are rooted in human nature, leading enterprise culture to be increasingly represented in cultural terms, connected to the self-understanding, values and attitudes located in individual and institutional activities (Hall, 1988; Keat, 1991). This was a recognition that structural change alone could not bring about the required cultural transformation, contributing to a phase of *cultural engineering*. In this phase a conscious attempt is made to initiate the economic and moral revival of Britain through a programme of sustained cultural change, which would release or create an enterprising spirit.

Despite the early recognition by politicians of the importance of the individual to the success of enterprise culture, many definitions of the term suggest that there is little connection between attempts to create an enterprise culture and individual business activity in terms of its development and day-to-day activity (e.g. Burrows, 1991a,b; Burrows and Curran, 1991; Goss, 1991). From this perspective therefore enterprise culture is an entity that exists outside government but is used by government as a means to counteract the dependency culture of the late 20th century, as well as providing a justification for a range of government policies.

A conceptual separation exists between the entity of enterprise culture and government use of it and those supposedly subject to it. This approach to understanding enterprise culture is taken up by other commentators such as Ritchie (1991), who in developing an understanding of enterprise culture again separates government and small business. This is done by arguing that they hold different standpoints and assumptions in relation to enterprise culture. From Ritchie's perspective, government is located in a revivalist-believer version of enterprise culture, which suggests that enterprise embodied in the small business is the key to the revival of the British economy.

In contrast, small business owners are located in a lived experience-subject version of enterprise culture and constitute and interpret the concept differently, drawing their understanding of it from their particular experience. From Ritchie's perspective, making do, getting by and doing the business characterise the enterprise culture of the small business owner, illustrating their survivalist instinct and objectives.

Ritchie's account provides the opportunity to observe a reification of enterprise culture as something that exists outside, with government and small business having a different relationship to it. In addition the two constructions of enterprise culture stand in opposition to each other, with the small business version short-circuiting government claims concerning the transformational role of the small business sector (Carr, 2000a). Research conducted by Blackburn *et al.* (1992) also argues that enterprise culture is not connected to the lived experience of small business owners; rather, it is understood as something that is connected to the political activities embodied in government aid schemes. Again it seems that small business owners are unable to make a connection between public notions of the enterprise culture, as expressed by government and politicians, and their own everyday experience.

What emerges strongly from conventional understandings of the enterprise culture is the notion that government and individuals in the context of small business and enterprise development are pitted against one another. Such an understanding of the relationship between government and small firms is problematic as the former's attempts to successfully create an enterprise culture heavily rely on the latter. In other words, it is clear that enterprise culture will not succeed unless individuals and businesses behave in a manner which is conducive to the market order.

Therefore it is crucial that a conceptualisation of enterprise culture be constructed which can highlight how the aptitude of individuals – in small business and elsewhere – as subjects and citizens is a central target and resource for the government in its attempts to create an enterprise culture – and not in opposition to it.

Creating the enterprising individual

To develop an understanding of enterprise culture that highlights the important connections between government, individuals and business, it is important that we first outline in more detail its institutional and ethical dimensions. Gibb (1987) associates enterprise culture with a range of enterprising traits and activities that are spread among the population, with individuals having a different mix and strength of these attributes. Such traits and attributes may be cultivated through education and training which itself should be enterprising in nature so as to allow the appropriate ethical transformation to take place. Carr (2000a) lists the following enterprising traits and activities:

- initiative;
- risk-taking;
- flexibility;
- creativity;
- independence;
- leadership;
- strong work ethic;
- daring spirit;
- responsibility.

In addition, the development of these attributes is heavily dependent on the institutional circumstances within which an individual is located, allied to the freedom and motivation allowed within this situation, which will impact on their use and cultivation.

Gibb argues that the institutional vehicle most likely to promote the development of these traits is independent business ownership. This he suggests is because such a context not only introduces individuals to the skills required (e.g. networking, knowledge of the independent business process and environment) for successful business ownership but also massages the range of enterprising traits outlined above. The promotion and development of enterprising skills and traits within a small business environment will from Gibb's perspective contribute to and support the existence of an enterprise culture. Thus for Gibb ethical reform requires the promotion of the enterprising attributes listed above within the context of an enterprising education system, while institutional reform centres on the promotion of the small business within which enterprising attributes will flourish.

Keat's (1991) explanation of enterprise culture also centres on the interwoven dimensions of institutional and ethical change. From his perspective the first strand of enterprise culture privileges the private commercial enterprise as the form of organisation in which the provision of goods and services is best facilitated. For

Keat (1991, p. 3) the commercial enterprise takes on a paradigmatic status, being the preferred organisational model for the provision of all types of goods and services. The privileging of the commercial enterprise has meant that a range of different organisations, e.g. hospitals, banks, government departments, schools and charities, have been required to reconstruct themselves along the lines of a private sector business functioning in a free market economy.

The second strand of enterprise culture centres on ethical reform that focuses on the types of conduct and practices, of both individuals and organisations, which display enterprising qualities. From Keat's (1991) perspective the picture of the enterprising individual which emerges is of someone who is firstly self-reliant and independent, taking responsibility for their own lives, and, secondly, achievement oriented, setting a range of goals and objectives that he/she strives to accomplish. Thirdly, the enterprising individual is optimistic and energetic, understanding the world as a place of opportunities that should be actively grasped. Finally the enterprising individual is someone who actively pursues the material rewards that result from success in a competitive world.

Individuals and businesses are strongly encouraged to involve themselves in activities which require the active development and nurturing of enterprising traits such as risk-taking, taking initiative and adopting an entrepreneurial spirit. It is hoped that with the promotion of such attributes individuals and businesses will be equipped with the virtues of enterprise, enabling them to contribute to an enterprising free market economy.

Keat's outline of the institutional and ethical dimensions of enterprise culture is, like Gibb's, intricately entwined. He suggests that it is within the institutional context of the commercial enterprise as a business entity that individuals are likely to demonstrate the ethic of enterprise (as an activity), i.e. display enterprising qualities such as risk-taking. In particular the small business as a commercial entity has been identified as the home of enterprise with numerous commentators, both political and academic, suggesting that small business will contribute in significant ways to a culture which values self-reliance and personal responsibility. However, a significant qualification needs to be made here. Despite the linkage that exists between the institutional and ethical strands of enterprise, there would seem to be a suggestion that commercial enterprises, in particular small businesses as commercial enterprises, are not always completely enterprising (Beaver and Jennings, 2000). Therefore they must be encouraged to thoroughly express enterprising qualities, a role which government has attempted to play, largely through the vast range of enterprise initiatives and policies put in place in countries such as the UK over the past 20 years.

The dimensions of enterprise culture

Although there are differences between Gibb's (1986) and Keat's (1991) analyses of the dimensions of enterprise culture, strong similarities are also evident. Both commentators place an emphasis on economic and cultural reconstruction, identifying institutional and ethical strands within the enterprise culture entity. Taking the institutional strand first, Gibb and Keat differ here in that the former focuses on the institution of small business, while the latter concentrates on commercial enterprises in general. With regard to the ethical strand, they both place an emphasis on enterprising attributes such as risk-taking, self-reliance and independence, recognising that a market order is possible only if the moral values suitable for it prevail.

Both commentators link the two strands of enterprise culture. Gibb suggests that it is within the context of the small business that enterprising attributes are nurtured, while Keat states that within the commercial enterprise in general individuals are more likely to display enterprising characteristics. However, despite the linkage that both commentators make between these strands of enterprise culture they identify, there is a suggestion that this is often severed. Both commentators recognise that small business and commercial enterprises in general are not always fully enterprising and therefore need encouragement to express enterprising qualities. This leads them to identify the requirement for an explicit enterprise strategy in which cultural engineering through education takes place. From their perspective education is used in enterprise culture to ensure that individuals are trained in the virtues of enterprise development and business ownership. Such training would ensure that individuals are equipped with enterprising qualities so that they are able to make the right choices and respond positively to the enterprise environment that is held out to them.

Commentators such as Gibb and Keat present a broad account of the dimensions of enterprise culture, highlighting an enterprise strategy of cultural engineering through education, so that individuals and businesses are equipped with the right enterprising qualities. As mentioned above, inherent within their account of enterprise culture is a recognition that the desired market order will not be achieved without the necessary moral values. Nevertheless, even with such recognition insufficient attention is paid to the actual mechanical means by which such a cultural transformation can take place, as well as the entities, particularly government entities, involved in this metamorphosis.

It is proposed here that, in order to facilitate a greater exploration how enterprise culture has been and still is actively produced, closer attention must be paid to the link between culture and government. A key reason for such attention is the recognition that, to enable such a cultural transformation to take place, the active intervention of the state is required (Marquand, 1992).

The lack of attention paid to the role of government in the actual physical creation of enterprise culture may be because a declared element of the enterprise culture project is a limiting of the role of the state. However, the paradox here is that the cultural revolution needed requires active state intervention and can only be achieved through the actions of a strong and intrusive state. To guarantee the desired market order, the state has been forced to engage in a project of social engineering as invasive as any past state activity (Marquand, 1988). Given this there is a necessity to move away from broad, static accounts of enterprise culture which only identify its various facets, shedding little light on the actual mechanics of enterprise culture production.

To achieve this we need to include a notion of government within our understanding of enterprise culture. This can be done by conceiving of enterprise culture in terms of norms, practices and techniques of conduct, which, in partnership with government, individuals and companies are encouraged to adopt, particularly if they want to access state resources. Thus it would appear that essential to any understanding of the phenomenon of enterprise culture is a focus on the link between culture and government.

Incorporating government into enterprise culture

Conventional accounts of the concept of enterprise culture fail to illuminate the connections between individual (business) activity, government and the wider enterprise environment created through the range of structural changes outlined above. Transforming the way we understand the relationship between business (for example small business) and government in enterprise culture will allow us to expose these links and make visible the impact of enterprise culture. Such exposure will emerge by paying attention to the institutional systems and moral techniques that produce enterprise culture. In other words the relationship between culture and government is highlighted through a focus on the cultural technology (i.e. institutional and organisational structures and policies) which produces enterprise culture.

Education is one significant area where the cultural technology of enterprise culture can be identified through attempts to promote enterprising traits such as independence, flexibility and self-motivation, as well as encouraging young people to enter into independent business ownership. Nevertheless, this is not the only form of enterprise cultural technology. Increasingly an emphasis has been placed on what individuals do once they are in business. For example the quality of small business has been identified as important, with a range of policies and initiatives put in place by government to promote this. According to Gavron *et al.* (1998) government policies have shifted towards advice and guidance rather than financial subsidies, to improve the calibre of new and existing business.

What is proposed here is the desire to make our understanding of enterprise culture more useful in a practical sense, by putting policy into enterprise culture theoretically, practically and institutionally (Bennett, 1992). Adopting this perspective, enterprise culture can be understood as a set of institutionally embedded relations of government, established during a particular historical period, which aim to influence and transform the mind set and conduct of a population.

Within the context of attempts to create an enterprise culture, the population being targeted are existing and potential businesses, with the aim of shaping and regulating their conduct through the growing advisory role of government. The necessary corollary of this orientation to enterprise culture is that it can be suggested that policies, as instruments of government, have a cultural dimension in the sense of influencing the way in which enterprise culture is produced. Thus in contrast to the conventional approach taken to understanding the enterprise culture phenomenon, it is suggested that there is a need for a new conceptualisation. This should focus on how the creation of an enterprise culture actively sets out to impact on the activities of individuals and the businesses they are involved in. Such an approach gives rise to the following definition of enterprise culture:

> ## Understanding enterprise culture
>
> This conceptualisation of enterprise culture concentrates on the links between the activities of government and the activities of the individual. This linkage can be understood in terms of the strategies and policies drawn upon by government, for the direction of the behaviour of individuals and business in enterprise culture. In other words the focus is on the range of policies and initiatives which aim to mould and shape entrepreneurial behaviour in business, both large and small and the response of individuals and business to this.

The impact of enterprise culture on business life

The understanding of enterprise culture that is presented here is one that focuses on the range of policies, strategies and initiatives which are used to shape, influence and regulate entrepreneurial behaviour. Such a conceptualisation of enterprise culture is commensurate with the growth in enterprise initiatives over the past decade. Currently in the UK there are over 200 central government business support initiatives, sponsored by five departments, which cost £635 million in 1995/96 (Gavron et al., 1998).

In addition, an understanding of enterprise culture that incorporates government initiatives and policies within it allows us to observe its impact on organisations large and small, as well as business life in general. In particular it highlights how a range of organisations have been actively encouraged to adopt an enterprising management style and embrace the need to think and manage strategically. What is argued here is that understanding enterprise culture, the position of the entrepreneur and businesses both large and small within it also implies understanding a way of thinking about the practice of management.

Over the past two decades notions of effective and best practice management have placed an emphasis on flexible, dynamic managers and organisations that can respond quickly, innovatively and decisively to the constant presence of change. These developments are seen as a move away from the bureaucratic structures and practices of the past, a form of management and organisation that has come under much criticism. Bureaucracies, it has been argued, are inappropriate for the future of management, whether in large or small organisations (Wood, 1989). Such criticism of bureaucratic management is associated with general post-Fordist economic restructuring within Britain and elsewhere.

In addition, enterprise culture and the emphasis that it places on enterprise and entrepreneurship can also be seen as a fundamental structuring element of these transformations. In this context the entrepreneur is assigned a privileged position, becoming the new culture hero of the Western world since the early 1980s, with managers being expected to manage as if they were entrepreneurs.

A key consequence of the privileged position given to the entrepreneur within enterprise culture is a re-negotiation of the relationship between entrepreneurship and management. Whereas in the past the entrepreneur and the manager were presented as discrete entities, with a very clear either/or relationship articulated between them, this notion of mutual exclusivity is not maintained within enterprise culture. From the perspective of the architects of enterprise culture, if an individual is to succeed in the marketplace of today and tomorrow, he/she needs to be an entrepreneur and a manager.

The notion of an inclusive relationship is emphasised, with a dialectic co-existence prevailing between entrepreneurship and management. This type of co-existence promotes enterprising qualities as discussed above, alongside a strong notion of rational managerial control. Thus individuals and businesses are encouraged to display enterprising traits such as risk-taking, independence and self-reliance and are also expected to perform competently a range of managerial skills including planning, organising and controlling. This combination of enterprising and management qualities is believed to enhance the strength of a business and allow it to exist successfully in a period of uncertainty and innovation.

The promotion of enterprising and management qualities highlights the essential paradox which exists at the heart of enterprise culture. This contradiction is that, while individuals and organisations are expected to be daring risk-takers, they are also expected to adopt this persona in a planned and rational manner, so that a significant material gain (profits, employment, etc.) will emerge from their entrepreneurial activity. This contradiction also exists outside individual businesses and can be understood as an attempt on the part of government to align the enterprising abilities of individuals and businesses with the aims and objectives of the enterprise economy within which they are located.

The essence of enterprise culture therefore is to nurture the individuals' desire for self-fulfilment and profit by encouraging them to be enterprising, while at the same time promoting the need for a rational, professional, managed and strategic approach to giving these desires a material reality. This essence manifests itself in an entrepreneurial management discourse that is operationalised through the enormous range of enterprise initiatives put in place by government.

Concluding remarks

Despite the popularity and power of enterprise culture and extensive government attempts to establish this phenomenon over the past two decades, a clearer conceptualisation of this concept has not been established. Conventional approaches to understanding enterprise culture have tended to ignore or underestimate its impact, as well as presenting exaggerated reports of its demise (Du Gay and Salaman, 1992).

In contrast, the key aims of this chapter have been to give this concept some solidity and in doing so to illuminate the highly significant impact it has had on business life and life in general in countries such as the UK in recent times. Many explications of enterprise culture have tended to downplay or ignore the role of government in creating this entity, despite the fact that it is unlikely to exist without strong and intrusive government intervention. The alternative approach suggested here concentrates on developing an understanding of the way in which the subjectivity and activity of individuals and business are directed and rationalised by government inspired enterprise initiatives, policies and strategies.

In addition, it is suggested that this rationalisation and direction have had an enormous impact on the practice of management in all kinds of organisations, public and private, large and small.

References and further reading

Beaver, G. and Jennings, P. L. (2000) 'Small Business, Entrepreneurship and Enterprise Development', *Strategic Change*, 9 (7), 397–403.

Bennett, T. (1992) 'Putting Policy into Cultural Studies', in Crossberg, L., Nelson, C. and Treichler, P. (eds), *Cultural Studies*. London: Routledge.

Blackburn, R., Curran, J. and Woods, A. (1992) 'Exploring Enterprises Cultures: Small Service Sector Enterprise Owners and Their Views', in Robertson, M., Chell, E. and Mason, C. (eds), *Towards the Twenty-First Century: The Challenge for Small Business*. Cheshire: Nadamal.

Burrows, R. (1991a) 'The Discourse of the Enterprise Culture and the Restructuring of Britain: A Polemical Contribution', in Curran, J. and Blackburn, R. (eds), *Paths of Enterprise: The Future of Small Business*. London: Routledge.

Burrows, R. (1991b) 'Introduction: Entrepreneurship, Petty Capitalism and the Restructuring of Britain', in Burrows, R. (ed.), *Deciphering the Enterprise Culture*. London: Routledge.

Burrows, R. and Curran, J. (1991) 'Not Such a Small Business: Reflections on the Rhetoric, the Reality and the Future of the Enterprise Culture', in Cross, M. and Payne, G. (eds), *Work and Enterprise Culture*. Basingstoke: Falmer.

Carr, P. (1998) 'The Cultural Production of Enterprise: Understanding Selectivity as Cultural Policy', *Economic and Social Review*, 29 (2), 27–49.

Carr, P. (2000a) *The Age of Enterprise: The Emergence and Evolution of Entrepreneurial Management*. Dublin: Blackhall.

Carr, P. (2000b) 'Understanding Enterprise Culture: The Fashioning of Enterprise Activity Within Small Business', *Strategic Change*, 9 (7), 405–14.

Du Gay, P. and Salaman, G. (1992) 'The Culture of the Customer', *Journal of Management Studies*, 29 (5), 615–33.

Gavron, R., Cowling, M., Holtham, G. and Westall, A. (1998) *The Entrepreneurial Society*. London: Institute for Public Policy Research.

Gibb, A. (1987) 'Enterprise Culture – Its Meaning and Implications for Education and Training', *Journal of European Industrial Training*, 11 (2), 3–38.

Goss, D. (1991) *Small Business and Society*. London: Routledge.

Hall, S. (1988) *The Hard Road to Renewal*. London: Verso.

Keat, R. (1991) 'Introduction', in Keat, R. and Abercrombie, N. (eds), *Enterprise Culture*. London: Routledge.

Marquand, D. (1988) 'The Paradoxes of Thatcherism', in Skidelsky, R. (ed.), *Thatcherism*. Oxford: Blackwell.

Marquand, D. (1992) 'The Enterprise Culture: Old Wine in New Bottles?', in Heelas, P. and Morris, P. (eds), *The Values of the Enterprise Culture*. London: Routledge.

Morris, P. (1991) 'Freeing the Spirit of Enterprise: The Genesis and Development of the Concept of Enterprise Culture', In Keat, R. and Abercrombie, N. (eds), *Enterprise Culture*. London: Routledge.

Ritchie, J. (1991) 'Enterprise Cultures: A Frame Analysis', in Burrows, R. (ed.), *Deciphering the Enterprise Culture*. London: Routledge.

Wood, S. J. (1989) 'New Wave Management?', *Work, Employment & Society*, 3 (3), 379–402.

12 Contemporary issues

Objectives This final chapter allows us to consider some of the current issues affecting the small business sector and enterprise development. Of the many possible themes that are worthy of inclusion, four have been selected that are considered to merit special attention. These are:

- the development and impact of the Internet;

- business creation and strategies for success – some new research and insights;

- international considerations and comparisons of entrepreneurship;

- innovation and high technology

The Internet

The three illustrations that follow offer an interesting overview of the power and influence of the Internet and its truly incredible effect on enterprise creation, management and development.

CASE ILLUSTRATION 12.1

Idealab – a case history of enterpreneurship on the Internet

Much has been written about the impact of information technology on the fortunes and operating practices of business and organisations in their seemingly relentless quest for competitive advantage. Information about customer trends, buying behaviour and payment methods, together with the response of enlightened management to cater for such changes in a pro-active, strategic manner, has taken Tesco to a 22% market share and record profitability, in an industry which as one commentator put it 'does not take any prisoners'.

There appear to be many examples where corporate management has embraced information technology systems to its strategic advantage and as a consequence has improved its operating context through, for example, raising entry barriers or improving the value chain to enhance a differentiation strategy (Porter, 1980, 1985).

Who would have thought, though, that 5 years ago the development of the Internet would radically transform business practices in many industries and create whole new opportunities for intellectual property development and entrepreneurial creation? This case history examines the formation and development of Idealab (http://www.idealab.com) by Bill Gross, described in the popular press as a 'high tech entrepreneur'. It seems fitting to begin this account with an introduction from Fast Company (1997) that states:

> Bill Gross, Chief Executive Officer of Idealab, has started 18 companies in nine months. On the Net, he says, 'time is more important than money.' Gross has been starting companies since he was sixteen but it was not until he met Steven Spielberg that he came up with his ultimate entrepreneurial idea . . . a company dedicated to ideas themselves.

Thus was born Idealab, a Pasadena-based think tank that conceives and funds new ventures on the Internet. Unlike many of the new Web enterprises, Idealab is more than an indulgence for its 39 year old founder. It represents a radical new model for starting and developing new companies that reflects both the volume and potential of ideas on the Internet and the challenges of doing business there. Gross launched the new company in March 1996, with the stated objective to develop 10 new businesses with a market capitalisation of some $100 million each that were capable of going public or to be sold by the end of the decade.

By November 1999, Idealab had started 18 different ventures, six of which are now fully operational. One of these companies, CitySearch, already appears to be enjoying considerable success, having achieved a strong market position against the formidable competition from Microsoft and America Online in the creation of online information services for urban communities. The creation of new companies would appear to be a process that comes naturally to Gross. He paid for his American college education (California Institute of Technology) by selling patented stereo speakers that he designed himself. Probably his best-known start-up is Knowledge Adventure, which is now placed as the fourth largest educational software company in the United States. Impressive though his business development track record may be, Gross is on record as stating that it does not really count for much when it comes to starting companies on the Internet, which is an entrepreneurial medium like no other. When asked what is the fundamental key to success on the Internet, Gross was in no doubt of his reply:

> Speed, is of the essence here. Time is more important than money. If a company cannot go from concept to launch in nine months, it's not going to make it. This is the toughest business in the world.

For readers of this case wanting to know of new ways and methods of achieving competitive advantage, the formula embraced by Idealab is constructed on four principles.

The first principle is to evaluate new ideas quickly – and thoroughly. Time is not wasted if a promising new idea is found to have no real commercial viability. The timetable set by Gross for Idealab is ambitious to say the least. Over the next 5 years, he aims to identify one new and potentially profitable idea per month and to launch one new company every quarter. The evaluation process is both professional and comprehensive with very little left to chance. Idealab has assembled a panel of 10 Internet luminaries as its commercial evaluation advisors. They include MIT Professor Sherry Turkle, an expert on the sociology of the Internet, Richard Wurman, creator of the very influential TED conferences, and Bob Kavner, the successful AT&T executive who now runs the On Command Corporation. To again quote Gross:

> These advisors don't just provide commercial insight, they also provide credibility . . . We have some amazing people working with and funding us.
>
> Once we persuaded Bob Kavner to become chairman of our board of directors, we got Goldman Sachs and AT&T as investors. Once you get those first few breaks, the rest is like a chain reaction.

The second principle is based around people, or rather the acquisition of a balanced managerial team capable of turning the new ideas into commercial and viable enterprises. Idealab companies, according to Gross, are fanatical about recruiting:

> The biggest difference between success and failure on the Internet is the selection and recruitment of the right people. We have eighteen companies in various stages of development and the only thing that is holding us back from having all eighteen companies fully operational is people. Our biggest challenge every day is where are we going to find really talented people to execute the ideas.

The third principle to promote speed in the selection and execution of new ideas is to provide the necessary support infrastructure that is so often missing in the new entrepreneurial venture and may well delay, or frustrate, commercial viability. Idealab has a central support staff that undertakes all the vital activities such as negotiating for office space, creating the required corporate identity and protecting intellectual property. For example, graphic designer Tom Hughes, who created the Macintosh logo for Steve Jobs, is responsible for creating the individual corporate identity and supporting marketing collateral for all of the companies in the Idealab portfolio.

> With the provision of these excellent and dedicated and shared resources, I can reckon being at least three times faster than someone starting a company in the normal way.

The fourth principle is to have an enlightened approach to ownership and control of corporate assets. Idealab does not take a controlling interest in its portfolio of companies. In return for the start-up capital that it negotiates, Idealab receives a 49% equity holding, the remainder being reserved for managerial investment and subsequent investors that may be needed to fund future business expansion. Gross puts this very succinctly:

> The way to create wealth quickly on the Internet is to spread it around.

There is no doubt that the Internet will continue to provide the medium for future new venture creation but the rate of commercial success is likely to be far outstripped by the rate of failure.

Speed, as an essential ingredient for both idea generation and exploitation, must be matched with strategic thinking, which as Moss-Kanter (1989, 1995) reminds us 'is a scarce resource'. Of the many ingredients that constitute Idealab's success to date, and let us hope in the future also, strategic thinking is embracing the concept of 'value chain management' (Porter, 1979, 1985, 1996). Gross not surprisingly does not use the strategic management vocabulary that readers of the

Journal of Strategic Change are familiar with but if the last comment on corporate success is left is him, it does seem to have a familiar ring to it:

> The way to get speed . . . and a successful business, is to create shared knowledge about this medium as quickly as possible . . . Your competitors won't share what they know, so you have to find long term allies and form lasting reciprocal relationships that improve the quality of business for everyone. I am trying to create a family of companies that are allied with one another in a commitment to increase the speed at which we do and enjoy doing business.

Source: Beaver (1998)

CASE ILLUSTRATION 12.2

Business strategy and enterprise development – the rise and rise of the Internet

At a recent business convention in America, the chairman of Intel, Andy Grove, confidently predicted that, if business organisations do not become Internet companies within the next 5 years, then they are sealing the fate of their own demise, because quite simply they will cease to exist.

This could of course, be pure marketing hype, another example of the exaggerated and arrogant claims that the information technology industry is notorious for. However, this prediction is being articulated by the corporate leader of the most profitable and dominant semiconductor firm in the world and arguably the most respected organisation among US technology companies (Brown and Eisenhardt, 1998). Allowing for a little poetic licence, this statement is probably correct.

Depending on the point of view, the Internet is either over-inflated or under-valued. What is in little doubt, however, is the capacity of the World Wide Web to function as the most amazing and innovative instrument of enterprise development.

The Internet is turning businesses and markets upside down and inside out. It is fundamentally changing the ways in which companies operate almost irrespective of their industry sector, market position or product mix. This goes far beyond the commercial decisions of buying and selling, or the development of E-commerce, and deep into the processes, management, structure and culture of the enterprise. The quest for competitive advantage and sustainable, innovative strategic positioning has taken on a whole new dimension.

Many businesses are using the Internet to make direct connections with their customers, some for the first time. Others are using secure Internet connections to intensify relations with some of their trading partners and using the Internet's reach and ubiquity to engage in deals and operations that were previously inaccessible.

Entirely new companies and business models are emerging in industries as diverse as road haulage and textiles, to bring together buyers and sellers in super-efficient new electronic market-places. Furthermore, the Internet is enabling organisations to reduce their costs – often dramatically – across their supply and demand chains, provide customer service and trading relationships in a different league, enter new markets, create additional revenue streams and re-define boundaries and ambitions for business development.

What the Intel Chairman was really saying was that, if in 5 years time an organisation is not using the facilities of the Internet to do some or all of these things, it will be overtaken and probably eliminated by competitors who are.

Several recent surveys have concluded that many senior managers no longer need convincing of the power and influence of the Web. One, undertaken by The Economist Intelligence Unit together with Booz, Allen and Hamilton in May 1999, found that, in their survey of 500 companies, more than 90% of top executives believe that the Internet will have a major impact on the conduct of business on the international stage.

However, it is refreshing to note that it is the managers of small businesses who are leading the way in the use of the Internet according to a survey undertaken by *Management Today* and British Telecom in January 1999. Their results showed that 93% of small firm professionals are linked to the Internet, compared with 76% in companies employing more than 500 people. Furthermore, small enterprises are also more likely than large firms to actively trade on the Internet, with 32% of businesses with 50 or fewer employees stating that they are receiving orders through the Internet, compared with 14% in companies with more than 500 people.

As readers of the *Journal of Strategic Change* are well aware, the research on and reporting of explanations and models of business growth and expansion are invariably on academic and managerial agendas. Despite the considerable advances in this area it is a sobering fact that:

> Most businesses are born to die or stagnate . . . no wonder that we are fascinated by those few that grow. It is also a natural instinct to pore over the remains of dead businesses to try to gather portents for the future.
>
> *Source*: Burns (1989)

The Internet seems to produce new businesses and business models with monotonous regularity. Some of these new firms will, in time, become the established names that everyone will be familiar with and some of them may well dominate their particular market sector or even industry. The qualities they share are a deep and sustained understanding of how technology can be deployed to serve their business strategies, a track record for implementing those strategies and a healthy surfeit of ambition.

Some businesses such as Amazon.com and E*Trade are already well on the way to achieving that kind of success. However, most – despite today's inflated market capitalisations – will simply fade from view, unable to translate revenue generation into the profitability that is necessary to sustain long-term success. The statement above from Burns may be 10 years old, but it is still relevant and equally applicable to the Internet.

Of the new business models and variants made possible by the Internet, it is the information intermediaries (known in the Internet jargon as *infomediaries*) that have the potential to be both highly profitable and difficult for rivals to dislodge. They can also dramatically improve the efficiency of even low-technology vertical markets such as road haulage or steel. Impressive though these aggressive entre-preneurial businesses may be, they are just a harbinger of what is still to come.

Lou Gerstner, the Chairman of IBM, made a presentation to Wall Street analysts (June 1999) in which he described the new dot-com companies as:

> Fireflies before the storm – all stirred up, throwing off sparks.

He went on to say that:

> The storm that is arriving – the real disturbance in the force – is when the thousands and thousands of institutions that exist today seize the power of this global computing and communications infrastructure and use it to transform themselves. That's the real revolution.

He added that although Amazon.com might be 'an interesting retail concept' (the latest Nasdaq valuation places a market capitalisation of Amazon at $31 billion, which by any reckoning is interesting), it would pale into insignificance against what Wal-Mart was planning. (The recent acquisition of ASDA as its entry to the UK has fuelled speculation of a major revolution in British shopping.)

Similarly, the signing of 8000 new accounts by Netbank.com may be impressive, but not compared with the ambitions of BancOne – arguably America's most progressive bank, in its change of corporate strategy from acquisitions and gains in market share to the provision of Internet based financial services.

There are many more examples but the thesis by Gerstner is simple and easy to follow. When a large and aggressive organisation moves some or all of its operations to the Internet, there is a ripple effect. The trading partners of the big company come under intense pressure to embrace E-business structures themselves. The big company, having invested heavily in E-business infrastructure, is determined to get a good return on it. Customers and suppliers who want to trade the traditional way will become increasingly marginalised, while those who adapt will simply win more business.

As both buyers and sellers reduce their costs and increase their efficiency by investing in the capacity to do business on the Internet, it is in their interest to persuade more and more of their business partners to do the same, thus creating a virtuous self-reinforcing circle.

Another factor that big organisations bring to the Internet is critical mass. IBM is a case in point. This year it expects Internet sales to total $15 billion compared with $3.3 billion last year. It is forecast that customers will visit the company's home page some 28 million times this year for E-service and support. These self-service transactions alone will save $600 million. Further, by electronically procuring more than $12 billion's worth of goods over the Internet this year, IBM will eliminate some 5 million invoices.

It is still much too early to judge the full extent of the significance of the Internet on the conduct and development of enterprise. The fascinating and as-yet unknown factor is how a networked, interconnected business community will change the way people work with each other. Sophisticated and rapid advances in Internet technology make an unprecedented degree of collaboration possible, but it is impossible to predict how far that will reach beyond the boundaries of individual firms and how people will adapt to constantly shifting agreements, joint ventures, federations and alliances. Another major unknown is how organ-isations will respond to ever more demanding and articulate customers with near-perfect market intelligence.

To conclude, E-business is much more concerned with business strategy and enterprise development than about issues of technology. There is no doubt that the early Internet companies have used their technological understanding (and absence of any historical and cultural baggage) to enter new markets and create positions that would previously have been closed to them. However, in the future simply having a novel business concept and being technologically smart is unlikely to be enough to go the distance. It has taken the large, established international and global players a little longer to get their Internet act together but they are getting there now and it is they and their customers, not the Internet start-ups, that will establish the pace, conduct and profitability of E-trade.

Source: Beaver (1999)

CASE ILLUSTRATION 12.3

The future of Small.Business@EnterpriseDevelopment.Com?

It has been stated above and by many other sources and industry comment-ators that a business without an E-commerce strategy will shortly be no business at all. The following statement taken from the promotional literature of Sun Microsystems takes this contention much further.

> A slick web site is the easy bit. The tough challenge – and the real opportunity that the Internet presents – is to find new routes to market, to optimise supply and dis-tribution channels and to price goods for a global marketplace. All businesses will rely on electronic outlets, which must be robust, available 24 hours a day and provide a guaranteed and reliable service.

The question that many enterprise practitioners would like to know the answer to is whether E-business is the biggest thing since the industrial revolution or whether the Internet is just another useful medium for accelerating business communica-tions. The answer probably lies somewhere between the two. The Internet goes far deeper into industrial and commercial business processes than does the telephone but it is not creating entirely new industries – at least not yet.

As stated above, it is still much too soon to judge the full significance of the Internet in the way that business is conducted even for allowing for the faster adoption of new technology that it both furthers and is part of. That said, it does appear that most of the pure technology issues now seem to be largely resolved, or at least well on the way towards resolution, as in the case of security, privacy and lack of bandwidth.

Because the key players on the Internet will (if the above account proves correct) be established rather than new businesses, the process will appear more like a highly telescoped evolution than a revolution. However, revolutions may come and go but evolution persists. The way in which the Internet is changing the process and opportunity for business creation and development may be less spectacular than some of its enthusiasts might wish but a good deal more profound.

Business creation and strategies for success

Much has been said throughout this text about the process of new venture creation and the management of successful and profitable business growth. The following accounts provide some provocative insights into this fascinating and difficult agenda. Why do some firms achieve rapid and profitable growth when others in the same sector stagnate?

CASE ILLUSTRATION 12.4

Seven characteristics that set apart the fastest-growing firms

Few people predicted the mobile phones boom as accurately as Charles Dunstone did. More than a decade ago he spotted the growing trend, quit his job selling for another company and, at 25, founded Carphone Warehouse. It is now Britain's largest independent mobile phone retailer and one of its fastest-growing unquoted companies.

Investors would love to be able to pick out small companies set for such rapid, sustained and profitable growth. It is the stuff of dreams for bankers and venture capitalists but finding such firms is often a matter of luck rather than judgement. However, Simon Philips at Bridgewater, a London management consultancy that has itself grown rapidly, claims that entrepreneurial success is less of an enigma than most people think. Philips believes that he has found a way of spotting fast-growing firms and has published his method in a book called the *Seven Principles for Sustained Growth*. The book is the result of consultations with more than 20 business leaders – including Dan Wagner, chief executive of Dialog, Mike Grabiner, the chief executive of Energis, Sir Christopher Bland, chairman of the BBC, and Chris Gent, the chief executive of Vodafone. Philip's aim was to gather together their experience to come up with seven principles that could be applied to all firms in any sector of industry and could be used to spot companies that are destined for rapid and sustained growth.

Philips states that he wanted to discover what makes the distinction between low-growth and high-growth companies and then be able to apply the criteria to any company in any sector. He was keen to discover why some firms trading in mature markets or in a recession could speed up their growth while other companies in booming markets failed to live up to expectations. According to Philips, the seven factors that are responsible for fast growth are as follows:

1 *focus* – one vision or goal and clear values to match;
2 *cohesion* – everyone is behind the vision with the top team leading the way;
3 *simplicity* – a principle throughout the organisation;
4 *pace* – a sense of urgency and dynamism;
5 *conviction* – confidence that ambitious goals are within reach;
6 *enterprise* – the freedom to innovate, grasp opportunities and even make mistakes;
7 *greatness* – not forgetting to be better in the eyes of customers and workers.

Philips says that Dunstone of Carphone Warehouse followed these seven principles almost to the letter. In doing so he has built a company that is now a household name with over 200 outlets in Britain and a similar number on the continent. In 1999, the company earned a place in the Sunday Times Virgin Atlantic Fast Track 100 league table for the second time, with sales that rose from £20 million in 1994 to £147 million in 1998, one of the biggest rises in the list.

CASE ILLUSTRATION 12.5

How to identify start-ups that succeed

A good niche market and the desire to succeed in being your own boss are the keys to success, according to a recent study of entrepreneurs.

In 1987 Chris Evans sold his family home and put his savings into one of the UK's first biotechnology companies. The bank turned down his request to borrow £10 000 and the venture capitalists that he approached said that he was far too young to start a company and had no track record. Today, and against all the odds, Evans is one of Europe's premier biotechnology entrepreneurs and has taken five companies public, once again proving that spotting successful entrepreneurs is extremely difficult. It is an art, not a science.

Small firm advisors are constantly trying to improve their success rate. A quarter of start-ups fail within the first 18 months and a further 35% fail after 5 years, according to Department of Trade and Industry figures. Part of the problem for backers is that it is hard to determine which entrepreneurs are likely to succeed.

BDO Stoy Hayward, the accountancy and management consultancy firm, has responded by commissioning research to identify the characteristics of entrepreneurs who started up in the early 1990s and have survived and prospered. A spokesman for the company stated that BDO were very keen to learn about the success factors and the fact that these firms are still trading is important to take into account.

BDO examined the personal qualities and motivations of entrepreneurs as well as how they raised finance to find the recipe for a successful enterprise. The research notes that the businesses that succeeded over the period of research were those motivated by a strong entrepreneurial desire and determination to create personal wealth.

According to the research, if these personal qualities were combined with the ability to identify a gap in the market, the chances of business survival increased. The research also identified other areas as contributing to a successful start-up. For instance, the type of finance and where entrepreneurs raise their capital were important factors in determining business longevity. More that 70% of successful start-ups raised their initial finance from personal funds and most of them combined this with a bank loan or overdraft. Just 18% sought financial help from parent companies, venture partners and business angels. The research states that businesses that started at the end of the last recession may have found it difficult to raise finance from other parties but those firms established in the mid-1990s were more able to obtain bank overdrafts and loans at an early stage. The research also identified an increasing number of successful start-up in the service sector in industries such as recruitment and selection.

Although the research is far from exhaustive, it goes some way towards identifying entrepreneurs who have a chance of becoming the next Chris Evans. A sure test is likely to be the arrival of the next recession. Successful start-ups are better planned and better prepared to weather any economic slow-down.

Source: BDO Stoy Hayward, London, 1999

CASE ILLUSTRATION 12.6

Entrepreneurs improve with age

A considerable number of the most profitable firms are started by people over 45 who have been made redundant. Their skill and experience gives them a head start over younger rivals. Britain has a new breed of entrepreneur and it is sufficiently strong to be attracting the interest of Government officials and industry lobbyists. That much is clear from a recent seminar in London involving representatives from the Treasury, the British Chambers of Commerce, the Federation of Small Businesses, the Banks and the academic world. They were meeting to discuss the growing numbers of men and women over 45 who are starting their own business. This band of entrepreneurs has attracted a number of labels. They have been described as 'third-age entrepreneurs' and as members of 'the golden-grey club'. However they are described, they have a growing value to the economy and are capable of creating value to the economy.

Contemporary research shows that third age businesses are fast becoming one of the most important and most successful parts of the start-up sector. A Lloyds TSB survey (1999) shows that a quarter of all new firms are now started by people over 45. The survey, which examined almost 250 000 bank accounts, showed that the third-age phenomenon is particularly strong among women – 26% of the women who started business in the UK last year were in the 45–59 age bracket. Similar research by Barclays (1999) confirmed that women established 40% of the 50 000 businesses polled on behalf of the bank. It also revealed that businesses run by entrepreneurs over 50 last longer and often outperform those led by younger people.

Other statistics from the Barclays study are also encouraging. Three-quarters of the respondent firms have been trading for at least 5 years, while half of those set up by younger people cease to trade within 4 years. It would appear that their success comes as much from the manner in which they trade and the different routes taken to business.

Third-age businesses have very different characteristics from companies started by younger entrepreneurs. For instance, they are more likely to be founded by people who make better employers, as they appear to suffer less stress than their younger counterparts do. Further, they are also more likely to stay trading past the critical first 3 years because of their superior experience.

However, not everything about older entrepreneurs is robust, as they are more likely to borrow on overdraft than younger owner-managers. This is something that could be linked to their personal wealth or old habits of borrowing. They are also less likely to set up in dynamic growth sectors such as high technology and biotechnology, preferring traditional areas of business where returns are lower and growth slower.

Participants at the London seminar were keen to find ways to encourage growth by harnessing the talent and experience of older entrepreneurs. Suggestions included the creation of a new form of business angel network, one that offers experience rather than investment. If this encouraged older entrepreneurs it could in turn, stimulate growth in small firms and improve the success rate of new enterprises.

International considerations

In his detailed and authoritative work on the small business sector, Storey (1994) states clearly and unambiguously that:

> The basic message to government is that, in its dealings with small firms, it needs to do less and better, rather than more and worse. The very clear message that comes across from discussions with small firms is that the key role which government can play is in creating a suitable macro-economic framework within which firms can prosper.

Storey then proceeds to outline the ingredients of a small business policy that should form the basis for a government White Paper on the objectives and targets of policy, arguing strongly that it would promote consistency in government perception of the small firm sector. His recommendations for government (Storey, 1994, p. 315) contain the endorsement that governments should:

> see small firm policy as integral with economic, employment and social policy, . . . with increased emphasis on . . . :
> - selectivity and targeting;
> - technology and science;
> - special groups;
> - financial assistance;
> - encouraging dialogue.

His recommendations implicitly recognise the role and value of the small business sector as a major contributor towards the health and prosperity of the economy but fall short of advocating entrepreneurship as a key instrument of social engineering and attitudinal change.

There are many writers and researchers that seek to promote entrepreneurship as the principal economic panacea and cite the economies of the USA and Canada as role models to be copied. The following illustration based on the research of the Kauffman Center in America presents contemporary evidence on the international value and perception of entrepreneurship and its contribution to employment generation, structural balance and wealth creation.

CASE ILLUSTRATION 12.7

Attitudes to entrepreneurship

One in 12 Americans are currently attempting to start a business and more or less everyone in the country knows someone involved in such a venture. Comparisons with Finland bring this figure into sharp relief where the phenomenon is considerably rarer with a rate of one in 67. Starting a new venture is regarded by most of the population as extraordinary and unusual. These are among the findings of the Global Entrepreneurship Monitor (GEM) study 2000, measuring and comparing entrepreneurial activity in ten countries undertaken by London Business School, Babson College and the Kauffman Center for Entrepreneurial Studies and Leadership (www.entreworld.org). Central among its findings was the discovery that, while entrepreneurship had moved rapidly up the public policy agenda in the last 10 years, there were substantial differences in the levels of activity between the countries studied. Paul Reynolds of Babson College stated that there is a sense in which it is legitimate in some countries like the USA but a cultural anomaly in many other countries.

The GEM study has analysed over the past 2 years the interplay between economic growth and entrepreneurship in the G7 leading industrialised countries plus Denmark, Finland and Israel. Some 1000 people in each country were surveyed together with a total of 300 specific experts in entrepreneurship. The USA, Canada and Israel emerged as the most entrepreneurial as measured by the percentage of people starting a business, averaging 6.9% across the three. Italy and the UK were classed as intermediate, at an average of 3.4 per 100. Trailing behind were Denmark, Finland, France, Germany and Japan, with an average of 1.8%.

The authors of the report conclude tentatively that about a third of the difference in a country's growth rate could be attributed to the variations in the number of business start-ups. They also estimate that another third is likely to be related to the activities of established firms, with the balance down to factors that include the interaction of new and existing companies. The data underline how no country with a high level of business start-ups is suffering a slow rate of economic growth.

The study also sought to unravel some of the factors affecting levels of entrepreneurialism. These include:

- *Perception of opportunity*. In the most entrepreneurially active countries, the level of perceived opportunity – suitably adjusted for actual opportunity – is dramatically higher.
- *Demography*. Men aged 25–44 are the most likely sector of society to start a business. The depth of that pool will be crucial to start-up rates. Meanwhile, the relative involvement of women varies considerably. In highly entrepreneurial countries, women participate at 58% of the rate of men. That falls to 31% in low category countries. Demographic trends will also influence business opportunity. It is much harder to establish a successful business in regions of zero or negative population growth.

- *Culture*. The extent to which entrepreneurs command respect varies greatly. In the USA, 91% of those surveyed said that starting a business was a respected occupation. In the UK, the rate was 31%, falling to 8% in Japan. While Germany languishes at the bottom of the table overall, 73% of those questioned said that entrepreneurs were respected. Apex Partners, which sponsored the UK and German part of the study, stated that their perception is that things have been changing dramatically in Germany in the last 2 or 3 years, in terms of attitude to risk-taking. The authors predict that such shifts in attitude may show through more clearly in future research.

- *Infrastructure*. The availability of equity finance was found to have an impact, as did that of good, reasonably priced professional advice. The potential for research and development transfer and the existence of flexible labour markets, were other notable factors. At the same time the study notes that most specific government policies were not stimulating the massive changes required to enhance the rate of entrepreneurial activity. The authors point out that there is plenty of other research confirming that such programmes are beneficial in promoting new business creation. They speculate that most initiatives are too small to have a significant influence on the economy. It also emerged that frustration with government programmes – perceived as poorly co-ordinated and/or opaque – is highest in the low category countries.

- *Education*. Countries with the most investment in tertiary education had the highest rates of business start-up.

The authors drew a number of policy influences from their findings. Michael Hay at the London Business School stated that there was a clear case for raising and supporting the total level of start-ups as this would demystify the process and further stated that governments should see it as a volume activity. By contrast, investment in tertiary education was a much longer-term project. At the same time, developing appropriate skills early in the education process was vitally important. Governments could also help by putting suitable infrastructure in place. However, the toughest hurdle appears to be adjusting attitudes towards entrepreneurship and its consequences, notably, disparity in incomes.

Adults active in business start-ups (mean percentage involved in start-ups)

Finland	1.49%
Japan	1.71%
France	1.81%
Denmark	1.96%
Germany	2.19%
UK	3.35%
Italy	3.5%
Israel	5.43%
Canada	6.89%
USA	8.42%

Kauffman Centre Research, 2000.

CASE ILLUSTRATION 12.8

The latest policy changes and thinking from the EU and the UK

Small firms and government

Governments may talk about an enterprise culture but the experience of many small firms does not always bear out the politicians' message. Throughout Europe small firms are in vogue. After many years of neglect from politicians there is a realisation that it is the small privately owned companies who will provide the jobs and much of the prosperity. In August 2000, the Feira European Council concluded:

> The European Council welcomes the recently adopted European Charter for Small Enterprises and underlines the importance of small firms and entrepreneurs for growth, competitiveness and employment in the Union. It requests its full implementation as part of the comprehensive framework for enterprise policy under preparation.

It would appear that the Europeans have digested the statistic that 75% of those employed in the private sector work for firms with less than 20 people. Only 10% of the EU workforce are employed by an organisation that employs more than 250 staff. According to Martin Manuzzi, a Brussels-based European advisor to the Institute of Chartered Accountants in England and Wales, the small business sector across Europe has more to unite it than divide it:

> Politicians are realising that small firms are powerful and flourishing. SMEs across Europe face many similar problems but maybe in continental Europe they are more used to working across border. In Europe, many multi-nationals are seen as faceless and un-accountable, whereas the economic strength of a community is often reflected in the well being of the local business.

It would be logical therefore to think that business policies were geared towards encouraging the small business sectors throughout the EU. However, the evidence from many entrepreneurs across the EU does not accord with the rhetoric of an enterprise culture espoused by the politicians. The accountancy firm Grant Thornton conducts an annual European Business Survey covering the principal SME sectors (see Table 12.1). The impact of both domestic law and taxation policies, together with regulation and bureaucracy, are the principal concerns of SMEs across the EU:

> European SMEs consider that the main short-term constraint on expansion plans to be domestic law and taxation, a shortage of skilled labour and a shortage of orders. While the main long-term constraints are domestic law and taxation, limited market demand and difficulties in accessing new markets.

Source: Grant Thornton (2000)

The European declaration follows a policy statement called 'Towards Enterprise Europe: Enterprise Policy 2000–2005' and the establishment of a new Directorate-General (DG) in January 2000. This covers the responsibilities for the former DGs for Industry and SMEs as well as innovation activities previously attached to the

Table 12.1 The percentage of companies that see domestic law/taxation policies and EU legislation as a short-term constraint on plans for development

	Domestic law	EU legislation
France	75	8
Italy	54	4
EU average	41	7
Belgium	37	6
Germany	36	10
Greece	35	2
Austria	28	10
Denmark	25	5
Portugal	24	4
Sweden	21	1
Luxembourg	20	12
The Netherlands	20	10
UK	14	13
Spain	14	2
Ireland	10	6

Table 12.2 EU enterprise policy: the main themes and objectives

- Promote entrepreneurship as a valuable skill

- Promote innovation and the ability to manage change productively

- Encourage a regulatory and business environment in which entrepreneurship can flourish

- Enhance the competitiveness of enterprises in the knowledge-based economy

- Improve the financial environment for enterprises

- Ensure the provision of business support networks and services to enterprises and facilitate the co-operation between enterprises in accordance with EU and national competition rules

- Improve access to markets for goods and services

- Promote a better understanding and better use of services, including business services

Information DG. The principal objective is to achieve an 'Enterprise Europe' – a sustainable economy based on knowledge and innovation, by 2005 (see Table 12.2). A statement from the new DG said:

Enterprise Policy seeks to create a climate of confidence among enterprises. Business start-up needs to be made easier and more attractive and the cost of doing business in Europe lowered. Further action is also needed to simplify the launch of new products on the Single Market. Many regulatory issues remain to be tackled as well, such as the effective protection of intellectual property and certain key sectors also require specific measures such as telecommunications where liberalisation needs to be speeded up.

Despite the above, there is strong evidence that governments are not pursuing policies that favour their SME sectors. A recent report from the Institute for Public Policy Research (IPPR), a British centre-left think tank, stated that many UK small firms 'are significantly underperforming' as a result, in part, of misplaced government aid. The report, *Agenda for Growth*, criticises the government for relying on a manufacturing model of business and failing to recognise the diversity of the small firm sector. Business Links statistics quoted in the report show that 46% of small businesses helped by government were from the manufacturing sector, yet manufacturing only accounts for 9% of the total stock of SMEs.

According to the authors of the report, policy solutions tend to adopt 'a one-size fits all' approach and do not take into account the impact of differences between small firms. The 'picking winners' approach to selectivity and preferential assistance in the small business sector, which has many advocates, has been criticised. IPPR's research has shown that small firms with a lifestyle motivation, as opposed to a growth orientation, does not have any necessary impact on the capability for business development or employment creation. The research also reports that much more could be done to encourage a greater proportion of small firms to embark on growth. The strategies for growth include the encouragement of owner-managers to recognise skill and business deficiencies by using customers to identify problems and the use of peer groups of micro-enterprises to enable firms to set goals and targets for their future performance and to devise and implement strategies to accomplish them. The newly formed Small Business Service (SBS) in the UK should also recognise the diversity of small firms and their operating contexts and ensure that all legislation affecting small firms is tested out over a range of business models. Andrea Westhall, one of the co-authors of the report, stated:

> The SBS will have to be highly flexible and responsive to the needs of different types of small firms and to rapidly changing market conditions. Support should be more directed to catalysing innovative approaches to addressing barriers to growth for different types of firm.

She continued:

> It will have to work more in partnership with other organisations. It cannot be a one stop shop but rather a first stop shop. Much more effort needs to be made to encourage tailored sectoral support.

These sentiments are endorsed in the UK by the Forum of Private Business (FPB). Research among their members (September 2000) found that only 19% had used the service of the local TEC in the last year and those that did thought that it was 'good to average'. Stan Mendham, the Chief Executive of FPB, said:

> We want to help the SBS hit the ground running so that it is successful for our members. The prize for getting it right will be that the rules are no longer written by big

business for the advantage of big business. However the SBS machine will be extremely difficult to manage and unless it is incredibly focused in its activities, it will collapse under its own complexity.

Patricia Hewitt, the Small Firms Minister in the UK, repeated the pledge (September 2000) that the government will 'think small first' when developing policies that affect the small business sector. Her response to the report by the Better Regulation Taskforce report *Helping Small Firms Cope with Regulation – Exemptions and Other Approaches* emphasised the government's commitment to the small firm sector and its interests:

> We are committed to building an enterprise society in which all firms can thrive and achieve their full potential. To help us achieve this we must make sure that the needs of small business are built in at the very start of the policy-making process.

Whether Mrs Hewitt and others can deliver on their promises to help rather than hinder the small business remains to be seen. As owner-managers and entrepreneurs know only too well, activity should not be mistaken for productivity. EU and domestic government policies towards the small business sector are strong on rhetoric but their contribution to productivity and value has yet to be proved.

Innovation and high technology

Introduction

There is a popular and romantic perception of talented entrepreneurs, often operating in high-technology sectors, developing innovative new products and processes that will transform their industry's, and even their country's, prospects. Thus they are perceived as the dynamos of technological development, social progress and economic growth. On the basis of the highly publicised successes of such modern high-technology firms as Intel, Microsoft, Apple, Hewlett-Packard and Xerox, all of which began as small entrepreneurial initiatives and grew rapidly into major corporations, it would seem that the perception has some foundation.

Of the many studies of successful innovation, most have attempted to identify the key factors that have contributed towards the success (often against all the odds) and longevity of such enterprises. Although there is a healthy degree of disagreement between some of the more notable studies, most would seem to agree that the following are of crucial significance:

- the commitment and motivation of key individuals, including the centrality and determination of the entrepreneur responsible for initiating the innovation;
- attention to key managerial activities and attitudes, such as the development of a strong market orientation, good internal communications, a sound and innovative strategy, good stakeholder management and the ability to predict and respond to environmental and industry changes.

The significance of innovation and the small firm

Policy-makers and academics rarely understate the importance of innovation. Indeed, innovation is an essential condition of economic progress and a critical element in the competitive struggle of both enterprises and nation states (Freeman and Soete, 1997). It has been estimated that over 60% of all economic growth is due to technological advance rather than improvements in labour productivity.

Small and medium-sized enterprises in their turn have a considerable contribution to make to the process of innovation generally and technological change specifically. While it is now accepted that there is no optimum size of enterprise that is particularly designed to maximise industrial innovation, intuitive common sense and considerable research evidence confirms that small firms have a distinct and crucial role to play (Storey and Sykes, 1996). A number of government reports such as the White Paper on Science and Technology (HMSO, 1993) have confirmed the potential from the encouragement of entrepreneurs engaged in innovation and technical advancement and the need to successfully transfer the technology in order for the commercial and economic benefits to be realised.

In a series of seminal papers, Rothwell (1983, 1984, 1988) noted that, although fundamental or radical invention occurred within large firms or large public laboratories, small firms were disproportionately responsible for near-to-market developments and initial market diffusion. In fulfilling this role, smaller firms enjoyed many unique advantages associated with a lack of bureaucracy, efficient and often informal communications, plus flexibility and adaptability through nearness to markets. By contrast, however, such enterprises faced severe constraints associated with a lack of technically qualified labour, poor use of external information and expertise, the unsuitability of original management beyond initial prescription, difficulties in attracting and securing finance and the high cost of regulatory compliance.

In essence, the advantages enjoyed by SMEs are fundamentally behavioural, while constraints relate to resource issues. There appears little doubt from the findings of contemporary research in this area that the amount and quality of available resources are a major determinant of the pace at which a technology can be advanced in a given time and how quickly marketing networks can be extended.

In examining the role of the smaller firm and its contribution to innovation and economic performance, it is as well to be reminded of the classic quotation from Edith Penrose (1959) who noted that:

> The differences in the administrative structure of the very small and the very large firms are so great that in many ways it is hard to see that the two species are of the same genus . . . we cannot define a caterpillar and then use the same definition for a butterfly.

The nature, composition and quality of management are central to the innovation and performance of any firm, where such achievement is defined and measured in terms of growth in sales, assets, profits, products and services, employment and even survival. In many respects the relationship between managerial quality and business performance is likely to be more pronounced in small firms than large ones. In the smaller firm strategic and operational decisions made by the owners, entrepreneurs and key players tend to be formulated and implemented more quickly and are less likely to be diluted or sabotaged by subordinates than decisions made by senior management in large organisations.

However, the decisions made by the key players in the smaller business, however professional and well considered, will have more of an uncertain outcome in the market-place, primarily because of limited market power, constrained resources and positional disadvantage (Beaver and Jennings, 2000).

As Penrose points out, 'a small firm is not simply a large firm in miniature'. Using her analogy, it cannot be assumed that a caterpillar is a small butterfly. Accordingly, those characteristics other than size which impact on the ability of the smaller enterprise to pursue and deliver innovative products need to be identified and examined. This is a central theme of this paper that is illustrated in the case examples that follow.

What then are the principal differences about those SMEs engaged in the innovation process?

First, they have different and special financing requirements that arise because of the need for seed capital and development capital. The process of research and development (R&D) can take some time before the firm has a commercially viable product with which to go to market and during this period there are no returns for the investors who are required to provide 'long-term patient money'. Access to finance and the presence of equity gaps are commonly cited as major barriers to innovation throughout the small business literature. Innovation often requires considerable front-end sunk costs, invariably beyond the scope of the firm's internal resources. This, allied with the frequent inability of the funding providers to adequately assess either the technological validity or the project viability, often militates against finance provision. In a recent review of public policy addressing high technology SMEs specifically and small firm innovation generally, Oakey (1997) concluded that 'All concerns are directly or indirectly influenced by shortages of capital'.

Second, the entrepreneur and the key players in the enterprise require distinct and different management skills and abilities (Jennings and Beaver, 1997; Beaver and Jennings, 2000). As a complex, inclusive process, innovation requires an eclectic base of managerial competence that all too often is sadly absent. Studies addressing the general fitness of many SMEs for innovation consistently point to the extent of poor management skills and also of poor marketing skills (Moore, 1995).

There needs to be a wider recognition and acceptance of several factors that are peculiar to the small business operating context. For example, the studies by Grieve-Smith and Fleck (1987), using a case study approach to examine the business strategies in small high-technology firms in the Cambridge area, raise several interesting managerial issues. They note that small enterprises can experience real difficulties in developing or obtaining the appropriate managerial talent, since they cannot provide the salaries and accompanying benefits that managers from large organisations can reasonably expect to obtain. Furthermore, their work illustrates several other important issues worthy of note. For instance, they refer to the founders of certain companies being conscious at the outset of the need to recruit external managers and to appoint these individuals from larger companies, to facilitate business growth and development. Additionally, they refer to the need to attract managers with additional skills to those already in the firm, to complement the expertise on which the company was based. This would suggest that the business founder(s) had the objective to construct a balanced managerial team as one of the prime drivers in attaining enterprise success and performance. It is also a factor that may well dramatically reduce the risk of business failure.

Recent research has also shown that many entrepreneurs become overly concerned with the procedural and technical aspects of their innovation at the expense of the capabilities required for commercial viability (Freel, 1998). The timing of decisions is often crucial, such as the trade-off between development costs and market revenues, as there are considerable first-mover advantages in the innovation process. Both of the cases in this paper illustrate this point particularly well.

Third, problems may well arise with the issue of technology transfer, which involves the commercial application of the research undertaken in a different context or location such as a laboratory that is part of a university. It is often argued that entrepreneurs engaged in innovation have different and special support needs and therefore special environments need to be established to facilitate successful technology transfer from the pure research in the university to the production and commercialisation requirements within the firm. The last decade has witnessed the establishment of many science parks attached to UK universities, together with a network of business innovation centres.

Fourth, there is compelling evidence to suggest that innovative SMEs do better when they are part of a community or cluster of like-minded firms that can participate in a supportive infrastructure which encourages their development and prosperity. Successful examples of such concentrations would be Silicon Valley in California, USA, and the Cambridge Phenomenon (the spin-off from technical developments in scientific research carried out at Cambridge University) in the UK.

Finally, several studies have found that firms that use and fashion their competitive advantage around information and external networking consistently achieved better results and were more optimistic about the future. Effective decision-making, especially at a strategic level, requires information. Furthermore, new information often provides the stimulus for change and progression. However, for many SMEs that do not have the functional specialists or levels of internal competence, information search and management activities can be prohibitively costly, misdirected and parochial. Forming networks with other organisations in the search for information is a mechanism by which small firms can ameliorate the problem of extending their knowledge base and strengthen their market standing (SBRC, 1992; Dodgson and Rothwell, 1989).

The following cases of Powderject and Bookham Technology are fascinating examples of the formation, management and rapid growth of relatively new entrepreneurial ventures using innovation in the fields of biotechnology and fibre optics and illustrate many of the above factors.

CASE ILLUSTRATION 12.9

Powderject plc

Company profile

Chief executive officer	Dr Paul Drayson
Market capitalisation	£415 million
Turnover 6 years ago	£0
Turnover 1997/98	£3.1 million
Expenditure on research and development	£9.7 million
Losses 1998/99	(£4.5 million)
Share price movements	1998/99 low, 194.5p
	1998/99 High, 902.5p
	Highest rise in a trading week, 197.5p
	(reason given: Swiss deal)

Pharmaceutical companies pump millions of pounds into research and development before seeing a profit. Powderject, which is pioneering needle-free injections, wants to keep costs down and make sure the public demands its products. Biotechnology has proved fertile ground for smaller company growth, but, as Paul Drayson the Chief Executive Officer (CEO) of Powderject knows all to well, growth is achieved only after big cash outflows on research and development. Drayson has to get the balance right between investment and cash management:

> My challenge is control the cash burn. I have to get the products to market within the timetables established. We are running a commercial operation, not a research institution.

So far, Drayson has kept the business on track. Despite losses of £4.5 million in 1998, Powderject's market value has risen to £415 million since it was founded in 1993 to commercialise the research findings of Brian Bellhouse, Drayson's father-in-law and director of Oxford University's medical-engineering unit. Bellhouse had invented a way of giving injections without needles. A helium gas trigger delivers a powdered drug with sufficient speed to penetrate the skin. Not only is the injection pain-free (it feels like a puff of air), it is also more effective than needles since the drug can be targeted more accurately. The company owns worldwide patents to this method, an attractive asset with the drug delivery sector growing at twice the rate of the pharmaceuticals industry as a whole.

Drayson's success may be due partly to his background, which is in industrial management rather than the research laboratory. In fact, he undertook his commercial induction in the biscuit market. By the time he was 30 he had set up a subsidiary for Trebor, the sweets company now owned by Cadbury Schweppes, developing a high-quality snack product. He sold the business for a substantial profit, learnt of Bellhouse's invention and invested his own money to start up Powderject:

> I had the experience of taking a product from concept to the supermarket shelf. It is an exhilarating feeling to see people buying something that you created and when you are running a biotechnology company, with such long lead times in bringing a product to market, it is important to remember what the goal is.

Powderject, which has been growing at 50% a year, went public in 1997 and has raised £35 million to fund its development. While Drayson has told investors how he plans to spend the money over 2 years, he recognises that corporate finance has to be managed carefully:

> The impulse, when you have raised a lot of money is to go out and spend it. But every pound we spend we have to earn back. My job is to make sure all those involved in the Powderject process get a good return for their investment.

Budgets are reviewed monthly and managers who do not meet them have to provide a convincing explanation. Drayson encourages a frugal atmosphere. There are no company cars and pension contributions and rewards are made up of basic salary and share options:

> I started my biscuit company in the recession. I had to go back to the bank manager and ask for an extension of my overdraft facility. I remember kicking myself for spending £2000 on office furniture that I could have done perfectly well without.

Drayson has had some difficulty in applying the performance measures he used for biscuits to biotechnology.

> I learnt biscuits through ratios. Sales to cost of sales, cost of sales to overheads to net profits, and so on. These disciplines are harder to apply in the more nebulous world of biotechnology.

As a result, he is working with accountants to build performance measures that can be applied to high-technology businesses where a lot of money is spent before any real sales are made. The model includes measuring such items as overheads per worker, current and potential sales per worker and product milestones achieved per worker. Drayson tries to maintain commercial focus by outsourcing early stage research to Oxford University. Drayson rewards scientists on the understanding that Powderject is allowed to commercialise any relevant findings. This reduces laboratory overheads and allows the company to use its own laboratory specifically for development.

The business earns money from partnerships with large organisations, which pay Powderject to develop their drugs for powder delivery. Payment starts with a fee when a deal is signed, continues with milestone payments as a drug passes through the various development stages and ends with royalties of 6–12% when it reaches market. Drayson's biggest achievement to date is a deal with Glaxo Wellcome to develop their genetic vaccines for hepatitis B, AIDS and cancer for powder delivery. At £180 million before commercialisation, this is one of Europe's biggest research and development collaborations. It is also a big endorsement of Powderject since these drugs will be developed for powder delivery only. While the partnership method has offered Powderject fast growth, it brings its own pressures. The company has grown from a staff of five people to 126 in five years and now has offices in Oxford, Wisconsin, and Palo Alto, California:

> We were a company of only 10 people when we set up the Palo Alto office. It was a risk but it was one of the best things that we have done. America's West Coast is way ahead of us in the area of drug delivery. It was a huge wake-up call for me about the

strength of the competition and I spend quite a lot of my time there to get a shot in the arm of entrepreneurial energy.

Half of Powderject's staff are now in the USA, the world's largest drugs market. Modern technology helps them to keep in touch. Powderject uses an Intranet, video conferencing and E-mail but Drayson knows that the phenomenal rate of growth creates problems:

> It puts a lot of strain on people to be adaptable, but if you start off with the right culture, the expectation of continual change, it can be managed.

Continual change is not to everyone's liking. As drugs proceed through clinical trials towards manufacture and distribution, Drayson has to hire new people over the heads of existing staff to direct these new and complex processes. He tries to manage this by involving existing staff in the interviewing process but knows that the rate of change does not suit everyone:

> When you are re-defining jobs and organisational structures rapidly, you will always lose some people. Sometimes a person who has done a brilliant job to a certain point, is just not suitable for the next stage. Then I look on it as my responsibility to help them as easily as possible into their next situation.

Drayson acknowledges that growth at this rate has a price:

> It places a strain on everyone to be adaptable. The company culture has to be one of continual change. Not everyone likes that.

The pace is necessary, considering that the drugs delivery industry that is worth $117 billion worldwide is growing at 15% a year: twice that of the pharmaceutical industry as a whole. Drayson has learnt something about how to accommodate growth from Auragen, its recent American purchase from WR Grace. As a subsidiary of a big company, Auragen had established procedures on many aspects of operations. Drayson comments:

> If you wanted to paint your office wall, there were rules to tell you what colour it should be. It is surprising just how much time these kinds of operational issue can take up when there is no settled procedure.

Drayson says that he has learned much from the Auragen rulebooks. His big challenge now is to build a brand that is solid enough to survive beyond the expiry of the Powderject patents. If he develops a brand that commands strong customer loyalty, it will be a potential barrier to entry for the industry. Drayson uses the example of the Intel microchip that is used inside personal computers and also the breathable fabric Goretex used inside well-known sportswear brands:

> If you buy a Ralph Lauren ski suit you are not just buying the brand and the design but also the Goretex label inside. It comes as a package.

Drayson's ambition is to establish Powderject as the customers' preferred form of taking powdered injections. To do this, he must make sure that the needleless injection is branded whenever it is delivered, so that the patient knowingly takes an anaesthetic for dental surgery or a Glaxo vaccine for cancer with a

Powderject device. Drayson is confident of achieving this ambition because of the growing trend towards patient choice in healthcare on both sides of the Atlantic. The Powderject technology itself assists in the process since it removes the necessity for an injection to be taken under medical supervision. With self-administration of injections, patient choice will play an important part in the creation of healthcare brands:

> As a lifetime asthmatic, I have a strong relationship with my inhaler. As a child I noticed that there were differences between inhalers – some were more effective than others – and if pharmaceutical companies had branded them more powerfully, I would have insisted on being given a particular type. This is the kind of position that we want Powderject to have in a few years time when the patents have expired.

Although the company is not expected to break even until 2002, its share value and turnover continues to rise. Drayson and his wife have a share in the company worth over £100 million. In June 2000 they sold £17 million of shares and gave £1.2 million of that to the Radcliffe Hospital in Oxford.

Epilogue

Getting the Powderject device to fire powdered drugs into the skin and work effectively is much more complex than the concept. After numerous delays and setbacks, Powderject reported in the first week of July 2001 that it is divesting its drugs business to concentrate on the traditional Evans Vaccines business that it bought in 2000. The company still hopes to use the Powderject technology for vaccines but nothing will be on the market until at least 2004. In the meantime the very nature of the company has shifted fundamentally. Drayson states that he has established the world's leading pure-vaccines company; however, 2 years and two owners ago, Evans was an unloved division of Medeva, the worst performing pharmaceutical stock in the FTSE 350. Evans' plant at Speke will require substantial investment while regulatory demands are rising all the time. Even if it is accepted that Drayson has done the right thing for the company, Powderject does not have the potential or charisma that two years ago enabled Drayson to sell £17 million shares at 800p. The Powderject dream has died.

CASE ILLUSTRATION 12.10

Bookham Technology

In the latter part of 2000, Bookham Technology has been one of the biggest victims of the technology shake-out. Its market value dropped from a peak of £6.5 billion, falling by £5.2 billion as its shares fell below the £10 price at which they were floated earlier in the year. Its appearance in the FTSE 200 Index was as dramatic as its disappearance some months later. In December 2000, the company, just 12 years old, was valued at £1.3 billion. The company was named after the Surrey town where the founder, Andrew Rickman, was born and grew up.

Company profile

Chief executive officer	Dr Andrew Rickman
Market capitalisation	£1294 million
Share price movements	2000 low, 879p
	2000 high, 5302p

The traditional image of a high technology entrepreneur is probably of an inventor with thick pebble glasses working away in the garage or a scientist making a breakthrough in the laboratory. Dr Andrew Rickman, the founder and Chief Executive of Bookham Technology, comes from a radically different mould. For him the business model was the priority and the product followed subsequently. Bookham Technology is the Oxfordshire-based company that developed a new approach to the manufacture of optical circuits that are used in telecommunications networks, based on fibre optics for speed. Rickman is a mechanical engineer by training and admits to having wanted to start and run his own business, in part as a result of peer pressure.

Rickman's independence extended not only to starting his own business but also to his views on how a new venture should operate. Working with Oxford Ventures, a seed-corn capital fund in the 1980s, helped refine these ideas. Rickman came to believe that the application of traditional venture capital fund approaches to such early-stage investments was for the most part counter-productive and that there were other ways for start-ups to find funding.

From this Rickman developed a business model for a new high-technology start-up, a company that produced an enabling technology with a fairly long gestation period, to create something of considerable value and longevity. The common Silicon Valley model of moving quickly to plug a short-term gap or seize a 6 or 12 month opportunity was rejected.

Rickman's aim was to eliminate many of the risks associated with staring a new business such as being a one-product company or a business focused on a particular market or customer. Such ventures invariably face the hurdles of developing the right product before anyone else and of getting access to that market. Instead, Rickman's approach was to address a much wide market need and then to focus on providing the right product solutions for specific market segments. He also took the view that marketing is a fundamental and crucial activity for a new business and estimates about a quarter of his time is spent talking to customers to ensure that the right product for the market was being produced.

With this model in mind, Rickman then developed his enabling technology. His interest in optical circuits meant that he knew they were being considered for a range of applications and he was also aware of the complexities of the current manufacturing process. Most of the components are produced on massive production lines where complex arrangements of miniature mirrors are adjusted and aligned manually. Rickman believed that it was possible to fabricate and adjust these components in solid state silicon in a similar manner to microchip production. Such an approach would reduce the number of errors associated with what was essentially a labour intensive process and make the final product more saleable.

Rickman founded Bookham Technology in 1988 and started a PhD in integrated optics at Surrey University, the most cost-effective way to fund initial research. At the same time he enrolled on an MBA programme at Cranfield Business School to develop his business skills. He then set about applying for grants and sponsorship as well as access to specialist facilities at the Rutherford Appleton laboratory. After several years of research, the company began to attract serous attention in the telecommunications market and significant investment in the business was accomplished. In 1997, the company launched its first range of products and moved to purpose-built premises. Since then it has won the support and financial backing from major players such as Cisco Systems and Intel and completed deals with significant telecommunications manufacturers and suppliers.

The years of hard work and research are now starting to pay off for the company. The rapid expansion in production capacity led to the establishment of a new facility in Swindon and to record financial results. Revenues for the second quarter (up to July 2000) were up 84% on the first quarter to £4.6 million, with losses falling by 18%. Such rapid growth has resulted in the substantial recruitment of new staff. The company has a payroll of some 600 people and this was set to rise to 1000 by the end of the year (2000). Such rapid growth needs careful management attention, not least to protect the key people from a massive culture shock. However, Rickman anticipated this and invested in the corporate infrastructure early on:

> The strategy was to construct an infrastructure for what could be a very substantial business. We have the goal of being the world's best place to work. My view is that the customer is our lifeblood but that is not the only reason for being here. We are here because we want to be here and we enjoy it. The customer will get a far better service if everyone here is happy, motivated and enjoying themselves.

The expansion is set to continue. The demand for optical components is outstripping capacity world-wide. Where Bookham has the advantage, according to Rickman, is that it can increase its output by 100% by increasing its staff by just 25% and since the public flotation the company is in a much better position to access the pool of available talent to support this growth.

The company's transition from the obscure to the high-profile business of today does give Rickman the opportunity to promote the importance of enterprising and innovation-led businesses and their impact on the economy and people. Rickman is also very keen to use his position to promote technology enterprises in general.

Concluding remarks

Innovation coupled with the ability to think and manage strategically are the key factors that distinguish and elevate the entrepreneurial firm from the small business venture.

The capacity to innovate can lead to substantial and profitable business development if that is the objective of the proprietor and the key players. When growth takes place, it invariably induces the crises that impose pressure on the existing management and facilitates further expansion if such crises are satisfactorily managed as the above cases illustrate.

However, it is a salutary fact that there are too many examples of entrepreneurs that have given up the uneven struggle with innovation and R&D in the UK. The Government White Paper on Science and Technology (HMSO, 1993) recognised the untapped potential that still exists from the failure to commercialise inventions and capitalise on British technology. One of the reasons for this failure must be the inhospitable environment and indifferent and confusing support infrastructure faced by the innovative entrepreneur.

This failure can only be reversed by a radical change in policy and approach that embraces all aspects of the support network and promotes the innovative enterprise to the position and significance that it rightly deserves and requires.

References and further reading

Beaver, G. (1998) 'Idealab: A Case History of Entrepreneurship', *Journal of Strategic Change*, 7 (3), May, 163–5.

Beaver, G. (1999) 'Business Strategy and Enterprise Development', *Journal of Strategic Change*, 8 (7), 371–4.

Beaver, G. and Jennings, P. L. (2000) 'Small Business, Entrepreneurship and Enterprise Development', *Journal of Strategic Change*, 9 (7), 397–405.

Brown, S. L. and Eisenhardt, K. M. (1998) *Competing On the Edge: Strategy as Structured Chaos*. Boston, MA: Harvard Business School Press.

Burns, P. and Dewhurst, J. (eds) (1989) *Small Business and Entrepreneurship*. London: Macmillan.

Burns, P. and Dewhurst, J. (1996) 'Small Firms Policy in Europe', in *Small Business and Entrepreneurship*, 2nd edn. Basingstoke: Macmillan, ch. 10.

Dodgson, M. and Rothwell, R. (1989) 'Technology Strategies in Small and Medium-Sized Firms', in Dodgson, M. (ed.), *Technology Strategy and the Firm: Management and Public Policy*. London: Longman.

EuroBusiness Monitor, September 1999.

Fast Company (1997) *Fast Company Magazine*, December–January.

Forum of Private Business, Membership Survey 2000.

Freel, M. (1998) 'Evolution, Innovation and Learning: Evidence from Case Studies', *Entrepreneurship and Regional Development*, 10 (2), 137–49.

Freeman, C. and Soete, L. (1997) *The Economics of Industrial Innovation*, 3rd edn. London: Pinter.

Gavron, R., Cowling, M., Holtham, G. and Westhall, A. (1998) *The Entrepreneurial Society*. London: Institute for Public Policy Research.

Grant Thornton (2000) *European Business Survey*.

Grieve-Smith, A. and Fleck, V. (1987) 'Business Strategies in Small High Technology Companies', *Long Range Planning*, 20 (2), 61–8.

Grieve-Smith, J. (1990) 'Small High Technology Firms', in *Business Strategy*, 2nd edn. Oxford: Basil Blackwell, ch. 11.

Hamel, G. and Prahalad, C. K. (1994) *Competing For The Future*. Boston, MA: Harvard Business School Press.

HMSO (1993) *Realising Our Potential: A Strategy for Science, Engineering and Technology*, Government White Paper on Science and Technology, Cmnd 2250. London: HMSO.

Jennings, P. L. and Beaver, G. (1997) 'The Performance and Competitive Advantage of Small Firms: A Management Perspective', *International Small Business Journal*, 15 (2), January–March, 63–75.

Kauffman Center Internet Web Site, www.entreworld.org (Global Entrepreneurship Monitor Study), London Business School and Babson College, USA.

Moore, B. (1995) 'What Differences Innovative Small Firms?', Innovation Initiative Paper 4, ESRC Centre for Business Research, University of Cambridge.

Moss-Kanter, R. (1989) *When Giants Learn To Dance*. London: Unwin Hyman.

Moss-Kanter, R. (1995) 'Entrepreneurial Organisations', *BBC2 In-Business*, November.

Oakey, R. (1997) 'A Review of Policy and Practice Relating to High Technology Firms in the UK', Working Paper 359, University of Manchester.

Oakey, R. (1994–98) *New Technology Based Firms in the 1990s*, Vol. 1 (1994), Vol. 2 (1996), Vol. 3 (1997) and Vol. 4 (1998). London: Paul Chapman.

Penrose, E. T. (1959) *The Theory of the Growth of the Firm*. Oxford: Basil Blackwell.

Porter, M. E. (1980) *Competitive Strategy: Techniques for Analysing Industries and Competitors*, New York: Free Press.

Porter, M. E. (1985) *Competitive Advantage: Creating and Sustaining Superior Performance*. New York: Free Press.

Porter, M. E. (1996) 'What is Strategy?', *Harvard Business Review*, November–December, 61–78.

Rothewll, R. (1983) 'Innovation and Firm Size: A Case for Dynamic Complementarity – or is Small Really Beautiful?', *Journal of General Management*, 8 (3), 5–25.

Rothwell, R. (1984) 'The Role of Small Firms in the Emergence of New Technologies', *Omega*, 12 (1), 19–25.

Rothwell, R. (1986) 'The Role of Small Firms in Technological Innovation', in Curran, J., Stanworth, J. and Watkins, D. (eds), *The Survival of the Small Firm*, Vol. 2. Aldershot: Gower.

Rothwell, R. (1988) 'Small Firms, Innovation and Industrial Change', *Small Business Economics*, 1 (1), 51–64.

Rothwell, R. (1994) 'The Role of Small Firms in the Emergence of New Technologies', *Omega Journal*, 12 (1), 19–29.

SBRC (1992) *The State of British Enterprise*. Department of Applied Economics, Cambridge University.

Storey, D. J. (1994) *Understanding the Small Business Sector*. London: Routledge.

Storey, D. J. and Sykes, N. (1996) 'Uncertainty, Innovation and Management', in Burns, P. and Dewhurst, J. (eds), *Small Business and Entrepreneurship*, 2nd edn. London: Macmillan.

Vossen, R. (1998) 'Relative Strengths and Weaknesses of Small Firms in Innovation', *International Small Business Journal*, 16 (3), 88–94.

Index